FROM MEMORY TO TRANSFORMATION

JEWISH WOMEN'S VOICES

FROM MEMORY TO TRANSFORMATION

JEWISH WOMEN'S VOICES

Edited by

Sarah Silberstein Swartz

&

Margie Wolfe

CANADIAN CATALOGUING IN PUBLICATION DATA
Main entry under title:
From memory to transformation : Jewish women's voices

ISBN 1-896764-08-8

1. Jewish women. 2. Women in Judaism.
I. Swartz, Sarah Silberstein, 1947– . II. Wolfe, Margie, 1949– .

HG1172.F76 1998   305.48'6'96   C98-932044-8

Edited by Rhea Tregebov

Front Cover: Photographic image by Elaine Brodie

Second Story Press gratefully acknowledges the assistance of the Ontario Arts
Council and the Canada Council for the Arts for our publishing program.
We acknowledge the financial support of the Government of Canada
through the Book Publishing Industry Development Program for our publishing activities.

Printed in Canada on recycled paper

Published by
SECOND STORY PRESS
720 Bathurst Street, Suite 301
Toronto, Ontario
M5S 2R4

Contents

INTRODUCTION

JUDAISM — as a religion and as a culture — is based on memory. The concept of *Zakhor*, remembrance, has been a major tenet in traditional Jewish practice and teaching. Memory has given us continuity, has enabled Judaism to survive through centuries of exile, upheaval and persecution. It is the transmission of religion, ritual, laws, culture and history that has kept us together as a people. Without this collective transmission of memory, Jewish identity would have vanished long ago.

Yet the transmission of memory, like history, is selective. For Jewish women in particular, what has been neglected may be as critical as what has been passed down. Communally, as a people, our legacy is rich. But for many Jewish women today, there is a keen sense of loss, of the lack of our own female history, heritage and traditions. We have few role models from the past; our achievements and contributions as Jewish women have rarely been acknowledged. Because Jewish culture, history and religion have come to us through a patriarchal vision, it is now our task as feminists to reinterpret this legacy through our own feminist lens. In the search for personal and communal identity, we find ourselves redefining what it means to be a Jew. As Jewish feminists we need to reconcile our heritage with the authentic experience of our own lives.

This anthology is an expression of a new social movement — Jewish feminism — that is transforming the secular and spiritual components of Jewish life. The women's movement, the Holocaust, the expansion of liberal Jewish theology and the growth of more diverse Jewish communities have compelled and enabled Jewish women to expand and reinterpret our role in the world, in the Jewish community and in our own families.

For many of us, change has become an absolute necessity. When feminism revolutionized the way we defined our roles in the world, significant numbers of feminists found no place for themselves in the traditional Jewish community. Some simply felt Judaism was irrelevant to their lives. However, an increasing number have joined in the struggle to articulate new ways of being a Jew, cultural and spiritual ways that enrich, empower and allow us to carry a new legacy of Jewishness to our children and grandchildren.

While this transformative process is exhilarating, the challenges are enormous. If our mothers or their mothers had been asked how they identified themselves as Jews, they would have given well-defined, pro-scriptive and prescriptive answers based on their religion and traditions, centuries old. Today, the issue of identity is much more complex. How can we define ourselves as feminists and still be part of the continuum of Jewish traditions? What part of the legacy do we question and what part do we retain in our search for identity? Moreover, the choices we make and how we proceed will not only affect our lives and those of our daughters and granddaughters, but of our sons and grandsons, our fathers and mothers as well.

From Memory to Transformation: Jewish Women's Voices explores many of the issues involved in this transformation. In it, we hear the voices of contemporary Jewish women — activists, rabbis, scholars, writers and artists, — as they explore a variety of compelling themes. They are voices in search of personal as well as communal identity.

This anthology had its genesis at a conference of the same name attended by five hundred women from diverse backgrounds with a broad range of concerns and priorities. The issues raised were so timely that the organizing committee invited presenters to develop their talks into essays for publication. This book is a rich sampler of current issues which we believe will prove a useful resource for women who are struggling to create fulfilled, equitable and enriched Jewish lives for themselves and their families. While this collection is not definitive, or fully encompassing, we hope that it will encourage further discussion and writing on the diversity of Jewish women's full range of experience. At the same time, we hope that the book will enable a broad audience of readers to gain a more complete understanding of the lives and aspirations of Jewish women today.

The individual articles are as diverse as the communities which produced them. We have included essays, the text for a stage presentation, the transcript of a panel of female rabbis, and photographs of work by Jewish women artists who explore the theme of memory and transformation.

Like most struggling social movements, Jewish feminism is searching for its roots, the historical underpinnings which bond women to their foremothers, while at the same time providing fuel for rebellion against past and current oppressions. However, we know so little of our women's history. It is a legacy of loss and amnesia. In her article "*Zakhor*: Memory, Ritual and Gender," Norma Baumel Joseph argues that, while remembrance is a requirement of Judaism, our heritage, as it has been articulated and taught, is a male heritage. Our foremothers have been lost, our women's lives, accomplishments and struggles buried (along with those of our non-Jewish sisters) under millennia of patriarchy. Unearthing our history — the total of our personal and collective memories — is integral to the transformation of our identities as Jewish women.

Moreover, while we are women, we are also Jews. Our oppression has been twofold and the challenge to historical memory is therefore also twofold. Centuries of religious oppression and anti-Semitism resulting in the Holocaust have not only vanquished millions but the memory and memories of millions. Certainly, more than any single event in recent Jewish history, the Holocaust illustrates the necessity of remembrance and the value of personal memory in sustaining culture and heritage. Sarah Silberstein Swartz, who talks about the recovery of family history during a visit to her family's shtetl in Poland, writes about this dilemma:

> I have felt very vulnerable in my quest for family history. A child of survivors, I am imbued with the importance of not forgetting. Yet there are no photographs and few witnesses to my parents' stories. Their only living child — born after the war — I am the sole carrier of their stories to be transmitted to my children, their grandchildren, born after their deaths. [...] How could I make real to my children a past that I myself have never experienced first hand? With no photographs nor witnesses to guide me, how could I conjure up the faces of lost family members, the images of a rich Jewish life in pre-war Poland ...

It is with this keen sense of urgency that Jewish feminists continue to explore memory in their search for identity. For many daughters of Holocaust survivors, family history has been a determining factor in how their lives have been shaped. Daughters of survivors and therapists Sandra Finkelman and Helena Feinstadt facilitate workshops with second-generation female survivors like themselves in which they explore their family histories.

Systemic, ongoing anti-Semitism in North America has also exacerbated the problem of lost memory. Traditional sources for relating heritage mostly kept Jews, along with other minorities, invisible. Authors Sharon Kirsh and Rhea Tregebov discuss what it was like to grow up in post-war Canadian cities with no literature reflecting their own history and experiences as Jews. Both have written books for young people with strong Jewish-identified autobiographical and historical components. Tregebov adds: "When we present Jewish children or children belonging to any minority with authentic images of their own culture, we not only arm them against prejudice, we nourish their sense of identity and worth, and protect them against the amnesia that a denial of cultural difference engenders." Kirsh further reminds us that, as Jews, we are entitled to our memories, our heritage. Children's author and illustrator Phoebe Gilman offers an evocative essay that demonstrates how memory can be embedded even in the seemingly timeless form of the folk tale.

Many contributors in this collection explore the search for identity through art and literature. Ethel Raicus and Shirley Kumove have translated the stories and poetry of Yiddish women writers whose works, until recently, have been inaccessible, outlining the biographies as well as the writing of these fascinating women. In her essay on women's roles in Judeo–Spanish Sephardic song, Judith Cohen provides a glimpse into this complex culture. The work of several contemporary women artists is described by Mimi Gellman, who investigates how these artists incorporate their concerns regarding memory and identity into their art. Artist Yvonne Singer relates her discovery that she is the god-daughter of Raoul Wallenberg and discusses how she has integrated this watershed fact into her work.

In the struggle for self-realization, Jewish feminists are examining and evaluating how personal and family histories affect identity. A committed feminist, Greta Hofmann Nemiroff insightfully questions whether her secular background and lifestyle allow her "to count as a Jew." We follow Nemiroff as she journeys through her autobiography, and reveals her evolving ambivalence and commitment to a Jewish identity. Judith Sloan's stunning performance art searches through the silences and distortions of family history to delineate how the truth can define an acceptable reality. Faigel Brown looks back at an unfaltering seventy-year relationship with her friend Shirley and comments on how these two extraordinary women and the world around them have changed since their friendship began.

We are strongly motivated to preserve our legacy, to retain and pass on the cultural memory on which our sense of community and history is based. Yet we also have a contradictory desire to move forward, to create a new context for ourselves. Writer and activist Irena Klepfisz muses over this dilemma and the possible strategies to reconcile these apparently contradictory impulses, recognizing that her Jewish identity and sense of continuity has been "inextricably intertwined" with her mother's generation. Klepfisz questions her place in history when this generation dies, adding: "I wonder [about these things] with increasing urgency as I ready myself to begin the Jewish generation relay race in which I've been entered."

In fact, the race has already begun. The search for history and memory are the first steps towards activism, the beginnings of the feminist transformation. Committed to entrenching a place for women within religious observance, scholars such as Norma Baumel Joseph are focused on redefining those aspects of Jewish tradition which are gender-biased. Women rabbis such as Elizabeth Bolton, Elyse Goldstein and Nancy Wechsler-Azen are reinterpreting liturgical language, creating new areas of study, establishing new models of leadership and making Judaism more women-conscious — often turning rabbinical practice on its head. And lay groups of women such as the Minyan of Crones are working with ingenuity and conviction outside of the rabbinate and the academy to create new women-focused rituals that honour the significant events in women's lives. This is change.

Jewish feminists are also changing traditional notions of home, family and community. Journalist Susan G. Cole explores the possibilities and challenges of lesbian parenting within a Jewish milieu. Helena Lipstadt discusses the importance of community and the struggle for acceptance for Jewish lesbians at a later stage in life. Yolande Cohen writes of continuity and change amongst Sephardic Jews in Montreal.

Beyond the home and family, Jewish feminists are taking the struggle to the "streets." Shlomit Segal reminds us that issues of poverty and economic injustice are absolutely consistent with the goals of Jewish feminism. Rachel Leviatan describes her work in Israel with young people who come from a world of poverty and deprivation.

While feminist activism is not a new phenomenon, *Jewish* feminist activism is in its infancy. Today, we are only beginning to define the links that the will help us transform our lives as Jewish women. Uncovering our collective and personal memories is leading us to new states of awareness. Long-time activist and author Melanie Kaye/Kantrowitz writes of her dream for a Jewish feminist movement, of her understanding that we are a part of a large coalition movement of groups: "We are not segregated ... We know our foremothers. Our leaders are not all Ashkenazic men in suits who belong to a synagogue. Our women lead. We recognize and embrace our diversity of race, culture, sexual orientation, observance and secularism."

Many within the traditional Jewish community might argue that this vision is too compromising, too inclusive. Certainly, a prevalent belief within Jewish orthodoxy is that strict adherence to literal interpretations of religion, ritual and practice is what has safeguarded Jewish life through the centuries. Today, we have a choice. We can walk away from Judaism, and give in to the dictates of Jewish orthodoxy. Or we can embrace Jewish continuity in the form of a more empowering Jewishness with expanded and diverse practices, interpretations and lifestyles. Jewish women can and will carry an enriched identity and legacy forward to those who will call *us* their foremothers.

We would like to acknowledge a number of individuals who have made this volume possible. First, the other members of the conference organizing committee: Nadya Burton, Frumie Diamond, Mimi Gellman, Ronnee Jaeger, Isabella Meltz, Kapri Rabin and Toni Olshen. Without their encouragement and support, this book project would not have been launched. We would also like to thank the Action Committee for Jewish Continuity of the UJA Federation of Greater Toronto with the participation of the Cultural Services Planning and Allocations Committee for recognizing the intrinsic educational value of this project with a Jewish Continuity Culture grant. Second Story Press gave us the go-ahead based on no more than a proposal and partial manuscript.

Rhea Tregebov, our editor, as always has been a wonderful source of calm, commitment and expertise. We appreciate her efforts very much. Also many thanks to Ellie Kellman for assisting us with the YIVO Yiddish translations.

It is important that we also acknowledge all those women who participated in "From Memory to Transformation: Jewish Women's Voices" — the conference — and its predecessor, "Jewish Women's Voices: Past and Present." Those thousand women provided the initial energy and inspiration for the book. Finally, we want to remember Shelley Duke, an avid and energetic supporter, who recently died. Her commitment, like that of Jewish feminists everywhere, is reflected in the pages of this book.

— Sarah Silberstein Swartz
& Margie Wolfe
Toronto, August 1998

PART ONE

LEGACY

'DI YERUSHE'/THE LEGACY:

A PARABLE ABOUT HISTORY AND 'BOBE-MAYSES,' 'BARSZCZ' AND 'BORSHT' AND THE FUTURE OF THE JEWISH PAST

ᑫᑌᑫ

Irena Klepfisz

Poet and essayist Irena Klepfisz weaves a parable of fact and fantasy, posing some important questions about ageing and the relationships between personal and communal history and between the past and the future. Dependent on the past generation to provide a sense of historical continuity, she asks: "What is history and where is my place in it?" Will the transformations we are enacting today become the Jewish feminist legacy of the future?

THIS IS NO *bobe-mayse*.* I never knew my grandmothers, both of whom died in the war, and it's only recently that I've gotten even a glimpse of what my *bobes* might have been like by watching my eighty-one-year-old mother, Mama Lo. Oddly enough, I too, though childless, am experiencing a state of *bobe*-hood. More and more, Mama Lo and I are sharing the aches and pains of getting old and older and bridging our

---

*Bobe-mayse: fantasy, fabrication (pejorative); grandmother's story (literal)

lifelong generation gap. Who would have thought? But then these are peculiar times.

For example, lately Mama Lo has been instructing me about "when the time comes ..." and showing me the desk drawer with her living will and the jewellery box with Elza's watch, not especially valuable, but the only physical link to my twenty-four year old almost-sister who committed suicide over thirty years ago. Occasionally, she walks me through the apartment, pointing to this or that. Sometimes she stares at her well-stocked bookcases of Ringelblum, Levi, Charlotte, Herman Wouk, Howard Fast and Jane Austen and George Eliot, at the framed reproductions of Chagall and Van Gogh, and at the *tshatshkes* of kittens, vases, miniature musicians (many of them presents from me). In a gesture of puzzlement (perhaps despair), she throws up her hands: "What are you going to do with ...?" she begins, then stops and changes the subject with a shrug.

Though she has experienced two world wars, poverty and serious illnesses, I suspect Mama Lo is admitting to herself for the first time that she has no choice but to accept her lack of control over her own life and mine. Knowing my forgetfulness and essential anarchism, she cannot feel easy about passing on the pots of sturdy jades and blossoming African violets. Actually, I'm not certain what she feels because I have no idea what it is like to be eighty-one, and also because, with iron-clad tenacity, Mama Lo has kept her inner life a locked vault. It is a vault to which she is not about to bequeath me the key. — History be damned, she is saying. — What is private is private.

So these days we are both silent about what we both know: that at some point, I will take possession of her possessions, dismantle her apartment, and, barring catastrophe, continue with my life for possibly two or three decades without her. In other words, my life as a daughter will come to an abrupt end and I will cease being Mama Lo and her generation's future and be transformed into a true *bobe*, the next generation's past.

Theoretically, legacies and inheritances are simple: some things we accept and keep, even if with great sadness; others we discard because they're inconvenient, useless, simply passé. A watch like Elza's — orphan child-survivor, dreaming poet, determined suicide — embodies so much public and private history that I've never been able to claim it for myself. So when the time comes, the watch will be transferred to my desk drawer. But I am determined eventually to bequeath it to someone, someone younger — not a relative, because I have none — but someone to whom its fierce and painful history will be important, and whose arm will display it like an honour, rather than a wound.

Mama Lo's other bequests will be more problematic. Should I, for example, keep a leaky pot — its white enamel worn, its rim dented — but Mama Lo's (and my own) sole physical link to Poland (post-war, of course, but Poland nevertheless)? What historical purpose will it serve standing on a shelf behind my Teflon pans, my well-used wok and bamboo steamers? Does such a pot belong in a museum and should I try to donate it? ("It's the very pot in which Mama Lo cooked her borscht — on *both* sides of the Atlantic. Believe me it tells the quintessential twentieth century Jewish story.")

And then there's the album with photographs of people I don't quite remember: a man and woman standing by the white brick oven in our Lodz apartment or a teenager kneeling by a sandbox in a park — ordinary people who, because of their imagination, stupidity and/or luck, just happened to survive. Should I ask Mama Lo to name them? I've no family, so what does it matter? Won't such an album inevitably end up in some "collectibles-barn" in Columbia County in upstate New York to be browsed through by eager weekenders trying to furnish their newly built A-frame with an aura of history? On the other hand, the album is part of *my life, my past* — one which my ageing brain has increasingly more trouble retaining, a past which, I confess, I've already distilled (or thinned — depending on your point of view) as I've tried to "get on" with my life.

The truth is that for most of my adulthood I've been braced against Mama Lo's disapproval, conscious I did not fulfill her wish and emulate her and her one-bedroom apartment in a three-bedroom one of my own fully furnished with a husband and children. Instead, I went off and settled into a wall-less, closet-less loft which I share with another woman who has no legal relationship to me, but with whom I also share my life.

Yet, for all my rebelliousness and alternativity, a part of my identity — the *Jewish* part— has been inextricably intertwined with Mama Lo and the life of her generation. *My* vaulted secret is that I've been a dependent Jew — dependent on Mama Lo's generation to provide me with a sense of *hemshekh*/continuity. They've been the visible *goldene keyt*/the golden chain to which I've wanted to hook the link I've been forging through my life and my work. With them gone, where am I supposed to hang myself?

To put it another way: *Vos iz geshikhte?*/What *is* history and what is my place in it? And how is time defined with any accuracy by human events? The Middle Ages. The Renaissance. The Age of Reason. How do we know when one age ends and another begins? I wonder with increasing urgency as I ready myself to begin the Jewish generation relay race in which I've been entered.

Take borscht, for example. Consider that beets were unknown to us at the time of the destruction of the Temple and were not among the hastily packed foods our *bobes* took into Babylon or later into the northwestern *goles*/exile. Then consider the centrality of borscht in modern Eastern European Jewish culture. By what process did this essential component of Jewish life emerge?

Borscht entered Jewish life many centuries ago — through the kitchen. The first Jewish mention of beets, I believe, occurs in *A bobe, an eydes/A Grandmother, A Witness*, a recently discovered collection which is bound to rival Glickl's *Memoirs*. Among its many fragmentary stories, *A bobe, an eydes* contains a series of tributes to a certain Gitl *bas* Frume *di frume** who, according to one *bobe-mayse*, lived in the later part of the thirteenth century in the town of Knin. Knin was far from her ancestors' beloved Ashkenaz, very far east in fact, in a region we nostalgically remember today as *poyln*/Poland — the cradle of *yidishkeyt, der yidisher oytser*/the Jewish treasure — but where, in Gitl's time, the buds of *yidishe geshikhte un kultur*/history and culture were barely formed, much less beginning to bloom.

It was some time during that Yiddish dawn that Gitl *bas* Frume *di frume* forged a secret friendship with Grushenka, even though Janek, Grushenka's brother, beat up Yankl, Gitl's brother, on a regular basis. One Sunday morning after sneaking out of church, Grushenka led Gitl (without Frume's knowledge), into her mother's Christian kitchen, where, for the first time, Gitl smelled the sweet, dark aroma of *barszcz*. "*Treyf!*" *undzer yidishe tokhter*/our young Jewish girl declared that night to her younger sister Chava, thereby conveying her understanding of

---

* Gitl *bas* Frume *di frume*: Gitl daughter of Frume the pious

the nature of the soup's bones and, indeed, its entire culinary context. But then, much to her sister's horror, Gitl added with *emesdike benk-shaft*/heartfelt longing: "*Ober es shmekt azoy gut!*/But it smells so good!"

Like other texts whose authors were neither official recorders nor note takers, but ordinary homemakers focused more on an event's ingredients than on its development and denouement, *A bobe, an eydes* gives scant information about the process of Judaization of the Polish *barszcz*. Perhaps once, perhaps more than once, the girl tasted the forbidden friend's forbidden food. In any case, at some point, after numerous visits and sniffs, much finger-pointing at the market place, two or three public tantrums, and repeated posings of the proverbial "*Ober, far vos nisht?*/Why not?*" — the impetus behind all creative leaps — Gitl convinced Frume *di frume* to act: ("*Dos meydl makht mir in gantsn meshige. Tog un nakht redt zi bloyz fun buraki un barszcz!*/The girl's driving me completely mad. Day and night she talks only of *buraki* and *barszcz!*") And so the frazzled mother peeled the bleeding vegetables into a pot of boiling water, added some *beyner, tsiker, knobl, un tsibeles*/bones, sugar, garlic and onions and, through trial and error — *tsu gedikht, tsu shiter, tsu zis, tsu zoyer*/too thick, too thin, too sweet, too tart — the soup looked, tasted and smelled exactly like the *barszcz* in Grushenka's mother's kitchen with the added advantage it could pass rabbinical inspection: *s'iz geven kusher*/it was kosher.

The rest *iz poshet*/is simple. By the first decade of the fifteenth century when Gitl's great-granddaughter, Frume *di freylekhe*,* was already a married *baleboste*/homemaker, the Slavic rooted *barszcz* had become *borsht*, the Yiddish word for the quintessential Jewish soup.

Given such history it is not surprising that today, near the end of the twentieth century, I am preoccupied with leaky pots, with Elza's watch (which, despite being idle for almost thirty years, began ticking the second I wound it), with photo albums and with the survival of borscht itself in Jewish kitchens dominated by woks and bamboo steamers. Nor is it surprising that I am preoccupied with Mama Lo's entire *yerushe*, including everything she lost almost sixty years ago so that when she debarked in *di goldene medine*/the golden land, Mama Lo had nothing but a goose-down *koldra* (which a year later caught fire from a faulty heating pad), some crumbling photographs, a pot pur-

* Frume *di freylekhe*: Frume the joyous/gay

chased in Lodz shortly after Liberation — and me. That year *poyln* was no longer a blooming garden, but a country-sized wall-less graveyard and Mama Lo's past *a vistenish*/a void, something which history and nature abhor and immediately engulf, thereby allowing the transformation of alien weeds into beloved indigenous flowers and *a treyf barszcz* into the embodiment of *a kushere heym*.

So when the time comes, I will have no choice. Somehow I will find my place on the historical continuum and try to observe and take notes. I will go to Sally and Linda's seder and recline on the Moroccan, Israeli and Native American rugs. Together we will retell the ancient story as it was passed from *bobe* to *bobe* and read from our Xeroxed Hagaddahs decorated with images of ancient goddesses and interspersed with the texts of witches' incantations, peace songs between Hagar and Sarah, tributes to midwives, toasts to the liberation of Palestinians, and praise songs and poems to Hannah Senesh, Yokheved and Gitl *bas* Frume *di frume*. At appropriate moments, my women friends and I will raise our cups of grape juice and greet Miriam the Prophetess, drink the vegetarian chicken soup, dunk the parsley in the bitter waters, chew the symbolic mortar and burn the sweet-scented incense. Each year we will substitute this for that and add that to this and sing and chant recalling the tears and losses and recite (in English, of course) "*hayntiks yor knekht, dos kumendike yor fraye froyen*/this year we are slaves, next year liberated women." And a few years from now, sometime around the year 2000, we will feel familiar, comforted and grounded in our tradition and look back upon the seders of our childhoods as the ancient ceremonies of another century and era — which is exactly what they will have become.

But until then, I am at Mama Lo's service. Whenever she wants to recall more vividly the *poyln fun ire kinderyorn*/Poland of her childhood and the sweetness of my *bobe* Rikla's *kikh*, a kitchen whose ashes and dust are now indistinguishable from those of the Second Temple — I will take Mama Lo to Second Avenue and Teresa's Polish Café and order borscht, the same *treyf barszcz* Gitl *bas* Frume *di frume* first smelled in Grushenka's mother's kitchen. As Mama Lo and I breathe in its dark, rich aroma, we will begin talking for the first time *bobe tsu bobe* about the miracles of our common past and the mystery of our separate futures.

WOMEN'S VOICES IN THE STORIES OF YIDDISH WRITER ROKHL BROKHES

❦

Ethel Raicus

In our search for Jewish women's history, Jewish feminists have redis-
covered the writings of Yiddish women from the past. Often complex
and controversial, these women and their works open our eyes to a time
and culture long vanished. Yiddish was the preeminent language of
Ashkenazic Jews in Eastern Europe prior to the Second World War, the
language most closely associated with Jewish women and their daily
lives, while Hebrew was the patriarchal language of study and prayer.
Ethel Raicus' commentary on the brilliant prose of Rokhl Brokhes pro-
vides us with powerful insights into the thoughts and experiences of
Jewish women of her pre-war Europe generation. We can only hope
that further research and translations of women's writing will continue
to blossom, so that Jewish women who are unable to read the original
Yiddish will have access to this important aspect of our legacy.

TODAY THE NAME Rokhl Brokhes is largely unknown even to those who
know and love Yiddish. What happened? Who was Rokhl Brokhes?
Brokhes was born in the city of Minsk, White Russia (present-day

Belarus), September 23, 1880. She perished there in the Minsk ghetto sixty-five years later. Brokhes had been starved and tortured by the Nazis, murdered and thrown into a mass grave. For approximately forty years, Rokhl Brokhes had been an acclaimed and widely read Yiddish writer. She had over two hundred short stories, novellas, theatre pieces and children's stories to her credit. Brokhes was only nineteen when her first short story, "*Yankele*," was published in St. Petersburg. It drew immediate attention to the gifted young woman, who was only sixteen when she wrote it. Brokhes was a prodigy; she had, by age nine, read with ease *Tanakh* and the works of Mapu (the first modern-Hebrew novelist) in the original Hebrew and was keeping a diary. Her father had been her teacher.

Volf Brokhes was a *maskil* [a disciple of the Enlightenment], a gifted — but impoverished — Hebrew writer who was never published. He died when Brokhes was nine, and soon after she went to work as a seamstress. Eventually she became a teacher of needlework at the Minsk Jewish Vocational School for Girls. However, from age nineteen on, her work appeared regularly in book form and in periodicals, including the *Tsukunft* [The Future] published in New York City. Her work was read in Russia, Lithuania and the USA and was translated from Yiddish into Russian, German and English until 1941. When the Germans entered Minsk, they destroyed the State Publishing House project to publish an eight-volume set of Brokhes's collected works. The first volume had already been typeset.

All disappeared, writer and writings, readers, her very name and memory. By 1990, Rokhl Brokhes had been resolved, to paraphrase Shakespeare, into a mystery. Until recently, the sum total of information about her came from the approximately seven hundred and fifty words in Zalman Reizen's *Leksikon fun der yidisher literatur, prese, un filologye* [Lexicon of Yiddish Literature, Press and Philology],[1] and the second edition of the lexicon, and any autobiographical information drawn from the one sketch and thirteen short stories by Brokhes that were available.

In 1995 other sources were found. Yiddish critic and writer Avrom Reisen's memoir, *Epizodn fun mayn lebn* [Episodes from My Life],[2] describes life in the literary circles of pre-Revolutionary Minsk. Reisen was a close acquaintance of Brokhes. Through Reisen's memoir, she becomes real and human, snatched from the intended oblivion of the mass grave. In *Epizodn fun mayn lebn*, Reisen describes seventeen-year-old Rokhl Brokhes as tall, slim, reserved, with a strong, well-modulated voice and bobbed hair. She was "big city" to the likes of Reisen. Her many admirers waited to be noticed. Among them were Reisen himself and Avrom Liessin, the famous socialist poet whose work was suppressed and who later became editor of the *Tsukunft*. Reisen describes his almost daily visits to her home and Liessin's poem of "longing for a distant beloved." He also describes a farewell theatre date with Brokhes and her mother's pleasure in it, knowing how much her daughter loved the theatre. Brokhes was then seventeen; Reisen, twenty-five. The above scenes bring to the mind's eye a woman who was meant to disappear and bring also the sudden, overwhelming realization that this disappearance was not to be. It has been prevented. There are still unanswered questions, but there is no longer a nothingness — a vapour.

By the end of the nineteenth century the great migration from Eastern Europe was on, and many writers emigrated to the USA and Palestine, Liessin and Reisen among them. Brokhes remained in Minsk all her life, except for a short period following her marriage to a dentist. There is no clear evidence as to who he was nor when they married. At some point, probably taking advantage of the relaxed domicile restrictions, Brokhes and her husband left the Pale to settle in the province of Saratova on the steppes of the Volga, several hundred miles southeast of Moscow. By 1920 the family was back in Minsk, driven by the dislocation and famine of the civil war that followed the Revolution. Of whom did the family consist at that point? Brokhes mentions "my children" in a sketch entitled "On the Volga Steppes with the Germans."[3]

By the end of the nineteenth century, Minsk had over 47,000 Jews, about 52 per cent of the total population. It was a vibrant centre of Jewish life. *Misnagdim,* anti-Hasidic sceptics, were strong; Hasidim were not quite as influential. The *maskilim* had founded schools there with curricula incorporating general subjects alongside the traditional. All brands of socialism argued their logic and vied for the allegiance of the emerging working class. Delegates from Minsk participated in the founding of the Bund, the Jewish Labour Association, in 1897, and Minsk Bundists were targeted in the 1905 anti-liberal riots. Zionists were a presence in Minsk from the days of the Khibat Zion movement in the 1880s, and by 1918 the General and Labor Zionists together were the majority in the community elections.

Rokhl Brokhes was there throughout all the tumult, but there is nothing overtly political in the stories we have from her — no depictions of Minsk, of political movements, of political activity. She seems to have lived in Saratova during the years of the First World War and the Revolution. Brokhes was cut off in that period from the Jewish literary community. She continued to write, however, if not to publish, but she must have done a lot of writing during that time for the State Publishing House to have planned an eight-volume set of her collected works. Where is the material now? Where are the manuscripts? We do not know.

Brokhes's voice was passionate, a cry for the deprived and the abandoned. She drew her themes from the poorest streets of the Pale where the Jewish masses were to be found in the greatest misery and despair. And she sought to draw them out of their darkness into the sun. Her voice was compassionate, but often enough, in the throats of her characters, the voices were harsh, coarse and almost unbearably cruel.

"Avremelekh" is a story about illegitimate infants abandoned to the angry care of old, impoverished "Bobe" [grandmother] Brayne. They are laid out in every imaginable receptacle, mewling in their hunger. She cannot feed them. Her miserable one-room shack is really a way station and she a Charon helping them to the next world. All the baby boys are named Avremele. A two-year-old boy from among them is brought to the home of a nursing mother to relieve her engorged breasts. He is in paradise: food, light and human warmth. Avremele charms them. They love him. But the cure for the woman is effected, and he is returned to Bobe Brayne — with sweet but total indifference. To make room for new charges, Bobe Brayne takes him to the populated area of town, puts a bagel in his hand and tells him that he should wait until she returns. Passers-by make no attempt to help the wailing child.

Earlier in the story, while Avremele is still nursing with the family, Bobe Brayne describes the *mamzeyrilekh* [the little bastards], the overcrowding in her shack, the poverty and her inability to feed them all. She doesn't know what to do with Avremele once his usefulness has ended. The listeners cluck their sympathy for the lovely child, but when Brayne suggests that one of them take him into their comfortable home, they panic. "You see," says Brayne, "no one wants him, but you tell me to take care of him." "We were only saying that Avremele is a beautiful child, that it's a pity ..."[4] is the answer.

"*Avremelekh*," published in 1940, is one of the last two stories we have of Brokhes. The other is "*Shpinen*" [Spiders], a many-layered story of a beggar, a female usurer and the beggar's wife, who is an absentee participant. There never was a surfeit of happiness in Brokhes's writing, but in these two stories there is an added cruelty that begs exploration.

In some of her stories the action is often an inner one or there is no action at all, without a climax. For example, the story in "*Tshad*" [Smoke] is quiet, and then simply drops away as a sailing ship might off the edge of a flat world. Dvoyre, the twenty-year-old daughter of an impoverished family, has had to work from childhood on. The parents worry about her chances for marriage, since she has neither a dowry nor even a decent dress in which to show herself. Dvoyre enjoys reading her Russian and Yiddish books, and she dreams of love.

A match comes along. He finds favour with everyone except Dvoyre; she cannot bear him near her. At her betrothal, she pleads a headache so as not to reveal her misery. Understanding the relief and joy of her parents at the prospect of her marriage, she decides to accept a man she cannot abide, whom she sees as the angel of death. And so, a soul goes under right there, surrounded by all who love her and wish her well. They sit sipping tea and talking about "important matters." Dvoyre thinks that "maybe that's the way it must be, till a person becomes accustomed ..."[5]

Brokhes's themes are inequity, entrapment, indifference, greed, remorse, hopelessness, hunger and sacrifice. Her passion, social justice, seems to hark back to influences stemming from the *Haskalah* [Jewish Enlightenment]. When the *maskilim* turned towards the Enlightenment, they brought with them their history, culture and literature. In seeking social justice, Brokhes seemed to leap backward, past the socialism and Marxism of her day. It was a sweeping search for a world corrected, made better. The wellspring of her passion, as it was for many socialists, seems to have been the *N'viyim* [the Prophets], learned as a child from her *maskil* father.

In the short story "*Di zogerin*" the *zogerin* [women's prayer leader] sits in the women's synagogue, behind the *mekhitse* [curtain separating the women's section from the men's], reading the service for the women, many of whom are illiterate. On request, she also intercedes on their behalf with prayers, both serious and trivial; a cure for the sick, a desirable *shidekh* [match], food for the table, that a petitioner's only cow be safely delivered of her calf. Then one day, in her grandson's presence, the *zogerin* explodes, yelling and cursing at the injustice of her situation:

> "No, I say; enough is enough! On their behalf I prayed, for their benefit I cried my eyes out. Enough! I say, no! May I be struck dumb if I will say one more word." She had a strong chin. She was a zogerin. A very good one and she argued, "*Reboyne-sheloylem*, kind Father, You alone know how I have prayed both summer and winter, never missed a *shabes*... On their behalf what have I not prayed for? Wealth, length of days, pleasure from the children..."[6]

She complains that she can hardly earn enough to feed her grandson, must beg for favours and is constantly humiliated. She ends her tirade with an angry declaration that she will henceforth pray only for herself.

This story can be interpreted in several ways. The *zogerin* can be seen as an overwrought woman driven to the brink of madness by poverty, marginalization, hopelessness; alive only when entering as some kind of adjunct into other people's striving. Her function once fulfilled and their goal achieved, she is deleted as though she had never been. Alternatively, the story can be read as being about a woman who has had a revelation, who has suddenly achieved centre stage in her own life's drama. The story could also be read as a metaphor for the artist's struggle to gain that sense of self, consciously or unconsciously, without which there can be no creative imagination. Or, finally, the story can be seen as a metaphor for the great debate of that time which was going on in Minsk, as elsewhere: will relief from the misery of Jewish life in Eastern Europe come within the context of a proletarian revolution, or can Jewish hopelessness be reversed only through self-conscious effort by Jews in a Jewish homeland?

Brokhes's story "*Misterye*" [Mystery] is a kind of fairy or folk tale. In a very large city at the end of a very long street that is sometimes so muddy that you could not cross it, there stands a little house, part of which is home to the *shames* [sexton or beadle of a synagogue], his wife and his daughter, Reyzl, and part of which serves as a combined synagogue and *besmedresh* [house of study]. Reyzl is a wig-maker. She is beautiful, wise, a doer of good deeds and she is lame. She is revered in the town and has received many offers of marriage, all of which she has refused.

At night, after her parents have gone to bed, Reyzl, having concluded her works of charity, gets down to her wig-making. It is then that she hears, coming from the other side of the house, the melancholy study-chant of the mysterious, ascetic scholar who has settled there. It is thought that he has left the noisy world (probably released by a wife) to devote his life to study. Reyzl imagines this woman as having grown in stature in her struggle to understand and to decide on such a sacrifice. This, in turn, leads her to speculate about the nature of inner growth. Fantasies less than spiritual intrude. But these go unrecognized, denied, rejected. Her thoughts on the different and the extraordinary run like this:

> She, the other woman, is after all his wife. If she was not as big as he, she had to become big and strong for his sake. And she envied that young wife, because what is the petty life of woman? And what significance have the lives of all those around her, who are preoccupied only with themselves? How devalued and workaday they appear as against this one. And how blessed is the one man or woman who can become that big, bigger than all and everything around them.
>
> But how is this achieved? Did the One on High ennoble them at birth and set them apart from all others, or did they by their own strength of will make themselves so?
>
> Then why should she not become an other and better one than she is ... than all the others if it is bound up with will alone?[7]

The story is rich in symbols and images, as well as Brokhes's rare allusion to events in the real world around her: "In the big world, big things were going on, but here in the street to the casual glance, there were almost no changes, other than that elderly people died; but then, others, as though to replace them, grew old."[8] "*Misterye*" continues:

Then, one night there was a noise at the synagogue door. Reyzl heard footsteps and when she opened her door, *he* [the ascetic] stood there, holding something in his arms. "A child," he said quietly, passing it from hand to hand, "someone has apparently abandoned it." At first there was consternation in the house. A little boy perhaps a couple of days old. Then came the questions: "Why us?" and "Is it our responsibility?" By the time of the first minyan [quorum for prayer] the next morning, the house was full. No one on the street was short of children, and nobody had bread to spare for another mouth.

There were neither offers to take the child, nor advice of any kind. So Reyzl was consulted, and she, of course, refused to give him up. He would remain in the house of the *shames*.

Reyzl was pleased and excited; her parents, remembering the children they had lost, considered it a godsend. The *shames* bought a little goat which was being led to slaughter for a coin; so there would be fresh milk for the child. (He had to borrow from Beyle the baker to make the deal!) But ... The house was transformed. *He* came often. *He* interrupted his studies, stood over the cradle looking at the child in wonder, and said quietly, "A dear, bright child." The child was between them and bound them together. And the bond was blessed with the brightness of the child and the joy that filled Reyzl's being.[9]

The text abounds in symbols and sublimations: the long road sometimes too muddy to cross; the beautiful but lame Reyzl; the study-obsessed ascetic, ready to turn his back on human contact; the little scapegoat, delivered from slaughter to become provider and nourisher; the extraordinary human being, who longs for the ordinary; the unwanted child who transforms the unfulfilled. The story is a *khad gadya* [traditional Passover song about a scapegoat being led to slaughter] in reverse that proceeds from malevolence to renewal. The doomed little scapegoat nourishes the rejected infant who brings happiness into bleak lives.

During the Soviet period Brokhes apparently wrote many children's stories. Five are known: four published in 1937 and one in 1939, well into the Soviet period. They are instructional and are informed by an idealistic conviction. They have warmth and the knack of bringing the story-teller face to face with the reader. These stories are meant to imbue the young with the dream of a world made good and, of course, with the desire to help make it so.

All together twenty-one short stories, five children's stories and several short segments of the memoir, "On the Volga Steppes with the Germans," have been discovered. It was the friend of Brokhes's youth, her admirer Avrom Liessin, later editor of the *Tsukunft,* who published so many of her stories. Surely there was correspondence between contributor and editor. Perhaps somewhere in New York packets and packets of letters may exist.

There is a monument on the mass grave that Rokhl Brokhes shares with who knows how many others. There are no individual names given, but the grave itself does have a name: *Untern barg* [Beneath the Mountain]. *Untern barg* happens to be the title of an early story by Brokhes and was probably the name of an industrial district in Minsk where the story is set. *Barg* also means a heap of earth. How unearthly, this hint of premonition. In the end, it is Rokhl Brokhes's voice that will be her monument. As her stories are unearthed one by one, they will, like her name, "be for blessing."

⚫

NOTES

1. Zalman Reizen, ed., *Leksikon fun der yidisher literatur, prese, un filologye* [Lexicon of Yiddish literature, press and philology], 3rd ed. (Vilna: Vilner Furlag fun B. A. Kletsin, 1927–29).

2. Avrom Reisen, *Epizodn fun mayn lebn* [Episodes from my life] (Vilna, 1929–1935).

3. Rokhl Brokhes, "In di volga stepes bi di taykhn" [On the Volga Steppes with the Germans], *Tsukunft* [The Future] (August 1926).

4. Brokhes, "Avremelekh," in *Shpinen* [Spiders] (Minsk: State Publishing House, 1940), 3–13. Translation by Ethel Raicus.

5. Brokhes, "Tshad," [Smoke] in *A zamlung dertseylungen* [A Collection of stories] (Vilna: Vilner Furlag fun B. A. Kletskin, 1922), 66–73. Translation by Ethel Raicus.

6. Brokhes, "The Zogerin," in Frieda Forman, Ethel Raicus, Sarah Silberstein Swartz and Margie Wolfe, eds., *Found Treasures: Stories by Yiddish Women Writers* (Toronto: Second Story Press, 1994), 85–86. Translation by Shirley Kumove.

7. Brokhes, "Misterye," [Mystery], *Tsukunft* [The Future] (August 1927): 192–196. Translation by Ethel Raicus.

8. Ibid.

9. Ibid.

DRUNK FROM THE BITTER TRUTH:

THE LIFE, TIMES AND POETRY OF ANNA MARGOLIN

ഏൟൟ

Shirley Kumove

During the major immigration to North America in the first decades of the twentieth century, Jewish women found many opportunities for growth and change, while still being influenced by memories of their Eastern European legacy. These first generation immigrant women were confronted with the dichotomy of the pull of old world ties and the push of new world promises. An astonishingly "modern" poet, Anna Margolin is representative of this generation of Jewish women who were born and educated in Eastern Europe at the beginning of the twentieth century, and who struggled for a vehicle of expression and livelihood in America. Worldly and sophisticated, Margolin wrote in Yiddish, her mother tongue, for the New York Jewish literary community of her day. In spite of the merits and acceptance of her erudite poetry in the international milieu of her time, her life ended in physical and emotional isolation, and her poetry became inaccessible to most people in its original Yiddish — another casualty in our lost Jewish women's history. Shirley Kumove recaptures the spirit of Margolin's life work.

ANNA MARGOLIN was born Rosa Lebensboym in Brisk (Brest-Litovsk), Belarus, in 1887. Her father, Menakhem, was an "enlightened" grain merchant, both pious and knowledgeable in worldly subjects. Her mother, Dvoyre Leye, was an unsophisticated woman, traditional in outlook. Rosa was their only child, and precocious. An apt and diligent student, she studied at *gymnasium* [high school] and was also tutored at home in Jewish subjects and in languages — Hebrew, German and Russian. By the age of fifteen she was enchantingly beautiful, extremely well read and fully developed as a woman. She had thick ash-blond hair which fell to her knees, large blue eyes and a musical voice. She was well aware of her physical appeal, and enjoyed youthful flirtations and love affairs.

Margolin came to New York for the first time in 1906, at age eighteen, to prepare herself for university. She had been sent to the USA because her father wanted to break up his headstrong daughter's current love affair. However, instead of enrolling at university as planned, she quickly immersed herself in the intellectual life of the Lower East Side. She soon began a tempestuous but short-lived love affair with Chaim Zhitlowsky, a Yiddish author, socialist theoretician and charismatic orator many years her senior. Around this time she wrote short stories which appeared in journals under a variety of pseudonyms.

By the time Margolin arrived permanently in the USA at the age of twenty-six, in 1913, she had already travelled extensively from Brisk to Königsberg, Warsaw and Odessa. She had spent two years in New York, visited London and Paris, returned to Warsaw, and spent two years in Palestine. Such an itinerary was unusual for a woman of her age and status. Her travels included meetings with leading anarchists in London and Paris, as well as marriage to Hebrew writer, Moishe Stavsky, which produced a son, Naaman. When the marriage broke up, Margolin left her infant in Tel Aviv in the care of his father. She never saw the child again.

When Margolin returned to New York in 1913, she became a columnist for the women's pages of the recently founded Yiddish daily newspaper, *Der tog* [The Day]. She wrote a weekly column called, "In The Women's World," and for a time she was a member of the editorial board. She wrote under her real name, Rosa Lebensboym.

The Yiddish literary and intellectual world Margolin had entered was male-dominated and fiercely competitive. Women writers were characterized by the critics as emotional and sentimental, compared only with each other, and not considered worthy of examination as part of the larger body of modern Yiddish literature. Their work was often characterized as "*vayberish*" [literally, female or feminine], a description which contained an implied insult. Margolin was particularly sensitive to the epithet "sentimental," and strove instead for "hardness," tending to veil or mask her own identity in many of her poems.

During the early decades of the twentieth century, Yiddish women writers in North America considered themselves emancipated and en-lightened. They created an extensive literature which ran the gamut from chronicling the domestic scene to the experimental and highly complex writing of Anna Margolin and others. They were first genera-tion immigrant women, part of the emerging female intelligentsia who experienced the profound contradictions faced by most women living in North America in the twentieth century. This society held out a heady promise, yet denied them full acceptance and recognition.

The Yiddish press in the USA was the incubator for many impor-tant writers who received their first journalistic and literary exposure in the pages of these newspapers. By the first decade of the twentieth cen-tury, New York City was becoming the liveliest and most populous Jewish centre in the world. From a single Yiddish newspaper with a cir-culation of under 4,000 readers in 1887, the Yiddish press in New York grew by 1915 to five dailies with a circulation of more than 500,000 readers. These newspapers were a major avenue for the dissemination of fiction, poetry, essays and criticism. The press published the work of most of the important writers, and also provided them with earnings as journalists and editors. This gave most writers a forum in which to ex-pound their opinions on a variety of subjects ranging from culture to Jewish history, literature, politics and world events.

However, the Yiddish newspapers provided limited opportunities for female writers. Even the "women's pages" were often filled with arti-cles by male writers masquerading under female pseudonyms. The women journalists were almost never assigned to report on economic or political matters, but were invariably consigned to the women's pages where they wrote about fashion, home decor and child rearing. Many of them, including Margolin, resented this restriction. In addition to her weekly column, Margolin wrote fiction and essays under her real name and under various pen names. She wrote with such style and flair that she soon came to the attention of the major Yiddish and Hebrew writers, many of whom refused to believe that her articles were written by a woman.

Margolin and other Yiddish women journalists did enjoy a measure of popularity. Perhaps their writing relieved the monotony of the crises and gloomy predictions that blazed from newspaper headlines. More likely, they served a useful marketing function for the variety of goods and services advertised in the women's pages. In any case, although women writers found an audience, their remuneration was less than what men received, they were not given editorial responsibilities to the same degree, and their work did not appear as frequently as did that of their male colleagues. The few women who held positions of influence were all too often the wives and lovers of the editors, publishers and writers. When these relationships broke up, the women frequently lost their positions at the newspaper, regardless of their journalistic or literary abilities.[1]

Margolin acknowledged the influence of other women's writing in a letter to her long-time companion, the Yiddish poet, Reuven Ayzland:

> If I have borrowed from anyone, it was not from men, never, only from women. And if my own work shows signs of other minds, other hearts — these are the minds and hearts of women I have encountered. I never forget them. They are always in my thoughts.[2]

When Rosa Lebensboym began publishing poetry, she took the name Anna Margolin; this was the name she used for the rest of her life. Her poetic debut occurred in the literary journal, *Di naye velt* [The New World], in 1920. Subsequently, her poems appeared in various publications.

It was in the summer of 1919 that Ayzland had come into her life. While she was still living with her second husband, journalist and psychiatrist Hirsh Leyb Gordon, in New Haven, Connecticut, it was Ayzland who kept her informed about how her poems were being received in the New York cafés where the Yiddish literary intelligentsia gathered:

> Last night, Anna Margolin was the main topic among the literati.
> A thousand hypotheses were offered about who might be hiding

behind the name, and the general opinion is that it must certainly be a man.[3]

Later, he wrote her again:

> Why people want Anna Margolin to be a man is beyond me. The general opinion, however, is that these poems are written by an experienced hand. And a woman can't write like that.[4]

Since her return to the USA, Margolin had had several romantic liaisons, including marriage to Gordon. Reuven Ayzland was also married. Ayzland's memoir claims that Margolin's threats of suicide forced him into a bitter divorce. His children became permanently estranged from him, and when he died they destroyed his papers. Whether he and Margolin actually married is not clear, but they lived together for more than thirty years.

In 1929, a collection of Margolin's poetry entitled *Lider* [Poems] was published in New York City. Outside of New York, Anna Margolin's book was well received. In Warsaw, leading writers discussed her with great admiration, and lectures were held to read and study her work. Such well-known writers as Bialik and Moishe Nadir praised her work. However, the reception in New York was lukewarm, and the book did not achieve the wide readership Margolin had hoped for.

In the early twentieth century, when Margolin began her career, Yiddish did not yet possess much of a literary tradition. Up to that point, Jewish culture and literature were focused primarily on study of the Bible and the Talmud in the original Hebrew and Aramaic texts. This was essentially a male activity.

Yiddish was the spoken language of everyday life and Yiddish literature consisted mainly of folk tales and religious tracts written for uneducated men, and for women and children. Yiddish made the leap from rather unsophisticated narratives and prayers to a modern literature without any transitional stages. This leap was inspired by the *Haskalah* [Jewish Enlightenment], and spurred on by the emergence of modern secular Hebrew literature in the nineteenth century. Two of the earliest modern Yiddish writers, Mendele Mokher Sforim and Sholem Aleichem, began their literary careers writing in Hebrew, but soon switched to Yiddish because it had a popular base. Yiddish literature was part of the ferment in Jewish life in Eastern Europe in which Jews were emerging from passive acceptance of tradition into more active roles in education, politics and religion. This change, and the accompanying social turmoil, was reflected in Yiddish literature. In one generation, Yiddish blossomed forth with the whole range of modern literature — novels, short stories, poetry, essays and journalism.

While Yiddish was the spoken language at home and on the streets, early Yiddish writers could acquire no formal education because Yiddish language schools did not emerge until after the First World War. Few Yiddish dictionaries and grammars were available, and there were hardly any literary models from earlier generations to guide them, or provide paths from which to depart. These first Yiddish writers, both men and women, were in effect literary orphans; they had to supplement such education as they had by their reading in other languages. Their style was heavily influenced by European Romantic and classical poetry, Russian Symbolism, German Expressionism and post-Expressionism. The lack of any literary tradition in modern Yiddish poetry as well as the experiments in foreign poetic forms may very well have been a liberating force.

Margolin wrote at a time when most Yiddish poets belonged either to *di yunge* [The Younger Generation], or to the *inzikhistn* [the Introspectivists]. *Di yunge* were a group of rebellious young poets who sought to transcend nationalistic and political themes and were influenced by aesthetics, symbolism and expressionism; the *inzikhistn* were influenced by psychoanalytic theory, and went in for experimentation with form and theme. Sometimes, the work of these groups was in harmony with mainstream poetic trends; sometimes they clashed. Margolin was well known in both circles and to some extent influenced by them, but chose to remain an outsider. In spite of her relationship with Reuven Ayzland, who was the leading theoretician of *di yunge*, Margolin held herself at a distance: "I am not a child of The Younger Generation, not a grandchild nor even a [literary] comrade. I was not a student at their school."[5] Few women published in Yiddish prior to the First World War, but afterwards there was a sudden outburst of literary activity by women writing in Yiddish in Kiev, Lodz, New York and other centres. Poetry was the leading genre in literary experimentation in Yiddish writing, particularly in New York, and women fit easily into this trend.

Margolin was well read in contemporary French, German, Hebrew,

Polish, Russian and English poetry. Enamoured of the poet Lorca, she undertook to learn Spanish. She was knowledgeable about the major literary trends, and was a formidable critic. She was influenced by Baudelaire, Verlaine and Rimbaud, among the French; Else Lasker-Schüler and Rainer Maria Rilke, among the Germans; and among the Yiddish poets, Itsik Manger and Avrom Sutzkever.

Dissatisfied with the major Yiddish journals for their neglect of serious poetry, Margolin privately published a Yiddish anthology titled *The Yiddish Poem in America* in 1923. The only woman she included was Celia Dropkin, perhaps because they shared similar concerns.

Restless and dislocated, Margolin was profoundly at odds with the world in which she found herself. She describes her poetic mission in the first epitaph she wrote:

> Say that until her death
> she faithfully protected
> with her bare hands
> the flame entrusted to her
>
> and in that same fire
> she burned.

This is the essence of her brief but creative career, and is central to Margolin's metaphysical dilemma. She suffered the plight of many creative artists who stick to their truths whatever the consequences.

The opening poem of *Lider*, "Once I was a Youth," assumes the voice of the unfettered male hero. Here she depicts herself as a young man in pagan Greece, ancient Egypt and Christian Rome. By so doing, she asserts that she will not be circumscribed by the rigid confines into which women have been cast. Perhaps she felt that only in a male voice dare she propose such transgressive acts.

ONCE I WAS A YOUTH

> Once I was a youth,
> heard Socrates in the porticoes,
> my bosom friend, my lover,
> in all Athens had the finest torso.
>
> Was Caesar and a bright world

built of marble. I the last,
chose for a bride
my proud sister.

Garlanded and drunk till late
in boisterous revelry I heard the news
about the weakling from Nazareth
and wild stories about the Jews.

What is radical in Margolin's conception of gender is her sense that both masculine and feminine attributes are available to the artist, that both men and women have dual natures constantly torn between the demands of intellect and logic on one hand, and emotion and passion on the other.

In re-imagining the confrontation between paganism and Judaism, Margolin evokes through her compressed images the clash of world views and opposing cultures, her voice intense and compelling. It is an irony of history, and of this poem, that it is a member of the presumably weaker, "wild" civilization who should survive to bear witness to this vanished world.[6]

In "My Ancestors Speak," Margolin reconstructs the generations of her own family and offers it as an encapsulated history of the Eastern European and immigrant North American Jewish family. Here we see the distancing from traditional values which the modern period exacted.

MY ANCESTORS SPEAK

My ancestors:
Men in satin and velvet
faces long and silky pale,
faintly glowing lips
and thin hands caressing faded folios.
Deep into the night they speak with God.

Merchants from Leipzig and Danzig
with clean cuffs, smoking fine cigars.
Talmudic wit. German niceties.
Their look is clever and lacklustre,

clever and self-satisfied.
Don Juans, dealers and seekers of God.

A drunkard,
a pair of converts in Kiev.

My ancestors:
Women bejewelled in diamonds like icons,
darkly crimsoned by Turkish shawls,
and heavy folds of Satin-de-Lyon.

But their bodies are weeping willows,
the fingers in their laps like withered flowers,
and in their faded, veiled eyes
lifeless joy.

Grand ladies in calico and linen,
broad-boned, strong and agile,
with their contemptuous, easy laughter,

with calm talk and uneasy silence.
At dusk, by the window of a humble house
they sprout like statues.
And coursing through their dusky eyes
cruel joy.

And a pair
I am ashamed of.

All of them, my ancestors,
blood of my blood,
flame of my flame,
dead and living mixed together,
sad, grotesque, immense.

They tramp through me as through a dark house.
Tramping with prayers and curses and wailing,
vibrating my heart like a copper bell,
my tongue shakes,
I don't recognize my own voice —
My ancestors speak.

Where most of the poetry of the 1920s written in Yiddish was conventional in its use of rhyme and observed the linguistic proprieties, Margolin, along with other Yiddish women writers, experimented with free verse, with incongruous and jarring juxtapositions of diction and sound. Her fierce, individualistic expressiveness was not at all concerned with the literary niceties. She boldly included in her poetry exotic imagery and erotic subject matter, including the then taboo subject of lesbianism. "My poems are not just mumblings, aromas, spiderwebs. A large part of them are texture — massive, rhythmic, broad; and the context — dramatic."[7] The literary climate of the 1920s in both American and European poetry was receptive to such innovation.

In "Odessa," Margolin evokes this beloved city in vivid images:

And can you remember
everything which has no name
is only a fragrance, a mystery?
And the breath of the steppe,
of the sun, of the tar?
The city lowered,
as if by a cord of silk,
down a thousand marble steps
into the singing sea.

Margolin's writing is imbued with ambiguity and discordance; often it is a construct of broken pieces. Many of her poems start out with comforting visions of home and belonging but are soon undercut by bizarre images of displacement and dislocation. The darkness is scrutinized, ominous powers are exposed, and incomprehensible forces challenged. One of the overriding concerns of Margolin's poetry is to undermine the established categories of the world she describes.

Restless and observant, Margolin's poems reflect the powerful tensions in the relationship between the sexes. She rejects the "feminine" voice traditionally assigned to women — coy, girlish, full of erotic yearnings, religious humility, sexual modesty and sentimental motherhood. Instead, she tells of disappointment, inadequacy and conflicted yearnings.

FULL OF NIGHT AND WEEPING

A silence, sudden and deep
between us,
like a bewildering letter
that announces a parting.
Like a ship going down.

A silence, without a glance, without a stir,
full of night and weeping
between us,
as if we ourselves
had bolted the door
to a Garden of Eden.

Margolin calls attention to the ways in which romantic love depends on coercion and loss of self-respect.

Among Margolin's strongest poems are those that reflect her yearning for the presence of God in the universe, that express her defiance of the impersonal, implacable and indifferent cosmos which she is determined to penetrate:

. I will shrug these still beautiful shoulders,
will, perhaps, still force these trembling lips
to smile, and will succeed.
Smiling and breathless
I exhale the weak smoke of my last cigarette
to the enormous iron mask of the heavens.

Anna Margolin was only too aware of the contradictions between her worldly pursuits and her religious faith. In one of her letters, she states: "But I haven't ever been able to be secular even though when I was very young I was a flaming anarchist. I have always talked to God and in times of sorrow, I admit I have given God hell."[8] Fiercely individualistic, volatile of temperament, Margolin lived a tempestuous, unconventional life. This complex individual threw herself into both intellectual pursuits and romantic attachments with great passion and had a succession of lovers, beyond her two marriages. Margolin's poetry gave voice to the powerful fissures in her life and in her times. Her writing focused on the conflicts resulting from her intellectual and spiritual yearnings for fulfillment as a human being, a woman and a creative artist; from sexual tensions; and from the distancing from traditional Jewish values which the modern period exacted. We can only surmise the effect that her separation from her child had on her writing.

After the publication of *Lider* in 1929, Anna Margolin increasingly isolated herself from the company of friends and colleagues. She ceased writing poetry altogether in 1932. Isolated, ultimately unable to withstand the storms raging within her, a virtual recluse, she suffered from depression, obesity, high blood pressure and other ailments until her death in 1952 at age sixty-five. Margolin was so intent on safeguarding the quality of her work that she insisted that her unpublished work be destroyed upon her death. Ayzland complied with her instructions.

Margolin's second and last epitaph was published in *Der tog* in 1932. At her request, this poem, minus the first two lines, is chiseled on her gravestone:

> She of the cold marble breasts
> and the slender light hands —
> She squandered her beauty
> on rubbish, on nothing.
>
> Perhaps she wanted it so, perhaps lusted after it:
> the unhappiness, the seven knives of anguish,
> to spill life's holy wine
> on rubbish, on nothing.
>
> Now, she lies with shattered face.
> Her ravaged spirit has abandoned its cage.
> Passer-by, have pity, be silent —
> Say nothing.

It is difficult to imagine the utter despair, the guilt, the isolation and the self-contempt which prompted Anna Margolin to pen these lines. However much her difficulties overwhelmed her daily life, in the realm of poetry Margolin showed the strength to preserve her own unique vision. In one of her last poems, she states her artistic credo:

DRUNK FROM THE BITTER TRUTH

The dark and the heavy — I take them.
Come strike and wound, wild anguish.
Drunk from the bitter truth,
I refuse all other wine.

The dark, the heavy, the used-up
shame me day in, day out;
I will burn it, bleed it, blaze them forth,
and transform them into the most refined glow.

From the dark, the heavy and the hard,
as if in service to a higher command,
I build illuminated steps to the sought-after,
dreaming and radiant God.

Anna Margolin's growing reputation rests on her one slim volume of poetry. Although she was neglected by male critics who dismissed her as a "woman writer," and her reputation suffered during the general decline of interest in Yiddish writing, now, after more than half a century of obscurity, her work has been rediscovered. A new generation of feminist scholars — Adrienne Cooper, Marcia Falk, Kathryn Hellerstein, Norma Fain Pratt, Sheva Zucker and others — are reappraising Margolin's achievement. Her poetry is once again available in a new Yiddish edition. Anna Margolin's poetry remains remarkably fresh and contemporary; her language original and personal; and her themes of anxiety, loneliness and search for identity and meaning speak to us across the generations with perhaps even greater relevance today than they did in her life time.

ALL TRANSLATIONS FROM THE YIDDISH BY SHIRLEY KUMOVE.

NOTES

1. Norma Fain Pratt, "Culture and Radical Politics: Yiddish Women Writers 1890–1940," *Female, Feminine and Feminist Images*, 131–152.
2. Reuven Ayzland, *Fun undzer friling* [From our springtime] (New York, 1954).
3. Ibid.
4. Ibid.
5. Ibid.
6. Sheva Zucker, *Ana Margolin un di poesye funem geshpoltenem ikh* [Anna Margolin and the poetry of the divided identity] (New York: YIVO Bleter, 1991).
7. Ayzland, ibid.
8. Norma Fain Pratt, *Anna Margolin*, video.

WOMEN'S ROLES IN JUDEO-SPANISH SEPHARDIC SONG

⊂⊛⊃

Judith R. Cohen

Sephardic Jews represent somewhere between 3 and 15 per cent of North American Jews; until recently, it has been too easy to overlook the rich traditions that originate from this segment of the Jewish population. Ethnomusicologist and performer Judith Cohen has spent many years exploring the musical tradition of Jewish women from Spain, Portugal, Turkey, the Balkans, the Middle East and North Africa — all part of the Sephardic diaspora. Cohen's work has brought attention to the rich cultural, social and religious experience and traditions of these women. For those who have been lucky enough to hear her perform her Judeo–Spanish repertoire, Cohen has also given us the gift of their song.

FOR MANY SCHOLARS, the main interest of Judeo–Spanish songs has been their historical and linguistic links to medieval Spanish literature. For many performers, Judeo–Spanish song has been a way to explore other aspects of their own heritage: their Jewish heritage for some, their

Hispanic heritage for others. As an Ashkenazic Canadian-born woman, my own interest in Judeo–Spanish songs developed almost accidentally: it grew out of my work in medieval Spanish music on the one hand, and on the other, from my travels in Spain, Turkey, the Balkans and Morocco. These places were, of course, all part of the Sephardic diaspora, though at the time, just after finishing my undergraduate work, I was not at all aware of this; in fact, I didn't even know who the Sephardim were.

After completing my MA thesis on women musicians in medieval Iberia's three cultures — Christian, Muslim and Jewish — I began to wonder about the music of the descendants of these medieval Spanish Jewish women, and realized that the musical, linguistic and historical backgrounds of all my travelling would form an ideal base for learning about this music. As a musician performing Balkan, French–Canadian, medieval and Yiddish songs, I was also eager to learn to sing the Judeo–Spanish repertoire, in the traditional singing styles of its various host cultures. As time went on, I also began to work on the relationships between Judeo–Spanish and pan-European balladry, again both as a performer and as a scholar. In 1996, I also began work on the musical traditions of the Jews who remained in the Peninsula as "New Christians," particularly in Portugal, in the mountain villages along the Spanish border.[1]

I will begin with an overview of the different genres of Judeo–Spanish songs and the role that they have played in women's lives, and then discuss some of the main changes which have taken place in the twentieth century, especially its last few decades. Women have continued to play the central role in the tradition, if not in the old context of direct transmission of songs from generation to generation, then in other ways, as performers, consultants and scholars. As the tradition becomes more and more removed from daily life, whether they will continue to play such a central role remains to be seen.

In the Sephardic diaspora, it has been women who have been the main singers and transmitters of Judeo–Spanish songs. Whatever languages the men had to speak in order to carry on with their professional lives, the women, whose lives in the Middle East and North Africa generally centred in the home, continued speaking Judeo–Spanish both to each other and to their children. "Judeo–Spanish" is merely a convenient umbrella term. The term "Ladino" refers to the language which resulted when the men translated Hebrew prayers and other religious texts into Judeo–Spanish for the women word for word, without regard to syntax. The day-to-day versions of Judeo–Spanish went by various names: *spaniol* [Spanish], *djidio* [Jewish], *djudezmo*, sometimes *ladino* and, in Morocco, *haketia*. Throughout these developments, this language, with its regional variants, was the main one women not only spoke but sang as well.

The origins of some of these songs can be traced back to before the Expulsion of 1492, when Jews still shared life in Spain with Christians and Muslims. Other songs of the Sephardim left Spain in later centuries, sometimes with Jews who left the country as New Christians and reclaimed their Jewish identity in safer havens. Still others were translated or adapted from songs of the various diaspora cultures, or were newly composed. The legacy of old Spain is found in some of the ballad tales, certain wedding song texts and especially in the language. Even when the songs are newly composed, the language has its roots in those of medieval Spain: Castillian, Portuguese, Galician–Portuguese and Catalan.

As the centuries rolled on, the language and the songs changed. Regional variants of the language became more settled; they had already adopted vocabulary and expressions from Hebrew, and now added more from local languages: Greek, Turkish, Slavic languages, Arabic. Later on, words from French and Italian crept in as well. Religious songs often mixed Hebrew and Judeo–Spanish in the same song. The song repertoire also developed and grew; melodies were adapted from local songs, ballad stories were translated into Judeo–Spanish. New songs reflected the new milieus — North Africa and the former Ottoman Empire. All along, women learned new songs, but kept on singing many of the old songs with their stories of medieval kings and queens, medieval battles, heroic and wicked characters larger than life. The melodies changed, and the Sephardim also learned new melodies wherever they lived. These ballad melodies were in turn "recycled" by men for use with Hebrew sacred hymns, a process documented from the sixteenth century on.[2]

Judeo–Spanish song is commonly classified according to the following genres: narrative ballads, or *romances* (pronounced ro-MAHN-ses), songs for the life cycle and calendar cycle, lyric love songs and recreational/topical songs. Until recently scholars concentrated on *romances* and, to a lesser extent, life and calendar cycle songs. These songs were available mostly on archival or documentary recordings, while most of the recordings made for the general public were of lyric songs. Thus there was a discrepancy between what was most studied and valued by academia and what was best known and enjoyed by a general audience. This also meant that the genres most closely associated with women — the *romances* and life cycle songs — were least familiar to the public. As well, the lyric songs are almost entirely from the area of the former Ottoman Empire, not from Morocco; Judeo–Spanish Moroccan songs were rarely heard on commercial recordings or in concert.

ROMANCES

The stories told, or rather sung, in the *romances* come from different epochs. Many go back to chronicles of early medieval Europe, or even further back, to stories traceable to the Thousand and One Nights. Some recount incidents of famous battles, or episodes in the lives of famous people — real, fictitious or a combination. Other *romances* were composed later on, at times coming into oral tradition from "broadside ballads," a form of inexpensive, often illustrated, publication sold by ballad-mongers which began in the sixteenth century and continued right through the early decades of the twentieth century. Some are translations or adaptations from forms such as the Greek *tragoudia* [literally "table song"; narrative ballad]. In many cases, Sephardim continue to sing *romances* that are no longer, or only very rarely, sung in Spain or Portugal; in other cases, the same ballad is still sung among Moroccan or Turkish Sephardim and on the Iberian Peninsula as well. The melodies, however, change; the same words, or very similar versions, will have very different tunes in their Moroccan or ex-Ottoman versions. Even when the song texts are old, the music is not that of medieval or, by and large, even renaissance Spain.

Most of the stories in the ballads are not specifically Jewish, though there are a number of ballads about Old Testament themes such as the judgement of Solomon, or the sacrifice of Isaac. The songs recount historical events, illustrate Christian–Muslim relations during the Christian "reconquest" of Spain from the "Moors," tell of betrayal, loyalty, seduction, heroism, murder, poisoning, adventures and wild coincidences. Full of taut action and pithy dialogue, the *romancero* [corpus of *romances*] seems an inexhaustible source of good stories, which in the days before television, radio and easily available books (to say nothing of the Internet) were a major source of entertainment, instruction and communication. Sometimes women altered the words, omitting references to Christianity, or changing violent endings to more accommodating ones; at other times they kept these references intact. One Moroccan woman I recorded in Montreal sang a tale of royal adultery on the part of a queen whose husband then cuts off her tongue, and chuckled almost gleefully at the ending. Women often comment on the songs after singing them, discussing the doings of sixth century Merovingian nobility or tenth century Spanish warriors' wives as if they were characters in a soap opera.

The *romances* are usually long, and the melody is repeated throughout. They are often sung in a fairly slow tempo, and in the former Ottoman Empire areas especially, may be performed with complex vocal ornaments and without a strict rhythm. There is usually no instrumental accompaniment, as women most often sang them at home, with their hands otherwise occupied, as they went through their long series of domestic tasks, alone or together with relatives. Young girls would sing them as they prepared their trousseaus, or, in Morocco, took turns on the *matesha*, the swing set up in the courtyard for pleasant spring evenings. Women sang as they rocked the cradle, and their children grew up with the stories of a long-lost Iberian world.

Today it is possible, but increasingly rare, to find women who still sing *romances*. On commercially available recordings of Judeo–Spanish songs, when *romances* are included, they are generally shortened, and instrumentation is almost always added, in deference to audiences no longer used to long story-songs, especially a cappella — and especially when they rarely understand the language. Few singers know how to perform the vocal ornaments, and fewer still, for the Ottoman ballads, can sing in the *maqam* system of subtle microtones.[3] Few, in fact, care to memorize the long texts which only a minority of listeners will understand. When men sing the *romances*, they generally know only the first few stanzas from having heard their women relatives sing them, and often from using the melodies for Hebrew texts. In Canada, the Moroccan Judeo–Spanish group Gerineldo (of which I am the "token Ashkenazi") has produced several recordings of Judeo–Spanish songs. These recordings included many *romances* drawn from documentary recordings which we made through our own field work, and which we sing in traditional style.[4]

Life Cycle Songs: Songs for Birth, Courtship, Marriage, Death

Like the *romances*, these are primarily a women's repertoire. Wedding songs (*cantares* or *canticas de boda*) are by far the most numerous of the life cycle songs. Each stage of the wedding had its own activities and each activity had its own songs; for example, "I'm showing you my new trousseau, mother-in-law and sister-in-law — there's nothing you can say I've left out!" or "The bride has come forth from the sea," a metaphor for the ritual bath, the *mikve*. Other themes include the mother's advice to the bride, or the bride's reflections on the life she is leaving and the new one awaiting her; sometimes there is frankly erotic imagery ("the bride lets down her hair, and the groom faints ... clouds move across the sky and wet the groom ..."). Wedding songs often borrowed rhythmic patterns from the host cultures, Moroccan or Turkish; in some cases, *romances* were adapted for the wedding context. Some women specialized in wedding songs, and formed semi-professional societies to sing for weddings and other joyful events, accompanying themselves on tambourines and other frame-drums. There is no one specific dance form; women from different areas of Morocco or the east danced at weddings in the basic style of the area.

There are fewer songs for birth, of which one is the well-known "Birth of Abraham" ("*Cuando el Rey Nimrod ...*"). One birth song, sung in Turkey and Salonica, includes lines describing the midwife calling out encouragingly to the woman in labour; this suggests the possibility of a woman composer. In any case, it was mostly women who sang these songs, as well as the laments, *endechas*, sung for the dead or on Tisha b'Av [commemoration of the destruction of the second temple]. *Endechas* are difficult to record, as most of the few women who still know them will not risk bad luck by singing them on an inappropriate occasion, and will not permit recording when it *is* the appropriate day to sing them.

CALENDAR CYCLE AND OTHER
PARA-LITURGICAL SONGS (*COPLAS*)

This repertoire is shared by men and women. It includes songs for Shabbat and the yearly cycle of holidays, as well as songs on religious themes not associated with any particular day. It also includes songs associated with venerated rabbis, and a few sung prayers in Judeo–Spanish. An important part of this group of songs are the Purim songs, *coplas de Purim*. Several of these songs are sung in a mixture of Hebrew and Judeo–Spanish. Outside the synagogue, and if it is not an actual holiday, men may accompany these songs on traditional local instruments such as the Middle Eastern lute (oud) or plucked or hammered dulcimer (kanun, santur). Moroccan women often sing the story of Sol Hachuel, a teenage Jewish girl who was martyred in 1834 for refusing to convert to Islam and marry the local governor. I've recorded women in Montreal who are descendants of her family. The Sephardic equivalent of the *Purimshpil* flourished in early twentieth century Salonica, and included several songs composed for these operettas.

CANTICAS: LYRIC/LOVE SONGS,
RECREATIONAL AND TOPICAL SONGS

This is the repertoire most generally heard on commercially available recordings, and is mostly from the former Ottoman Empire area. It is here that women's role is less clear, as many of the recordings are of male singers, including the very earliest ones, from the early twentieth century. The songs' function is social rather than ceremonial or ritual, and their origin is more recent than the *romances* and many of the life and calendar cycle songs. They range from the most romantic, sometimes melancholy themes, through narratives of tragedies such as the Great Fire of Salonica (1917) or use biting social commentary. Rather ironically, these are the songs people often think of as hearkening back to pre-Expulsion Spain, simply because they usually haven't heard the oldest ballads and other song texts. The *canticas* may be sung unaccompanied, or with a variety of instruments; from the late nineteenth century on, for example, several women in the former Ottoman Empire areas learned the mandolin or a similar instrument.

The origins of these songs are diverse: nineteenth century Spanish compositions, popular urban songs from France, Greece or Turkey, Argentinean tangos, or the Charleston or foxtrot! In the 1920s in Salonica, song texts — often parodies — are attributed to Sadik el Gozos, Leon Botón and Yacob Yona, and the *cantadera* [semi-professional woman singer] Bona la Tanyedera is frequently mentioned. In Tel Aviv, I recorded a group of older Turkish and Rhodesli women who met weekly to sing together in Judeo–Spanish; they had used a well-known tune as the basis for their collective composition of a new song describing their group's activities, and sang it to open the meetings. It is unclear who created the adaptations of these tunes to Judeo–Spanish texts, though in some cases composers are identified.

CHANGES IN CONTEXTS AND TRANSMISSION

It's difficult to actually date changes, but particularly with the "new diaspora" of the twentieth century — the move from North Africa and the Middle East to the Americas, Western Europe and Israel — contexts and transmission of traditional songs have changed and continue to do so. The old model of oral transmission from mother to daughter, in the context of domestic tasks and social gatherings, has all but disappeared, along with the contexts themselves. Even this oral transmission, with the increase in literacy fostered by the schools of the Alliance Israélite Universelle (a French philanthropic society) from the late nineteenth century on, was supplemented in many cases by notebooks where women wrote down words to their favourite songs. Many of these notebooks have been preserved and are an invaluable source of texts, often in long, detailed versions.

Senior citizens' clubs have become a new venue for singing; I've recorded *romances* and wedding songs sung during bingo games. At these social gatherings, women may casually jot down words to songs for each other, or pass around letters from far-away friends who have written down song texts for them at their request. Another new source of transmission is what is often referred to as secondary orality: learning from recordings, often of popular Israeli singers such as Yehoram Gaon, so the songs are no longer sung in traditional style. Some women have found new roles coaching non-Sephardic performers in singing style and pronunciation, or actively searching their own memories to provide songs and information for ethnomusicologists like myself and, through us, for sound archives and documentary recordings.

Most professional performers of Judeo–Spanish songs are not themselves Sephardic. They are from a variety of backgrounds — Ashkenazic North Americans wanting to learn about other aspects of their Jewish heritage; Spaniards wanting to learn more about their country's Jewish history; Early music specialists wondering about the connections of Sephardic to early Iberian music. Israeli performers often have a mixed background which includes Sephardim, or may themselves be Sephardic but from families where the language and songs have disappeared for a generation or more. Many of the non-Sephardic artists — often women — have played a central role in bringing Judeo–Spanish song to a wider listening public, though not in traditional style, and often performing a very limited aspect of the repertoire, until recently mostly the lyric love songs. In the late twentieth century, several documentary recordings have become available, and performers have begun to work more from them, and from sound archives, often consulting ethnomusicologists. Two recent women performers from Israel are Ruth Yaakov and Esti Kanen Ofri, who have both worked seriously on learning the Balkan/Turkish Sephardic tradition.

The main performers from within the Moroccan tradition are the Canadian group Gerineldo previously mentioned. Esther Roffé in Caracas and Henriette Azen in Paris are the only other Moroccan performers I know of. Both women have recorded albums, in Azen's case totally a cappella. Roffé rarely performs abroad, and Azen's age and uncertain health make it difficult for her to work outside local community settings, though she continues to record and write about her family's repertoire. In the former Ottoman areas, the legendary Victoria Rosa Hazan was one of the early recording artists; she lived her last years in the Brooklyn Sephardic Home for the Aged, where she continued into her nineties to sing and to coach and advise younger performers. In Israel, Berta/Bienvenida Aguado (Turkey), Dora Gerassy (Bulgaria) and

Kobi Zarko (Salonica/Turkey) have performed and recorded songs from their family's traditions. Aguado in particular has been the model for a number of younger singers, as she is one of the last women to sing in the old highly ornamented, *maqam* style and is an accomplished, tireless, singer. Younger performers form the eastern Sephardic communities include the well-known Pasharos Sefardis ("Sephardic Songbirds") led by Karen Gerson. Flory Jagoda (Bosnia/Washington DC) is both a performer and composer; her songs are among the very few which have entered the repertoire, in many cases as traditional songs whose singers are unaware they are her compositions. Jagoda also keeps the chain of transmission going; her own adult children perform with her, and she has begun to teach songs to her grandchildren as well. More recently, story-teller Matilda Koen Serrano (Italy/Israel) has composed lyrics in Judeo–Spanish, set to music by Israeli composer Haim Tsur, in a light, popular style.[5]

SCHOLARSHIP AND JUDEO–SPANISH SONG

Academic studies of Judeo–Spanish song have changed considerably in the last two decades of the twentieth century from a focus on *romances* and strictly musicological and linguistic concerns to broader perspectives focusing on new contexts and repertoire, social circumstances and gender studies. There are only a handful of ethnomusicologists specializing in this tradition: they include the meticulous transcriptions and musicological analyses of pioneering scholar Israel Katz (USA); as well as Edwin Seroussi (Israel), Shoshana Weich-Shahaq (Israel), Ankica Petrovic (Bosnia), Miguel Sanchez (Spain), Pamela Dorn-Sezgin (USA), Nikolai Kaufman (Bulgaria) and Henrietta Yurchenco (USA), and my own studies (Canada). Seroussi has made important contributions, drawing on his knowledge of rabbinical responsa on women's singing and his research on early sources of melodies in Israel and Sephardic communities in Western Europe, as well as twentieth century song repertoires and styles. Weich-Shahaq has carried out the most extensive field recordings, and written widely on social and contextual aspects of Judeo–Spanish song, as well as its links with Spanish peninsular traditions; she has also played a crucial role in dissemination through documentary recordings and advising contemporary performers. My own work has included gender roles, social contexts and recordings. Recently, I have focused on Spanish festivals which attempt to "revive" a medieval Jewish past and on the Crypto–Jewish communities along the Spanish–Portuguese border. Much of the innovative academic writing on Judeo–Spanish song has been carried out by women. But academic studies are published mostly in academic journals — perhaps we need to take steps to see that our work and that of others appears in more broad-based and accessible venues.

To this general overview of women's role in Judeo–Spanish song, I would add that the Sephardic communities I have interviewed generally react quite positively to different performance styles, and to non-Sephardic performers, as long as the songs are treated with respect. Interestingly, many older women reacted more negatively to mispronounced texts than to innovations in vocal style or instrumentation. But, unfortunately, the future of this repertoire does not seem to lie in its traditional transmission. It is up to those of us who want to sing it to do so in the most honest ways available to us. Although recordings and printed sources can always be used as backups, and innovations are part of any tradition's development, I feel that doing something in a new way should be based on knowing something about the old way. Many cities have substantial Sephardic communities, and before it is too late, where at all possible, the best way to learn songs from any tradition is from the people who sing it and talk about it, as long as there are people left to do so.

⊂⊚⊃

SELECTED BIBLIOGRAPHY

Cohen, Judith. "*Ya salió de la mar*: Traditional Judeo–Spanish Wedding Songs." In Ellen Koskoff, ed., *Women and Music in Cross-Cultural Perspective*. Greenwood Press, 1987.

"Women's Role in Judeo–Spanish Song." In Maurie Sacks, ed., *Active Voices, Women in Jewish Culture*. University of Illinois, 1995.

"A Bosnian Sephardic Woman in Kahnewake, Quebec." *Canadian Woman Studies/les cahiers de la femme* 16/4, 1996.

"Sonography of Judeo–Spanish Song." *Jewish Folklore and Ethnology Review* 16/1–2, 1996.

Seroussi, Edwin. "The Growth of the Judeo–Spanish Song Repertory in the Twentieth Century." *Proceedings of the Tenth World Congress of Jewish Studies*, D2. Jerusalem, 1990.

"Sephardic Music: a Bibliographical Guide with a Checklist of Notated Sources." *Jewish Folklore and Ethnology Review* 15/2, 1993:56–61.

Weich-Shahak, Susana. "Sephardi Folk-Songs." forthcoming, *New Grove Dictionary of Music and Musicians* (new edition).

NOTES

1. Women were central in maintaining and transmitting prayers and rituals among the New Christians of Spain and Portugal. Even today, in Crypto–Jewish ("Marrano") communities in Portugal there are still women who maintain the traditions and perform wedding ceremonies, even though the "visible" wedding is carried out by a rabbi, a priest or the State. This was largely because of the need for secrecy over the centuries of the Inquisition under which public services or large gatherings were impossible. Gradually, secrecy became built into Crypto–Judaism, even when the danger was, at least officially, over. Today, these women tell me their daughters don't want to learn the long prayers and rituals, and, with the advent of rabbis, mostly Orthodox, and conversions to mainstream Judaism (also mostly Orthodox) this unique instance of women playing the central role in Jewish religious and ritual life is dying out.

2. While this process is documented and the names of many Judeo–Spanish ballads are given, their melodies are not notated, so we don't know what the actual music was.

3. *Maqam* is the complex melodic modal system used in Middle Eastern music, ordering both musical pitches (the "notes" of Western music's scales) and the melodic patterns associated with them. Microtones are intervals smaller than the

half-tone, which is the smallest interval which a piano can produce. They are an intrinsic part of the *maqam*, and are very difficult for those unaccustomed to it to identify and reproduce accurately.

4. Gerineldo was founded, and is directed by Dr. Oro Anahory-Librowicz, in Montreal, originally from Tetuan, Morocco. Other members are Solly Lévy (Tangier/Montreal), Kelly Sultan Amar (Melilla/Casablanca/Montreal) and myself (Montreal, grandparents from Lithuania); Moroccan–Israeli Charly Edry often joins us on violin.

5. This is not the place for a full discography; see my "Sonography" (1996).

DAUGHTERS OF
HOLOCAUST SURVIVORS:

SOME CENTRAL ISSUES

꧁꧂

Helena Feinstadt & Sandra Finkelman

Daughters of Holocaust survivors are different: different from sons of survivors, different from other children of immigrants and different from other Jewish daughters. Their roles as caretakers and transmitters of the past — culturally induced roles for all women — have been heightened because of their parents' war-time experiences. The heritage they have received from birth is inextricably linked with their sense of self, sense of responsibility, and commitment to remembrance. Daughters of survivors and therapists Helena Feinstadt and Sandra Finkelman discuss their experiences working with others like themselves, the direct heirs to a legacy that Jews have pledged never to forget.

AS A THERAPIST I had been working with survivors of various traumas. I began to wonder about my own history growing up with traumatized parents and how this related to my work. What did I have in common with other daughters of Holocaust survivors who were therapists?*

---

* In order to ensure anonymity and confidentiality, quotations are compilations.

In 1991, four of us — the authors as well as Zelda Abramson and Esther Kohn-Bentley — all daughters of Holocaust survivors and psychotherapists in private practice, began meeting biweekly to discuss our experiences as daughters of survivors, both personally and professionally. These discussions uncovered many similarities and areas of instant recognition and identification, but also many differences. Our parents' experiences before, during and after the war had all been different. These factors, in combination with differences in personality, would naturally result in differences in home environment and child-rearing practices, and would in turn have an impact on how we learned to view and cope with life.

One thing that began to stand out for us during these meetings was the difference we perceived in the impact on daughters versus sons of survivors. The burden of care-taking and responsibility seemed to be carried more by daughters. Given the gender learning that takes place while growing up and the natural tendency of girls to identify with their mothers and boys with their fathers, and given that it is socially more acceptable for women to focus on emotions and men on actions, it seemed to us possible that daughters tended to be more connected to their mother's fears and cautions, and sons to their father's "heroic" experiences of the Holocaust. Parents may give different messages to their daughters and sons about how to be in the world. It is difficult to separate out general gender differences from differences that are amplified or modified by our parents' Holocaust experiences.

After meeting together for a couple of years over tea and goodies, we found that we had benefitted immensely from our shared stories and experiences. As therapists, it became important for us to create a similar opportunity for other daughters of survivors to come together and share their experiences and so we began to develop workshops geared specifically for them. We were aware that mixed gender groups for children of survivors were already available, but felt that the quality of connection and sharing would be different in a group solely for women. A women-only group would provide a safe environment where women could speak openly and honestly.

In exploring the impact on our lives of growing up in a family of survivors, we need to recognize how difficult it is to separate out the contributing effects of a variety of influences: the Holocaust, our status as immigrants, our parents' personalities, being Jewish and being female. Our exploration does not separate out the impact of the Holocaust from these other influences.

THE PROCESS

In creating an opportunity for women to come together and share their experiences, it was also important to structure an experience that would facilitate maximum connection. We chose a variety of vehicles to achieve this: experiential exercises, writing exercises and small and large group sharing.

We would begin each workshop with the history that brought us together, asking a few questions which allowed us to see who we each are, our commonalties and our differences. Our goal in asking these questions was not to find answers but simply to identify points of connection. We explored this non-verbally, in a circle, stepping forward to indicate our position in response to questions asked: Who is herself a child survivor, child of survivors, grandchild of survivors? Whose parents are both survivors? One parent a survivor? In our workshop experience, mostly we were children of survivors, with one or both parents as survivors.

We also identified the group members according to the different ways a parent survived the war — in ghettos, in concentration camps, in hiding, passing as a non-Jew, in Russia, in the Resistance. Participants were asked to what degree stories were shared, and in what way. Was it the heroism of survival that was emphasized or the torture of victimization? Along the continuum of total silence, and hearing stories nonstop, where did each person's experience lie? We would have the women actually position themselves physically along an imaginary line with total silence at one end and nonstop stories at the other. We found that women positioned themselves fairly evenly along this continuum, reflecting the broad range of experience people had. "Hearing from the woman next to me that her parents recounted the war endlessly, as mine did, made me feel that my growing up was not that crazy."

We also asked participants to identify those who grew up not knowing that they were Jewish or that their parent(s) were survivors, but then found out later in life:

I suspect my father is a survivor. He will not talk about his life prior to coming to Canada at all. I know he spent some time in France after the war. I know he was born somewhere in Poland. The amount of silence, the amount of mystery surrounding his life makes me have this strong suspicion. He feels a stranger to me and I feel cut off from some strong element of who I am.

Whenever we touched on the point of having siblings or half-siblings that died during the war, the emotion of the moment was clearly profound for all present. We asked participants to consider whether this circumstance created a greater sense of loss, of being a replacement. We also discussed the special burden placed on the only child, or the eldest and the significance of birth order. "As an only child, I have always felt a huge burden of responsibility towards my parents. I felt that it was all up to me to make their lives okay. Now as they are ageing, I particularly feel the absence of a sibling with whom I could share the care-taking."

Some other areas we touched on in terms of identifying parallel experiences growing up were the language spoken in the home, and the degree of religious upbringing.

We would then move to the present to identify current commonalities, asking whether parents were still alive, whether our significant relationships tended to be with other children of survivors, other Jews, or with non-Jews. Each situation has its unique challenges. The discussion would also investigate Jewish identity and individual career choice. In terms of this last question, what quickly stood out was the high proportion of individuals working in some form of helping profession. Our traumatized parents had groomed us to learn to take care of them, thus developing in us antennae to help others. This early learning of empathy and compassion, coupled with a desire to make the world a place where such horrors would not be repeated made the choice of helping professions not surprising.

We felt that writing was a safe way to allow women who were new to exploring this topic and were new to the workshop environment, as well as those more experienced, to express themselves in privacy and containment. After having a chance for this personal reflection, women then had the opportunity to share these reflections with others. Some of the issues we addressed included what it meant to be Jewish; what impact being a "daughter" (of survivors) had on our being partnered or not; our feelings about our parents' ageing and mortality; the legacy of the Holocaust and its impact.

These questions allowed for lively discussion and sharing. For many women, this was the first opportunity to talk of these issues with other "daughters." Having one's own experience echoed was powerfully validating. Witnessing the intensity of interaction in discussing these different issues, it became clear to us that there was a need to explore some of these themes in greater depth. In longer workshops we chose to explore growing up in a family of survivors, relationships as adults with our parents, other relationships, Jewish identity and Holocaust legacy and taking care of ourselves.

GROWING UP IN A HOLOCAUST FAMILY

> I wasn't allowed to learn to ride a two-wheel bike. My mother was afraid that I might get hurt. I knew this was because I meant so much to her. Another loss could not be risked. I felt that I was being held back. I felt embarrassed around my friends. I finally learned to ride on the sly when I was twelve, but only got my own bike when I was seventeen.

While the specifics of survivor experiences varied widely, many common themes were present. Most women spoke of growing up with overly protective and fearful parents. Every life possibility was met with remonstrations: "what if," "be careful," etc. Taking risks, taking on challenges and new experiences was often discouraged; straying from the familiar and familial safety was seen as dangerous. This quality of over-protectiveness, however, tended to focus on the physical world and our physical well-being. Emotional protection was often seriously lacking. In this regard, it was often the child who was left with the responsibility of parenting the parent. Due to the horrific experiences many parents had as children, parents were unable to empathize with and relate to their children's problems. Often our problems were minimized and invalidated since they could never measure up to what our parents had been through.

The total picture, however, was not all negative. Many women spoke of having tremendous respect for their parents' courage and ability to begin and provide a new life for their families though they had often started from nothing and in unfamiliar surroundings.

> I often think about my parents coming to Canada with a child with very little money and no understanding of English. Within a short time they were in English classes, my brother was in school, and my father was working in a factory. Sometimes I am amazed at the life they created; they had friends, a nice home, a small store. My father became the manager of his factory. All this starting with nothing and knowing no one. They were role models for me for the possibility of creating my own life, relationships, learning, work and personal interests. I learned how to be strong, especially in the face of difficulty.

RELATIONSHIPS AS ADULTS WITH OUR PARENTS

> My parents were both in the hospital, each at a different hospital at opposite ends of the city. I found myself taking cabs from one to the other, compelled to be in two places at once. My two brothers who lived in the same city felt things were taken care of. They called me for occasional updates on our parents' health and I did not even find this strange.

Care-giving for elderly parents is one of the areas where gender difference seems to really stand out. Many women spoke of taking on the major responsibility of caring for ageing and ill parents. This is reinforced by familial expectations. Sons are often not expected to help, and exempt themselves from this responsibility. "I'm single and my father expects me to move in with my mother to take care of her after he passes away. He can't see that I have my own worthwhile life to live. Even so, I find myself sometimes thinking that I owe it to her."

Even as adults, the need to be approved of, and the need to meet with parental expectations continues to be a struggle. We need to examine how we can live our own lives and how we can balance our need to do what is right for ourselves with our need to be "good daughters." This dilemma is how to separate from our parents yet stay connected to them, how to live lives that reflect who we are, including ourselves as daughters. Many women spoke of wanting to make their parents' lives easier because of their horrific suffering. Yet we, too, can be overly protective of our parents. For example, many women spoke of not sharing their problems as a way of protecting their parents. Our incredible compassion for our parents and their suffering presents a huge challenge. The dilemma, again, is how to balance our need to express our compassion for them, yet take care of our own needs.

OTHER RELATIONSHIPS

> Having partnered with someone who is not Jewish, I was really looking forward to meeting other "daughters" in the same situation. How were they coping? Even though I have an excellent relationship, I feel like a traitor. I wanted to know whether others felt the same sense of guilt that I did.

We have wondered about the impact that growing up with the Holocaust has on our relationships. We wanted to examine whether our tendency in relationships has been to be with other children of survivors, other Jews or with non-Jews. We also wanted to look at whether we are drawn to other children of survivors because of the instant understanding we hope for; whether we relate only to Jews because of the legacy of the Holocaust. For those who choose non-Jewish partners, we wanted to determine whether they were plagued by a sense of guilt. For some of the women, these are incredibly pressing issues. The pain in resolving them, and the eagerness to connect with others who share these struggles, is very apparent.

Because of the typical desire not to disappoint our parents and to try to meet their expectations because of all they have been through, it is our sense that any deviation from marrying a nice Jewish man can be even more of an emotional challenge for daughters of survivors than for other Jewish women. Divorce, being single, being lesbian, partnering with a non-Jew or someone of colour, being a single parent by choice and so on also represent greater emotional challenges.

Many women spoke of growing up with other children of survivors. For them it was a shock to realize that not everyone grew up in families of survivors and not everyone was Jewish. We found that women's experiences in their choice of friends were varied and unique. Some spoke of having only Jewish friends. For some, it was only with other Jews that they felt safe and comfortable. For some, the message that you could only trust other Jews became the driving force in choosing friends. Others did not feel this need. In fact, some women spoke of rebelling from their legacy by associating primarily with non-Jews, especially in teenage and young adult life. This was a way to fit in with mainstream society, to be accepted, to be normal.

In partnerships, again experiences were varied. For example, some women would only consider a Jewish partner, while others were more interested in the individual; their being or not being Jewish was of little importance. We found this to be true in both heterosexual and lesbian relationships.

We wondered if, as "daughters," there were particular patterns of relating. What role do we take on? Are we the constant listener and caretaker? Do we tend to have a need to be in control and take charge? We found that there was a tendency to be nurturers and caretakers in our relationships; an extension of our role with our parents, as well as a culturally induced role as women.

JEWISH IDENTITY AND HOLOCAUST LEGACY

> As a daughter of Holocaust survivors, I feel that I should want to learn about Jewish liturgy, join a synagogue, be active in the Jewish community. I feel the importance of aspects of this, but I haven't found a way to integrate my feminism, my connection to Buddhist philosophy and my Judaism.

As daughters of Holocaust survivors, many women feel the need to find and express a Jewish identity. Finding this self-expression raises questions: How do I, as a feminist, identify as a Jew? How does being a daughter of Holocaust survivors inform my Jewish identity? Do I consider myself Jewish in a cultural, secular and/or religious sense? Where can I go, in community, to tap into and express my Jewishness? These questions present a particular challenge to women whose current Jewish identity deviates from that within which they were raised.

Many women spoke of the importance of their Jewish identity as a way of honouring the legacy of the Holocaust. This legacy carries, for some women, much bitterness as well as hope. One woman described this bitterness as "living with the Holocaust growing up, and now wanting to be free of it to have my life." Other women feel the Holocaust legacy motivates them to political action, in the form of fighting for the rights and freedoms of all people. Many women felt the need to preserve Yiddish language and culture, as well as to forge new roads into Jewish learning and expression. A common theme in this area was the importance of not forgetting and finding positive ways of educating others.

The third generation plays a special role in terms of legacy. For many this begins with the importance of having children. Many "daughters" feel a particular responsibility to have children, in order that the Holocaust legacy not die with their generation. For others the issue of what they teach their children about the Holocaust becomes crucial. How do "daughters" pass on the legacy without fear and burden? How can the legacy be passed on to provide the next generation with strength and determination of self?

TAKING CARE OF OURSELVES

> Every Sunday I feel pulled. I think about visiting my parents to give some relief to my mother, who is taking care of my father, who had a stroke. Yet Sunday is the one day I can really take for myself since I work the rest of the week. Most of the time I end up visiting them and convincing myself I can handle another week of no day for myself.

The issue of self-care is one of struggle and determination for many "daughters." As women we have been taught to care for the needs of others. This is often a felt strength and a way we connect to others. As daughters, partners, friends, wives and mothers, we can so easily take care of the other; yet we yearn so strongly to take care of ourselves. Although this is a theme felt by many women, we feel that daughters of survivors in particular are placed in the position of nurturer and emotional caretaker at a very early age. Given this training, learning to honour the need to take care of ourselves takes on a special significance and urgency.

For many of us, taking care of ourselves means becoming comfortable setting up boundaries between ourselves and our parents or others we feel bound to nurture. For many women, taking care of their own needs can make them feel that they are abandoning others. This goes back to the issue mentioned earlier of living our own lives. For many, taking care of our own needs means adopting a set of coping strategies which facilitate meeting these needs. Many women in the workshop spoke of the need to remind themselves of the entitlement to have their own lives. We constantly need to remind ourselves of our parents' strength and their abilities to survive. We must keep in mind that they will survive without our constant protection and care. Many women talked of the difficulty, as perpetual nurturers, to let themselves be taken care of by others.

What is very important to us as facilitators is to create a space for seeing possibilities for moving forward in one's life and honouring strength. We feel that the interactive format that we have created for "daughters" to speak and be heard allows for an empowering validation not only of one's experiences, but also of these possibilities and strengths.

RETURN TO POLAND:

IN SEARCH OF MY PARENTS' MEMORIES

༄

Sarah Silberstein Swartz

One of the touchstones we have for discovering our personal and family history is memory. We need to make sense of our own remembrances and the stories we hear from others in order to understand our relationship to the past and the present. This is an important part of the ongoing search for identity, as each individual seeks her own unique legacy. We need to know from where we came, before we can figure out where we belong. For children of Holocaust survivors, the search for memories is more complex and elusive. Sarah Silberstein Swartz travelled to Poland looking for her personal legacy — to the shtetl [village] where her parents spent their pre-war lives.

"Memory, even when it is so close to experience — or perhaps especially when it is that close — is multiple and contentious. The past depends on the angle from which it is seen and from which it has been lived."
— from Eva Hoffman, *Shtetl: The Life and Death of a Small Town and the World of Polish Jews*

TWO SETS OF MEMORIES

My father, Menachem Silberstein, tells his story (USA, c. 1969):

> It was May 5, 1945 when I was liberated from Mauthausen in Austria. I came back from over two years in concentration camp. Everyone was dead: my parents, my six brothers and sisters, my wife, my daughter and son — all my close family, killed by the Nazis.
>
> The war was over. Where should I go? I decided to return to Poland — first to Warsaw, and then to Vishogrod, not far from Warsaw, the Jewish town where I was born and raised, the town where my family and I lived until we were forced to flee to the Warsaw ghetto. In Warsaw, I went through the lists of Jewish survivors who had registered at the Jewish office; I looked for names of relatives and friends who had signed up that they were still alive. There were very few.
>
> In Vishogrod, I searched for what had been and was no more. All I had left were my memories. The town was empty; there were no more Jews. All our homes, our stores, our buildings were demolished, boarded up or occupied by Poles. The cemetery was deserted — deserted and desecrated; the Nazis had destroyed all the gravestones. Our beautiful old synagogue had been torn down to the ground by the Nazis a long time ago.
>
> When I went to look for what had been my home, I was stopped by a bunch of Polish hooligans. "You're back," they yelled. "Since Hitler didn't finish you, we will." They surrounded me, tied me up with rope and bound me to a drainpipe where they left me. It took me a long time to undo the rope. Shaken, I fled back to Warsaw. That was the last time I saw Vishogrod.

Mieczyslaw Biernat tells his story (Vishogrod, Poland, 1996):

> I remember your father, Menachem Silberstein, from before the war. He was a dapper young man, very well groomed and striking, very determined. He was older than me by about fifteen years. My family knew his family because we owned a bakery in Vishogrod. Silberstein and his family owned and ran the flour mill where we bought our grain. He was an important man in the

community, your father; he sat on the town council, one of several Jews.

When the Nazi soldiers came to Vishogrod in October 1939, things changed for all of us, but especially for the Jews. First, the Jewish homes were looted by the Nazis. Then the Jews in town were moved to a confined area, a ghetto. Next it was decreed that Jews wear yellow patches on the front and the back of their clothes. One day, a group of about thirty Jews who weren't wearing their patches were rounded up and brought to the courtyard of the Gestapo headquarters, where they were beaten. I could see them from the window of the bakery, which was next to their headquarters. Then the Nazis let everyone go — everyone but your father. They wanted to make an example of someone, someone whom everyone in the community knew and respected. They chose your father.

The Nazis stripped him down to his undershirt. They took a piece of rope and tied him to a drainpipe. It was a cold autumn evening and he stood there shivering, out on the street where everyone could see him. Hours later they took him down again. He was shaking, blue from the cold. I'll never forget it ...

Did both these events happen to my father? Or were they one and the same encounter? Who were the perpetrators — the Nazi soldiers or the Polish civilians? Did it happen during or after the war? And whose memory was more accurate? My reconstructed memory of my deceased father's story or that of Mieczyslaw Biernat, the Pole who still lived in Vishogrod fifty years after the war, steeped in his memories? The paradoxes in these two parallel stories were to haunt me throughout my journey to Poland.

The Legacy of Memory

Memory is complex; a selective, fragile and elusive process. A step or two removed from reality, it seems very real to the people doing the recalling, modified by their own lenses of personal experience, perspective and words. Memory shifts and is transformed with each telling — different for the listener than for the speaker. Add to this an exchange of stories, a change in context and setting, a major step away in time, barriers of language, of culture, of understanding — and the degrees away from the "truth" become even greater.

Along with their heart-breaking war-time experiences, my parents told me stories about their "normal" lives before the war, mostly about Vishogrod, the small Polish town where they both were born and grew up. Because they died when I was in my twenties — over twenty-five years ago — and because my environment is so different from theirs, it has been hard for me to recall these stories, even to believe that their experiences in a fairly peaceful pre-war Poland actually occurred. In my mind, the emphasis has always been on the horrors of their Holocaust experiences. Yet my deepest roots are based in their pre-war life. My ancestors came from this shtetl where Jewish life had existed since the thirteenth century. Had history been different, I might have been born in Vishogrod myself.

I have felt very vulnerable in my quest for family history. A child of survivors, I am imbued with the importance of not forgetting. Yet there are no photographs and few witnesses to my parents' stories. Their only living child — born after the war — I am the sole carrier of their stories to be transmitted to my children, their grandchildren, born after their deaths. The responsibility for this transmission has seemed onerous and at times impossible. How could I make real to my children a past that I myself have never experienced firsthand? With no photographs nor witnesses to guide me, how could I conjure up the faces of lost family members, the images of a rich Jewish life in pre-war Poland, the landscape of a picturesque small village that I had never seen with my own eyes? How could I remember things I had never experienced?

In my own life experience, I have never felt that I had roots in any one place. Mostly I identify as a diaspora Jew — a Jew from nowhere or, in my better moments and perhaps more accurately, from everywhere. A child of survivors, I have not yet found a place where I belong — not in Germany, where I was born, nor in the USA, where I grew up, nor in Canada, which has been my home for the past thirty years. As an only child with few blood relations, I have had to form a new family — with chosen friends, with my own two daughters. Now I long for something from the past.

I am in search of my parents' memories — stories which I heard throughout my childhood, some of which I have perhaps myself embellished. I want to connect with my eyes to a place which will give me roots, just as my ears connect with the strains of the Yiddish language and the melodies of Yiddish folksongs. These are my links not only to an extinguished world, but to my own childhood home. I want a connection with the past, even though all the players are dead. A half-century old, I am still looking to belong.

EXPERIENCING POLAND

I had daydreamed about travelling to Poland for a long time. I even thought of a trip to Poland as a "return," which was absurd, since I had never set foot in Eastern Europe. Armed with information that I had been collecting for months from the small network of *landslayt* [people from the same town or region], and from the Vishogrod memorial book my father had helped publish before his death, in the spring of 1996 I was ready to search out my roots.

Yet, as I sat in the plane to Warsaw looking at the emptiness below, I was overcome with my own hesitations. The decision to visit Poland had been a difficult one for me. I was afraid about what I might find, or perhaps even more afraid of what I might *not* find. My greatest fear was of finding nothing, of not relating at all to the people and the landscape, of feeling alienated. No ties, no connections to the world from which my parents came. Because of the Holocaust and the resurgence of Polish anti-Semitism after the war, there were few Jews left in Poland.

There are those Jews who refuse to dialogue with Poles because of our mutually painful pasts — Jews who will not travel to Poland, or, if they do, whose anger over events of the past cuts the fragile links of communication. Numerous survivors have told how they were betrayed by their Polish neighbours during the Holocaust. Many Poles, on the other hand, believe that they have been unfairly judged by the world. Both communities see themselves as victims of history.

Dialogue with individual Polish people was paramount to my experience, though I was well aware of the irony that all my links to the pre-Holocaust Jewish world were through Poles. Since the Jewish community no longer existed in the shtetls of Poland, the only source of information about my parents' generation was the gentile population.

I found it hard to believe that *all* Poles were anti-Semitic. To regard these people as the enemy would have been to cut off living access to my past. On this trip, I was committed to listen, to try to understand and not to prejudge.

When I arrived in Warsaw, I was amazed at its strange familiarity. Here was an entire city speaking the "secret" language my parents had used when they didn't want me to understand. As in childhood, though I couldn't understand individual words, I was able to comprehend the gist of conversations. Other childhood senses were also awakened. Eating in inexpensive student milk bars, I savoured food I remembered from my mother's kitchen: cold beet borscht with boiled eggs and radishes, mushroom-filled kreplach topped with fried onions, cucumber salad with dill in heavy cream.

Warsaw was my entry point, but my real destination was Vishogrod, seventy-two kilometres west of Warsaw, located on a hill above the Vistula River. The name "wyszogrod" means city on the heights; a castle had been built on this hill before the thirteenth century. In the fourteenth century, the castle was fortified with a high stone wall by Casimir the Great, Polish ruler and friend of the Jews. In 1364, he published a decree that gave Jews "freedom to trade, the right to import and export merchandise and to lend money." In the mid-eighteenth century, a large stone synagogue was built. Legend has it that the synagogue was built of stones from the ruins of Casimir's original wall, sold by the Prussians to the Jews of the town in 1798.

Before the Second World War, the town had a population of 6,000 inhabitants and 3,200 (approximately 800 families) were Jews. Most shops and businesses in town were run by Jews. On market days, Poles from the surrounding countryside came to the *rynek* [marketplace], where they exchanged their farm produce for wares sold by Jews. According to the memorial book, "there was an invisible, deep and absolute interdependence between Jews and gentiles, between the rich and the poor, workers and idlers, villagers and town dwellers." In the 1920s, eight out of twelve members of the town council were Jews. In the 1930s, the vice mayor was a Jew.

The Nazis invaded Vishogrod in 1939. The Jewish population was dispersed, some escaping to the Warsaw ghetto or further east to Russia, others deported to concentration camps. Few returned. In 1948, there were five or six Jews in Vishogrod. Today there are 3,000 citizens of Vishogrod, not one of them a Jew.

It was spring in Poland, as I rode through the countryside with Yarek, my driver and translator. The landscape was lush and green. My parents had often reminisced about the deep Polish forests with their tall, graceful evergreen trees and the expansive fields of wildflowers where families went on picnics during the day and young lovers went on se-cret rendezvous at night. They had described the walks along the *ste-genes*, the winding paths above the sandy banks of the Vistula, and across the old wooden bridge that connected the heart of Vishogrod with its small islands, where cattle grazed.

My father had come from a Hasidic family where his father, a fol-lower of the Ger *rebe* [religious leader, teacher] prayed and studied full time, while his mother ran the family hardware store and cared for their seven children. Menachem, the first-born son, began to work in the store at the age of twelve and soon rebelled against his father's religios-ity. As a teenager, he joined a group of young Zionists who met weekly at the town library. Marrying his first wife, Frida Kronenberg, the daughter of the wealthy Sini-Meier Kronenberg, was another form of rebellion. He joined his father-in-law in the family business — a flour mill erected in 1929 and owned by several partners — and became a merchant. I had heard countless stories about the mill, including the story of how some family members had used it as a hiding place from the Nazis before they escaped to the Warsaw ghetto.

The first place I sought out in Vishogrod was the mill; it was a physical affirmation of my family's past. I knew it was located on the way into town. After we passed the sign that read "Wyszogrod" on the main road, Yarek followed a short dusty dirt road towards a sprawling brick building. There, pulled up to the front door, were two large trucks being loaded with bags of flour. A modern sign on the building stated this was the Vishogrod mill. At the very top of the three-storey building chiselled into the bricks and showing the wear of time was the date of the building: 1929.

The owners of the mill, two brothers, greeted us. When our driver told them I was the daughter of the pre-war owners, they allowed me to wander through the building by myself. As I walked around the cavernous building, I paused and slid my fingers up and down the thick sandblasted wooden posts which separated the many bags of flour from the huge containers of unprocessed grain. The noise of the machinery mesmerized me, as I walked up the staircase to the highest point of the building. Through a tall window overlooking the town, I looked out in the sunlight, over the surrounding rooftops, over the countryside. The mill was in fine working condition — well taken care of, immaculate, esthetic. I picked up a handful of grain and put it into my pocket — a keepsake — and went back downstairs.

I can only speculate about the emotions that the appearance of a daughter of the former Jewish owners aroused in the current owners. However, Yarek reassured the two brothers that I was not here to re-claim the mill; I was only interested in my family's history. The owners replied with apparent equilibrium that if I wanted to take the mill back, they would understand. If they returned the property to me, they would be compensated by the government. They knew how I must be feeling; their own family had owned a large farm which had been con-fiscated by the government during the Communist era. Their empathy, where one might have expected hostility, was surprising. My own suspi-cions gradually subsided as the brothers spoke.

Through our translator, the brothers explained that after the war, the mill had been owned by the state. Run co-operatively, it had been neglected and unproductive. When the communist government fell, the brothers, who came from several generations of millers, had bought it and converted it from steam to electrical power, cleaned it up, ac-quired new equipment and began producing again. The owners invited us to their office for a midday break. There, we sat at a table and shared hot tea, vodka and ice cream. I imagined my father and his father-in-law in this same room discussing business many decades ago. I pulled out photos of my two daughters. One of our hosts said he too had two daughters. "We have that in common," I said. "That and the mill," he replied. We finished our ice cream, shook hands and wished each other good fortune.

With his first wife and two small children, my father had lived in a house adjoining that of his father-in-law. Made of brick, rather than wood, it was considered one of the more prestigious residential buildings in town. They had lived on Plotsk Street, but when we came to this street there were several brick buildings. We got out of the car and looked around; people returned our stares.

An elderly couple walked by. The man wore thick glasses and used a cane; the woman led him by the elbow. He was clearly blind. When the man heard us speaking in English, he stopped and asked in Polish if we were Jews. I was taken aback. Was this a hostile question? What business was it of his? Then I realized that given the size of the town, we were immediately recognizable as strangers. And given that few tourists come to Vishogrod, the logical assumption was that we were Jews.

"Yes," I replied. "Both my parents lived in Vishogrod before the war. My mother's name was Regina Zlotnik. My father was Menachem Silberstein. He lived on this street. Do you know their names?"

"Yes, I knew the Zlotniks. They lived across the street from us on Rembovska." Then he stopped for a moment. "I recall your father's name, too. He worked with his father-in-law, Kronenberg, who owned a flour mill. I knew them because my family owned a bakery and we bought our flour from their mill."

"I believe my father lived on this street with his wife and two children. Would you happen to know which house was his?"

"Yes, I know which house was his," and he gestured further down the street to a brick building with an enormous arched wooden door. "Silberstein and Kronenberg lived side by side in the two homes attached by the large wooden door. Now my brother and I live there. In fact, my wife and I live in the part of the building that was your father's home."

My heart raced as I built up the courage to ask whether we could visit. My overwhelming impulse was to see the inside of this house. We introduced ourselves. Mieczyslaw Biernat and his wife Sofia would be glad to invite us into their home. As we followed them, they told us that Sofia's mother had purchased their house in 1958 from a man named Stankiewicz, a Jew married to a Polish woman, who took her name and acted as an "agent" for many Jews when they decided not to return to Vishogrod after the war. The Biernats thought that my father had probably given this man his power-of-attorney to sell the house. My father had told me nothing about this. I knew that there were many swindlers after the war who acted as "agents" for Jewish properties. In any case, I decided not to pursue the matter further. I was too grateful for this serendipitous opportunity to see where my father and his family had lived.

It was a tidy little house, modest but well kept, three rooms plus a kitchen, heated by a tiled old-fashioned coal burning stove. The walls were adorned with crosses and pictures of Christ and the Madonna and with photographs of the Biernats in their younger years. It was very hard to imagine my father living here. From my father's stories, I had envisioned the house as rather grand. But no matter; I was very moved at being surrounded by the same walls which had embraced my father's first family.

We were invited to sit down at the dining room table and Biernat began to tell us stories about Vishogrod and my family. I wanted to show him the photos of my parents which I had brought with me to verify that we were talking about the same people. But, of course, he was blind. In contrast, his memory was very sharp. He painted his own vivid pictures of what life was like in Vishogrod before the war, mentioning minute aspects about Jewish rituals, celebrations and life cycle events. His keen interest in Jewish life seemed to stem as much from nostalgia as from a natural curiosity. And his commentary was both charming and knowledgeable.

On Friday afternoons, the poor Jews in town would ask for money at the Jewish shops and were given several *groshn* [coins] to buy fish for the Sabbath meal. Biernat was impressed by this expression of solidarity — something he felt didn't exist amongst the Poles.

Biernat recounted how on Friday nights after the first star appeared, the *shames* [beadle] would walk the streets and shout, "*Makh tsu di tir!*" [Close the doors for the Sabbath]. Sometimes he would shout, "*In shil aran!*" [Go to the synagogue]. Astonishingly, Biernat recited these phrases in perfect Yiddish, in the familiar dialect of my parents. "Do you speak Yiddish?" I asked in surprise. "No," Biernat answered, "we all spoke Polish in Vishogrod. But these are the words as I remember them spoken."

His natural curiosity as a youngster sometimes got him into trouble. Biernat described how gentile families would perform tasks forbidden to the Jewish families on the Sabbath. Just before the Sabbath, Jews would bring a huge pot to his family's bakery to be kept warm. He recalled one day opening the lid of the pot to look inside and almost getting his nose burnt on the steaming cholent, a traditional potato and carrot stew prepared before the Sabbath and left on the stove. As a child, he had seen a mezuzah [a parchment scroll containing a biblical text] on a neighbour's door frame and torn it off. He'd then pried it open and taken out the paper with Hebrew writing. A Jewish woman had seen his prank and had gone straight to his mother, who later gave him a spanking.

Biernat had been good friends with my mother's youngest brother, Leybl Zlotnik, who was the same age as he. They had played in the street together. When they were young it was hide-and-go-seek; when they were older, they were on competing soccer teams, the Jewish Maccabia team versus the Polish team. Their parents never allowed them to go to each others' homes because of their religious differences.

This seemed typical of what I understood of pre-war Jewish/Polish relations in Vishogrod: friendly in the street, separate in the home. I wondered whether this was at the core of Biernat's fascination with the Jewish community: it was all around him yet so inaccessible. How intrigued he must have been by what went on behind the doors of his friend's house, especially because it was forbidden.

Biernat then talked about the war. Leybl's sister, Ruzhka, he explained, had come to his family from the Warsaw ghetto in early 1943. Ruzhka had pleaded with his mother to hide her and two other family members. She had money and could pay them well. But his mother refused. Hiding Jews meant the death penalty for Poles. Instead she gave Ruzhka some bread and sent her away.

I had sat listening to Biernat's story but, perhaps because of the shock of the entire encounter, it took me several moments to realize that Ruzhka, this woman who had been turned away by Biernat's mother, was, in fact, my aunt Ruth. Ruth, who survived the war and who is still alive, and who to this day refuses to talk about the past. And the two relations whom she had been so desperate to save were none other than my own mother and Ruth's husband, my uncle Monyek. I knew the three were in hiding together for most of the war. My mother had the financial resources, gold coins sewn into the lining of her dress, and my aunt had the bravery to seek the hiding places.

How many neighbours, gentile friends, had my aunt had to approach before she found a safe refuge? I couldn't help feeling embittered on her behalf. It was a terrible risk for a Polish family to take in a Jew. But they, unlike my family and other Jews, had the opportunity to exercise some choice over their fate. Surely Biernat must feel some guilt over this incident, even though he had been a young man at the time.

Absorbed in my own emotions, it took me, again, some time to note that Biernat was repeating the story in an uncharacteristically agitated manner. I realized that he did not know the outcome of the tale — whether Ruzhka and the other two had lived or died. "Ruzhka lived through the war and so did the other two people — my mother and my uncle," I blurted out.

"They all survived?" Biernat asked, his face suddenly ashen. How often in the last fifty years had he wondered about the destiny of those fugitives who had been sent away? Perhaps he *had*, after all, felt some responsibility for his mother's decision. In any case, his immediate relief was evident. It was clear that it was not only I who was benefitting from our interchange.

Mieczyslaw Biernat was seventeen when the war began. When the Nazi troops occupied Vishogrod, they set up headquarters across the street from my father's house. The Biernat family bakery stood adjacent and, from its windows, the young Mieczyslaw could watch the action in the Gestapo courtyard. When he told his story about my father being tied to a drainpipe by the Nazis, I had to hold back my tears. Why had I never heard this before? How many other painful stories existed which I had never heard?

Only a few days later did I recognize in Mieczyslaw Biernat's account echoes of my father's story of his return to Vishogrod after the war. The similarities struck me as too great to be coincidental. How likely was it that my father had been strung up on a drainpipe twice in his life — once by the Nazis, then again by the Poles? I began to doubt Biernat's account, as well as Yarek's translation. Was there only one true version? And, true or false, what did each story mean? Was Biernat lying or covering up Polish anti-Semitism by making the Nazis the only enemy? Was my father's recollection a composite of two events, an inadvertent expression of his lack of forgiveness for his gentile countrymen? Or was the least likely possible: that both stories were true and that my father suffered two parallel assaults during his life time?

My father's account had one great disadvantage: I could not check it out with him. Whose memory could I rely on? The living or the dead? But how could I give Biernat's account precedence over my father's?

I was so disturbed by all these possibilities that I decided, since I had another week in Poland, to revisit the Biernats — this time with a trusted friend who was fluent in both English and Polish. When we arrived the second time, the elderly couple greeted us as though we were old friends. Sofia Biernat had baked a *babke*, a Polish specialty, in our honour. A beautiful bouquet of lilacs in unusual shades of purple and blue stood in the middle of the dining room table. Our dialogue continued.

Again I asked Biernat about my father's experience with the Nazis. It was in the fall of 1939 when my father was tied up and left in the cold, he repeated. I then told Biernat my father's story, the one that had occurred *after* the war. He did not know that story. He had heard that Menachem had come back after the war but he never saw him. Biernat vehemently confirmed that his story was true; he had seen it with his own eyes. He stuck to his story with great conviction. And as I listened to it, I believed him — for that moment.

THE SECOND VISIT

The following spring, exactly a year later, I returned to Vishogrod. An indomitable force was pulling me back.

When I enquired at the local public library about a book on Jews, I was told that the local "expert" on Jews was Dr. Teodor Slominsky. I had been given his name the year before, but he had been too busy to see us. Before I could waver, the librarian arranged an appointment.

Teodor Slominsky's house was situated amongst flowering fruit trees on a quiet street. His family had it built before the war. Though the Germans had taken it over during the occupation, his mother and sister had reclaimed it when they returned after the war. A man in his eighties, he still practises medicine from his home.

Dr. Slominsky was considered the local "expert" on Jews because he had written a paper entitled "The Causes of Deaths of Jews in Vishogrod in the Last Three Hundred Years" which he had discussed on a television programme. He assured me that very few Jews had died of tuberculosis, though he wasn't sure why this should be the case. I wondered whether he was aware of the irony of his statement: The main cause of death in the last three hundred years within the Jewish community of Vishogrod — and all of Europe — had been murder by the Nazis. No medical treatise was necessary to establish this fact. I felt the tension within me mount. I was, however, here to hear him talk about his memories of the Jews of Vishogrod. I was determined to suspend my misgivings in order to learn what I could.

Slominsky didn't know my father's family, but he did remember the Zlotniks. His father had at one time been business partners with my grandfather. My maternal grandfather, Wolf Zlotnik, and Slominsky's father had gone bankrupt together in 1923, during a major financial crisis of that year in Poland. I remembered my mother telling me how quickly her family went from wealth to poverty. A wheelbarrow of money became worthless overnight. Wolf Zlotnik, Slominsky recalled, was short and stout and had a short, tidy beard. And he had a beautiful daughter. My mother, Regina, perhaps?

Slominsky talked about his friendship with Leybish Freyzinger, the last Jew to reside in Vishogrod after the war, who had died in the 1980s. Slominsky explained that he and Freyzinger had been in Auschwitz together and had continued their relationship in Vishogrod after the war. Slominsky had been in Auschwitz. Suddenly his expertise on Jews took on a different meaning for me.

The youngest in his family, Slominsky had been sent to the neighbouring city of Plotsk to be educated. Because he was a Polish intellectual and his family was wealthy, the Germans had deported him to Auschwitz in 1940. He rolled up his left sleeve and showed me his tattoo. It was a very low number, a sign of early internment. He explained that he had managed to survive for five years in the concentration camp because he worked in the barns and had access to the corn feed for the animals.

Slominsky retrieved from the back room an identification photo of himself as an Auschwitz inmate and an official letter signed by Freyzinger stating that Slominsky had helped Jews at the beginning of the war by supplying them with flour and medical help. He treated this letter as his badge of honour. An official statement such as this served as important documentation of one's allegiance during the war. Here was documentary proof that Slominsky was not an anti-Semite.

The most interesting item that Dr. Slominsky brought out, however, was an old red brick wrapped in newsprint. "I want to show you something. This," said Slominsky, "is a brick from the Vishogrod synagogue." Then he went on to tell the apocryphal tale I already knew: these bricks had been purchased by Jews from the ruins of the castle wall which dated back to the fourteenth century. To me, the more believable, and far more extraordinary, feature of this relic was that this man had kept the brick in his possession for over fifty years.

Slominsky explained that after the synagogue was destroyed by the Nazis in November 1939, the Germans living in Vishogrod had used the bricks as retainers for their gardens. When Slominsky saw this profane use of the bricks, he had immediately claimed one and hidden it away for safe-keeping. I was very moved that he was sharing this relic with me. How many people had he shown this brick besides me? He obviously wanted to make a connection, a *Jewish* connection — as had Biernat. My feelings towards Slominsky softened further. He was a much more complex person than I had initially thought.

Back in Warsaw, I contacted Marie Yolande, Slominsky's daughter. She was a few years my junior and had grown up in post-war Vishogrod. She spoke fondly of her childhood there. She and her husband still spent every weekend with their four children in her father's house in Vishogrod, experiencing something of the idyllic country life that my parents had spoken of.

I was invited to join Marie Yolande and her family for a weekend in Vishogrod. Their English was impeccable; they had spent four years in the USA. It was a relief to speak without a translator. We talked about our families — our children and our ancestors — and our relationship to this little town. And for the first time on this journey, I felt I was communicating with peers. We spoke the same language in many ways and Vishogrod was our bond.

It was pouring rain, but we strolled along the *stegenes*, the paths above the river, watching the boats as they sailed in the mist beneath the old wooden bridge. I took my companions along a hidden dirt road, formerly called the *shil gesl* [the little synagogue road], leading to a lovely communal garden of flowers and vegetables, on the spot where

I knew the synagogue had once stood. This was new knowledge for them and they were very moved. In the drizzle, we walked together, first through the Catholic cemetery where Marie Yolande's mother was buried, then across the street through the gates to the field where the Jewish cemetery had been. We felt compelled to share our legacies. At the end of the day, we promised to meet again.

In Memoriam

Across the road from the Catholic cemetery stands what is left of the *besoylem* [Jewish cemetery] of Vishogrod. Unlike its Catholic counterpart across the way, there are no gravestones. Instead there is a row of four remnants of stones with Hebrew writing. There are also several memorial stones which were placed there after the war: one erected by the Brzozowskich family from the USA to honour their relatives, another erected by what was left of the Jewish community of Vishogrod in 1947.

The gates and the major monument which grace the cemetery as one enters were erected in 1989 by Alex Gmach, a survivor who, on his return to his hometown of Vishogrod, found an empty cemetery. The monument reads in Polish and in Yiddish: "This cemetery was disturbed by the Nazis in the years 1939–1945. Even the dead were not given peace."

This piece of land feels like holy ground; it is very quiet, intensely serene, a field of mowed grass and dandelions with some small trees. Like the plot where the old synagogue stood and where a communal garden now grows, this place demonstrates the respect with which the townspeople regard these remnants of Vishogrod's Jewish past. Neither the synagogue plot nor the cemetery land has been built over with modern edifices. Instead both places are communal spaces, tended by the townspeople.

As I walk on the grounds of the cemetery, I am overcome with mixed emotions. This should have been the resting place for my family; instead they were turned to ash in the crematoriums. I walk alone on the overgrown path to the end of the cemetery, across the overgrown grass dotted with dandelions. I look for small stones, as I often do when I go to visit my parents' graves in New York. But here in

Vishogrod all I find are granite pebbles on the ground, pieces of broken tombstones. Yet, how much more authentic and intimate this ruin of a cemetery feels to me than the sprawling, manicured one on Myrtle Avenue in Queens, New York, where my parents are buried. In some strange way, I feel more connected with the spirit of my parents in this Vishogrod cemetery. I leave three stones on the monument: one for my parents, one for my father's two murdered children and one for the rest of my family whose lives were curtailed by the Holocaust.

I am reluctant to leave the town. I desperately long for a tangible item to hold in my hands to pass on to my daughters. We stop at a corner store for a drink. Then I see them — the memorial candles made in Vishogrod. Red wax in a decorative glass, they are probably meant for Christian church rituals. I take them home as *yizkor* [memorial] candles, in memory of my family. In Vishogrod, I have found something to call my own.

I feel affirmed. In spite of its ironies and paradoxes, my search has been worthwhile. I know there is no absolute "truth," but I now have my *own* memories.

This article is dedicated to Ellie Kellman, my supportive travelling companion, and to Aron Gmach, my Vishogrod *landsman* [countryman], without whose invaluable memories this journey could never have been made.

FURTHER READING

Epstein, Helen. *Where She Came From: A Daughter's Search for Her Mother's History.* Boston: Little, Brown and Company, 1997.

Hoffman, Eva. *Shtetl: The Life and Death of a Small Town and the World of Polish Jews.* Boston: Houghton Mifflin Company, 1997.

Karafilly, Irena F. *Ashes and Miracles: A Polish Journey.* Toronto: Malcolm Lester Books, 1998.

Naves, Elaine Kalman. *Journey to Vaja: Reconstructing the World of a Hungarian–Jewish Family.* Montreal: McGill–Queen's University Press, 1996.

Richmond, Theo. *Konin: A Quest.* London: Jonathan Cape Ltd., 1996.

Steinlauf, Michael C. *Bondage to the Dead: Poland and the Memory of the Holocaust.* Syracuse: Syracuse University Press, 1997.

PART TWO
IDENTITY

A FEMINIST, FIRST:

SPECULATIONS OF A SECULAR JEW

❧

Greta Hofmann Nemiroff

Greta Hofmann Nemiroff has been a respected, active member of the women's community in Quebec and Canada since the earliest days of the feminist movement. Without hesitation she calls herself a feminist, an identification she has proudly chosen. In this essay, Nemiroff examines her ambivalence towards her birthright, her identity as a Jew.

DO I COUNT AS A JEW?

A FEW YEARS AGO I received a call in my Montreal home from a francophone sociology professor, who was conducting a study on leadership within Quebec's "cultural communities." She wished to interview me. I imagined that she had categorized me as a feminist active in the English-speaking community in Quebec and Canada, although I have also been active in francophone feminist circles within and outside of Quebec. My interlocutor, it turned out, wished to interview me as a "leader" within the Jewish community. I was quite taken aback. I explained that

I had never been active, let alone assumed a leadership position, within the Jewish community. Indeed, never in my fifty-odd years had I been an active member of a Jewish organization. "Not one?" she asked. I recalled only that as an adolescent I had taught arts and crafts in YMHA day camps for three summers, but even there I had little to contribute to Jewish cultural activities.

My then-husband, was he a Jew, she asked? Yes. My three children, she asked, did they identify themselves as Jews? Yes. Well then? Well, we were secular Jews who were attentive to the possibility of pogroms, but we did not celebrate our Jewishness in any of the traditional ways, opting out of participation in Jewish ritual and organizations. How did we define ourselves as Jews? We simply *were* Jews; even our mode of retaining marginal Jewishness was within a long-standing Jewish tradition, I explained. There could be no Jewish heaven without a room for people like us: atheists, agnostics, eclectic intellectuals, artists, iconoclasts, eccentrics, non-joiners, political radicals, people engaged in endless and noisy discussion, who were argumentative, sentimental, witty, furious and fatalistic. I don't think I made it into her study; in any case, I never heard from her again.

My Jewish identity, such as it is, is generally informed by the values and proclivities articulated by many secular and ambivalent European and North American Jews in their pursuit of modernity. However, my Jewish identity was also formed through the specific reality of being born and raised in Quebec in the mid-twentieth century. I have been viewed as "the other" by both Jews and non-Jews: perceived as a Jew or kike by the non-Jewish majority of my Montreal youth; a most contradictory conflation of prejudices made me a "dirty German Jew" during the Second World War; since my parents did not belong to any religious congregation, observant Jews like my then in-laws did not welcome me as one of their own, either; at the age of thirty-seven, I was suddenly informed by the state that I was something called an "allophone," a political invention useful in dividing opposition within Quebec to its secession from Canada. Now it appears that when the francophones refer to "*les anglais*," Jews are to be included. Where before they shamelessly discriminated against us, the real "*anglais*" now welcome us to swell their declining numbers. I strenuously object to being herded into a group of the very people who indulged in anti-

Semitic discrimination fifty years ago, the fading Anglo–Scottish establishment which ruled most of the anglophone educational institutions I
was obliged to attend. Having been born in Quebec, I do not accept
being called an "allophone," a category created for people who were
born somewhere else. It was my parents, after all, who immigrated to
Canada and settled in Montreal in 1929.

They came from Vienna, a place which never failed to inspire nostalgia in them, notwithstanding the Holocaust which laid waste their
families. They came to Canada for better opportunities than those offered in post-Versailles Austria, and this economic decision saved our
lives. My father was a chemical engineer and my mother was an accomplished crafts woman in puppeteering, book-binding and ceramics. In
Canada at the time, there were no Jews in engineering, my father was
told, so he spent his first years as a mechanical draftsman in Welland,
Ontario, while my mother ran a rather insolvent Viennese bakery in
Notre-Dame-de-Grace. Eventually my father was able to get a job in
engineering in Montreal; he rose to the vice-presidency of two companies.

My sister, Herta, was born in 1933 and I was born in 1937. We
lived a *yeke* [bourgeois German Jew; stuffy and upright] middle-class
life in Notre-Dame-de-Grace, far to the west of "real" Jewish neighbourhoods around St. Laurent Boulevard, immortalized by Mordecai
Richler. My parents lived within a community of Central Europeans in
permanent exile, an intelligentsia of ambivalent secular Jews, some of
whom celebrated Christmas but quietly repaired to *shul* [synagogue] on
Yom Kippur. They transplanted their very eclectic Central European
intellectual life to Canada, transmitting their cultural icons to us, the
sparse next generation. I attended my first and only Sabbath services at
the age of fifteen when a high-school friend invited me a few times to
the Shaare Zion Synagogue on Cote-St-Luc Road. I was both bemused
and unmoved by the experience. My sister and I were permitted to stay
home from school on some of the High Holidays "out of respect" and
in solidarity with other Jews, but that was as far as our "religious education" extended.

When I attended a public high school with a large population of
the children of working-class Eastern European Jews, I had to revise inherited and indefensible familial attitudes of Viennese Jewish snobbery

against the *Ostjuden*. These people were regarded by the more firmly rooted Viennese Jews as interlopers from the farthest reaches of the Hapsburg empire. In a period of urbanization and economic growth, Jews from the eastern outposts of the Hapsburg Empire converged on Vienna from the 1870s on; by 1939, they had created the largest Jewish community in Western Europe. It was during this period that both my grandfathers came to seek their fortunes in Vienna from small towns in Hungary. The children of atheists, my sister and I are at least three generations removed from observant Jewry.

My family, then, were the ambivalent and ambiguous kind of Jews used as examples in arguments against Jewish assimilation: did not the "assimilated" and converted Austrian and German Jews end up in the gas chambers along with everyone else? What good did their self-marginalization and pretence of assimilation do them? This was irrefutable: members of my mother's family, including her parents, had converted to Catholicism and Protestantism, and it had done them no good at all. With very few exceptions, those who didn't escape the Nazis were murdered by them.

A MONTREAL CHILDHOOD

I was named after two women who were to perish in the Holocaust. Grete Holm, a cousin of my mother's, was a cream-puff operetta singer with a superb voice but bad taste in men. Her career was said to have been mismanaged by her non-Jewish husband, who divorced her around the time of the Anschluss (the March 1939 German invasion and annexation of Austria). She and her mother perished together at Auschwitz. Dr. Grete Blum, much admired by my mother, was a medical doctor and the older sister of my mother's best friend, Mitzi. It was only well into the 1960s that we learned how she and Mitzi died. Throughout the war, they had been hidden with seven other Jews in a basement in Vienna. While the allies were entering Vienna, some youths from the Hitler *Jugend* [Youth] flushed them out and slaughtered them in the street. There is a memorial to these symbolic "last Jews of Vienna" in the Jewish cemetery, a vast unkempt sea of graves on the outskirts of Vienna. The inextricable relationship of my name to those redoubtable women, a central source of Jewish identity in my life, is confusingly tied to the horror of their deaths as well as to their high achievements. For this reason, I have always thought of myself as a tertiary survivor.

My early childhood was played out against the backdrop of the Second World War, which reduced my parents to whispered confabulations over Red Cross lists trying to find out who had survived. A stream of refugees stayed with us; every evening we listened to the news on our RCA Victor radio. My mother was so pleased that her mother, who lived with us, survived long enough to know that there had been victory in Europe. Malvine Iranyi, my grandmother, fell into a coma on the night of VE day, May 1945. She died a day or two later. In 1967, exactly a century after her birth, I wrote about her death in a short story entitled "The Day the War Ended." With my heart, I always recall the title as "The Day the World Ended."

The Holocaust itself was part of my earliest consciousness of the world around me. Later on, my mother liked to recount that when she came to the garden to tell me that the war was over, I observed that now we would not have to go to a concentration camp. My mother, shocked that I knew about the camps, assured me that there were none in Canada. (She was wrong. There were "internment camps" throughout Canada for Japanese, German and Italian nationals and Canadians.) If Hitler came to Canada, I said, he would build camps, perhaps beside the Presbytère in St-Sauveur-des-Monts where a chain-link fence surrounded the playing field. How would the Nazis find us, my mother asked, fascinated by the world according to her seven year old. Our neighbours would direct the Nazis to us because our garden was nicer than theirs. That way they could take down the fence and create one large garden for themselves. My world picture included gratuitous denunciation as a given. This knowledge has layered itself around me with the same adherence as my name, Greta.

In the later years of elementary school, every Thursday afternoon after school I was taxied across the city to the Jewish Immigrant Aid Society (JIAS) on de l'Esplanade, where my mother and her friends, Mesdames Stone, Meier and Marston, volunteered at a "Clothing Room." They handed out coffee, tea, recycled clothing and conversation to hundreds of Jewish refugees from Europe. I did my part by measuring the waistlines of pants and skirts, then writing their sizes on tags which I would affix to the garments. I remember the fusty smells of old dry-cleaned wool and strong brewing coffee, intermingled with the crescendos and cacophony of people recounting their tragedies. The refugees spoke numerous languages, but they tended to converse in German, the lingua franca of both the concentration and displaced persons' camps. Because German was my "first language" at home, I understood the terrible tales, to which I faithfully listened with a mixture of fear and fascination. How could they still be alive, I wondered, as they spoke of crawling out of mass graves over the dead bodies of their families, or after waking up in a *lager* [camp] beside the stiff starved and icy bodies of a mother, a father, a sibling?

These are the two terrible truths I learned at the Clothing Room: The first is the great "why me?" Why was the great gift of life given to me and denied my betters and my beloveds? In a modest and childish way, I too knew the guilt of "there but for the grace of something (there was no God in my family) go I." To this day I feel my immense good fortune in my parents' early immigration; at the age of three, I would never have survived the first "selection."

The second lesson was that suffering does not necessarily ennoble people. Sometimes people had to wait a few weeks until there were winter coats for them. Although a scrupulous list was maintained, there were sometimes fist fights over the few coats that turned up. "Hitler should have got you," adversaries would fling hatefully at one another, sometimes tearing the coats into shreds in the process. This did not shock me. There is an inexorable logic to the combination of triumph at survival with profound guilt, and then the displacement of that guilt into anger at other survivors ... all fuelled by the ceaseless struggle of keeping afloat. The rawness of post-Holocaust behaviour taught me everything I have ever had to know in order to survive.

The Clothing Room at JIAS also taught me about the secret needs of women, my mother and her friends. They were portly mittel-class mittel European housewives living under their husbands' benevolent but nonetheless controlling thumbs. Their days and evenings at JIAS doing good works got them out of the confines of their homes. One day a week they kept evening hours, after which they would repair to a club or a café where they would decorously sip cocktails appropriately called "Pink Ladies." They even had their own taxi driver, easy-going

Mr. Nathan Creatchman, who smiled at their foibles as he conveyed and retrieved them, returning them home in good time. While the Clothing Room was a sad locale for the recounting of horrifying experiences, it must have been cathartic for the survivors; it was deeply disturbing, I think, for my mother and her friends, all of whom were empathic women. It was also a launching pad for daring sorties into the real world, away from the control of their husbands. Nothing very risqué happened to them in these establishments ... except perhaps in their minds; I have never forgotten the hilarity of their adventures and the frisson these recollected outings set off in sparks of wit and brightness of eye.

It must also be said that in my childhood and youth, Montreal was a city rife with ethnocentricity, racism and anti-Semitism. Since the public schools were either Catholic or Protestant, all Jews and "others" (Eastern Orthodox, for instance) went to English Protestant schools which were presided over by the Scottish oligarchy which ran the Protestant School Board of Greater Montreal. Catholics either went to English or French Catholic schools. Those of us who "went on," often went to McGill University which had a *numerus clausus* [maximum quota system] in various faculties well into the 1950s. Its scholarship and bursary handbook informed me that most honours and monies were reserved for white, Christian males. I never felt at home at McGill, and two degrees later, I still feel a tightening in my gut whenever I enter the Roddick Gates.

This past autumn, I thoughtlessly did not check the date before assigning the students' papers in my Humanities course at Dawson College. Some Orthodox Jewish students drew my attention to the fact that the date I had indicated for the submission of papers was Yom Kippur [the Day of Atonement]. I apologized and extended the due date for everyone in the class. One of the Jewish students then observed that in any case there would not be a class on Yom Kippur. I explained that since I would be there, the class would go on. I could see that the students who had raised the issue were surprised that I would teach on Yom Kippur. After class they approached me to ask if I were Jewish, to which I responded that I was a secular Jew. I explained to them that, since I do not observe the holiday, I felt it was more respectful to work than to use it to avoid work. With great authority, they ruled that if I did not observe Yom Kippur, I could not be a Jew. They added that if I did not believe in God, I certainly could not be a Jew. I staunchly protected my right to define myself as a Jew, arguing that many people who saw themselves and were regarded as Jews would agree with my beliefs. As the discussion progressed, they agreed that Jewishness was more than a set of beliefs and rituals and that it also involved shared history and sensitivity to the ever present possibility-of-pogrom. Reluctantly they granted that I could indeed call myself a Jew; I myself was surprised at how strongly I defended my very weak Jewish identity. I realized that despite my hatred of oppression and racism, I have felt much more genuine defending feminism than I felt insisting that I too am a Jew.

PERSONAL IDENTITY AND FEMINIST VISION

There has never been a time in the history of my own self-consciousness when I have not been aware of my femaleness. In my youth I wanted to hear and read stories only about girls and women: a direct literary trajectory marked my progress from *The Snow Queen* to Nancy Drew and *Susannah of the Mounties*, through Wonder Woman comics to annual readings of *Jane Eyre*. The fictional characters who attracted me were strong girls and women who somehow transcended the contingent roles assigned to them. They realized their ambitions and desires through their own initiatives and talents rather than through the more traditional narrative routes of love and magic.

How could it have been otherwise, given the women in my family? Both my grandmothers were fairly well educated for their class and time. Henrietta Hock Hofmann, my paternal grandmother, was born in Vienna in 1857; Malvine Loeb Iranyi, my maternal grandmother, was born in Vienna in 1867. Both women efficiently ran large and complex households. When her husband's illness forced him into an early retirement, Malvine created a small business producing and selling cake mixes in attractive rococo packages.

My mother, as mentioned above, studied puppetry, book-binding and ceramics. Eventually she taught ceramics and crafts at St. George's School in Montreal. My father's sisters, all born in the 1890s, were distant but strong influences on my sister and myself. "We were six girls at home," Aunt Kaethe sighed to me in London in 1975. "*Hélas*, not one of us was beautiful!" Although four of the Hofmann daughters were to marry, only one had a child; all six of them worked in the paid labour force. Three sisters became business women, one became a medical doctor, and two earned PHD's in Berlin since those options were not available to women in Austria. Perhaps they were influenced in their choices by their mother and her sisters, all of whom had intellectual interests and had to be nudged into marriage by their father's exercise of patriarchal prerogative. Two women cousins of my aunts also earned an MD and a PHD. The aunts I knew best were Dr. Hedwig Fischer, a dermatologist who ended up in practice in Syracuse, NY; Dr. Else Hofmann, who became a docent at the Metropolitan Museum in New York; and Dr. Martha Hofmann, a poet and educator who returned to Vienna after the war. They were all autonomous, highly intelligent polyglots with a wide knowledge of history, literature and the arts. My sister, Herta, says she was influenced to become a doctor by our visit to Aunt Hedwig in 1943. She was taken with Hedwig's autonomy and capacity to support a large white clapboard house in a lovely garden, all presided over by a full-time housekeeper. "No one ever told her what to do," she told me many years later.

I, on the other hand, was somewhat ambivalent about my aunts. I admired their vast knowledge and energetic intellectual lives, but I was somewhat repelled by their self-absorption, eccentricity and incredible vanity. Their loneliness made them demanding of attention, but they were also generous in their interest in us, the only two girls of the next generation. I do not know if they were conscious feminists, but I am certain that they considered themselves more than intellectually equal to men. On their account, the message silently conveyed to me by my parents was that I had to surpass my aunts by having a successful career, marriage and children. In short, to become what the women's movement would later describe as a "Super Woman." It is no coincidence that both my sister and I married at nineteen years of age and had children in our early twenties.

The accomplished women of my family created a climate of expectation regarding my own capacity to become a full actor in all aspects of our society. I was to experience overt anti-Semitism and sexism as a student at McGill University, at Boston University, and in the workplace.

When I began seriously reading Black, gay and feminist writers in the 1960s, I experienced recognition and excitement at these intellectual and political expressions which validated many of my own concerns and perceptions. I felt the first intimations of a community to which I could belong.

The 1960s brought *La Révolution tranquille* [the Quiet Revolution] to Quebec. It was not my revolution, but like all Quebec women, I was to benefit from the broadening of women's rights in Quebec society. In autumn, 1970, with Sister Prudence Allen (then Christine Garside), I co-taught the first Women's Studies course offered in a Canadian university at Sir George Williams University, now Concordia University. There were very few texts or books available then, and as we went along we learned much from the students who filled our classes to capacity. The dialectics of the classroom informed our development of a feminist framework through which to research and to teach.

We taught de Beauvoir and newer texts of this period, all of which were based on critiques of patriarchal institutions and belief systems, including Judaism and Christianity. Over the years, I worked with students who staunchly defended orthodoxy as protecting the rights of Jewish women and exalting their status. From my distance from religious practices, I have not been convinced by arguments that religious orthodoxy has women's interests and rights at heart. Feminist scholarship in religious studies has, on the whole, reinforced my opinion that the "great" monotheistic religions, developed by men for men, are built on a foundation of misogyny. I am heartened by Orthodox women's groups in many religions, which are re-examining and reinterpreting basic religious texts from a feminist standpoint.

Some of the first American women to publish in "second wave" feminism were Jews such as Betty Friedan, Andrea Dworkin and Robin Morgan. However, their focus was on women's oppression qua women, not as Jews. The 1970s and even the early 1980s were a period of "sentimental feminism," whose prevailing credo was that all women shared common cause and common solutions. Many feminist writers and activists who popularized this view were white, educated and middle-class. In both the Canadian and American women's movements, it took the multiplying voices of women of colour, immigrant women, lesbians, working-class women and disabled women to force white middle-class women of all persuasions into a *prise de conscience*, the realization that no one could speak for all women and that our priorities and solutions were shaped by what de Beauvoir would call the "*facticités*" of our lives. These self-critical insights provoked a period of vehement denial on the part of some white women, leading to a highly charged environment of accusation and counter-accusation. Many groups within the women's movement began to establish their own hierarchies of oppression; this led to some very painful public and private moments among feminists. In the long run and in true post-modernist fashion, feminists who wanted to form a critical force politically had to accept their individual and each others' multiple identities and standpoints. Clearly we must work within the variables which combine to form personal and group identities, mediating and negotiating our differences into positions of coalition rather than adhering to notions of a monolithic entity called "women."

In the 1980s, Jewish women who attended the United Nations Women's Conferences and NGO (non-governmental organizations) forums in Copenhagen (1980) and Nairobi (1985) reported serious and painful confrontations between Jewish and Palestinian women. However, at the Fourth United Nations International Women's NGO Forum in Huairou, China, in 1995, numerous Palestinian, Jewish and other women joined together with the Women in Black for an international demonstration of solidarity. Certainly Canadian Jewish feminists do not form a homogeneous entity: we experience alienating distances based on class, sexual orientation, religious beliefs and irreconcilable political ideologies. It is not clear on either a local or an international basis that all differences between feminists can be reconciled. The complexities and contradictions within feminism, locally, nationally and internationally, will continue to impel feminists to investigate new ways of resolving our differences. To date, women's movements are much more likely to work towards inclusive, nonviolent and democratic solutions to problems of resourcelessness and domination than are those "men's movements" best exemplified by the nation state, its military apparatus and its major political parties.

As feminists struggle for a safer and fairer world, our knowledge of how power works has increased. As a feminist and a tertiary survivor, I have been deeply moved by research which addresses the different ways in which men and women experienced numerous aspects of the Holocaust. While the male voice has dominated much Holocaust discourse since the end of the war, works such as *Different Voices: Women and the Holocaust* have contributed immeasurably to our understanding of the complexities of that experience, illustrating the specificity of women's history during the Holocaust. I was especially moved by an article which addresses the possibility that Jewish women survived longer than men in the concentration camps. In speculating about explanations of this phenomenon, the author considers that "'Women's work' — activities centering around food, children, clothing, shelter, social relations, warmth, cleanliness — may be regarded as the only meaningful labor in a time of such dire necessity [...] Because of the different material conditions and social relations that characterize their lives, women are able to create or recreate 'families' and so provide networks for maintenance that may be related to survival rates."[1] Such an analysis of women's agency runs counter to the demeaning media stereotype of the "Jewess" as a supine victim, passively accepting her fate beneath the iron heel of National Socialism.

I am disturbed by the current commodification of the Holocaust, that huge industry of cultural production which recreates a "holocaust" sometimes far removed from the realities of the time. While Jews often insist on the "uniqueness" of our holocaust, it is perilous to be blind to similar contemporary sites of genocide in Bosnia and Rwanda–Burundi. Shamefully, popular Jewish versions of the Holocaust do not usually acknowledge the persecution and genocide visited upon Europe's gypsies in the name of the same Nazi fantasy of racial purity. The intonation, "never again," has been crassly used far too often to justify Israeli landgrabs and brutality towards Palestinians. I felt intense shame in witnessing on the TV news a group of Orthodox Jewish men singing and dancing as they evicted a Palestinian family from the house and the land they had farmed for generations. It is an abomination to the memories of Holocaust victims to cite their horror as justification for inflicting suffering on others.

My political and emotional identity has been formed by the fact that I am female in a world which has continually demanded that I act against my own best interests in the name of propriety, religion, family, social cohesion and the ideology of sacrificial motherhood. I have suffered abuse in my life because I am a woman and because I am a Jew. The faces, the voices and the tales of the refugees remain vivid in my mind. I am disturbed that most of my identification as a Jew emerges from so much pain and injustice. That is the peril of assimilation: no happy memories of Jewish belonging or experiences of joyous ritual and ceremonial occasions inform my fragile Jewish identity.

As a feminist, however, I recall innumerable joyous occasions with other feminists at March 8 celebrations, at conferences and in courses I have taught. I remember celebrations of triumph when we have won rights or triumphed in a skirmish against the patriarchy. My beliefs fall within the general range of feminist thought; I understand women's situation from my own experience ... something I cannot replicate with a Jewish consciousness based on the absence of God and the opaqueness of Jewish ritual. While I am a Jew by birth, I am a feminist by choice. The fact that I am writing this essay for a book such as this is proof of my longing for a satisfactory convergence of these two themes in my life.

PRESENT LOCATIONS

In spring, 1995, at a panel I chaired in Toronto, I ran into one of the women who had taken our Women's Studies course at Concordia University in the early 1970s. We had a brief conversation and exchanged telephone numbers. A few months later she invited me to take part in a Jewish Feminist Conference she was helping to organize in Toronto in early 1996. I was intrigued but hesitant, given my own marginal Jewish identity. We finally agreed that I would give a workshop dealing with some of the tensions of being a feminist and a secular Jew.

I welcomed the chance to attend this conference in the hope that the two life themes of Jewishness and feminism would somehow converge through this experience. I enthusiastically attended an Oneg Shabbat [Friday evening celebration] presided over by Rabbi/Cantor Elizabeth Bolton, who had also been a student in our Women's Studies course at Concordia. Despite all my good feelings, however, and the great artistry and warmth with which she conducted the Oneg Shabbat, (a mixture of music and story-telling in Yiddish, Hebrew and English), I felt disconnected from its contents. Often I simply did not know what she was talking about and felt little visceral recognition of her material. I felt fondness for Liz and pride in her talent and warmth, but I could not forge an identity from her excellent material.

Whenever I hear Norma Baumel Joseph, the keynote speaker, I learn a great deal. Perhaps through her I would find a bridge to a Jewish feminist identity which had so eluded me. As usual, her speech was dynamic, interesting and provocative. She was speaking of *Zakhor*, the biblical commandment to remember, and how it plays out in "History and Herstory." I had never heard of *Zakhor* before, nor of many of the subjects she covered. She inveighed against the patriarchal view of Jewish history and asked, "How could we have let some one write us out for so long?" She claimed that a symbolic "she" who represented her and us, her audience, led the Jews out of Egypt, stood at Sinai, and was present all through Jewish history. "I was there," she intoned, "I was the woman who tried to rebel against Moses' unique authority. I was excluded, but the people wouldn't go without me and they waited."[2] How moving her voice and words were! Her call to expand our understanding of Jewish scriptures to include those women whose presence and experiences were silenced and suppressed was most appealing to me, as it would be regarding any religion. However, I had to ask myself whether or not I was there. Did I feel that connection? The answer was no: I was not at Sinai and in a sense I was not even here at the conference in the way my esteemed colleague would have wished for me as a Jewish feminist. I felt somewhat bereft, but I was also increasingly fatalistic about my ability to find an appropriate Jewish niche for myself.

I didn't expect many people to attend my workshop, entitled "Jewish Feminist by Default? Mapping Intersections for Feminists who are Secular Jews," especially since I was beginning to feel increasingly distant from the Jewish experiences which surrounded me. However, there was a good turn out and our discussion persuaded me that I may not be quite as marginal as I think. There are many other secular Jewish feminists trying to forge identities uniting the ephemera of secular Jewish identity and their feminist consciousness where they live and breathe. I am comforted that some other Jewish feminists need neither God nor ritual to construct their identities as Jewish feminists. They were comfortable refusing to harmonize their thoughts and actions with the verbal monopoly of Jewish men. Like another speaker, Melanie Kaye/Kantrowitz, I too "... am not willing to leave the Jewish world to the men," not even my very minimal part of it.

My comprehension that there are other Jewish feminists on my general wave length was a kind of "breaking the silence" experience. As such, it brought me some comfort but no concrete sense of community. I know, however, that self-definition is never static and that mine will undergo many refinements before my life is over. I recall a Montreal Jazz Festival in the early 1990s where I stood in a huge crowd of Jews, Quebecois, anglos and tourists of all stripes. We were watching a klezmer group produce those inimitable sounds lately resurrected largely from the memories of ageing Holocaust survivors. "*Bon soir,*" announced a young woman who fiddled, sang and acted as emcee. "We are Jews from New York." The crowd roared its welcome in French and English. As I stood there that balmy Montreal evening listening to klezmer far removed from the Schubert lieder which accompanied my childhood life, I recognized that Quebec itself is changing with dizzying speed and in several directions at once. I don't believe that even forty years ago any group of Jews would have been so daring or so warmly welcomed on the streets of downtown Montreal. This happy thought did not totally transform my complicated relationship with Quebec, but I did file it away to be updated for the duration of my life.

A Tenuous Link

One brilliant August Saturday in 1988, I searched for the memorial to my namesake, Grete Blum, and her companions in the Jewish cemetery on the outskirts of Vienna. So removed am I from Jewish practices that it never occurred to me that the cemetery would be closed on a Saturday, my last day in Vienna. The Jewish cemetery is part of an immense public cemetery divided amongst the Catholics, the Protestants and the Jews. After being rebuffed by the closed gate to the Jewish cemetery, I noticed that the stone wall separating it from the Protestant cemetery abruptly ended a few hundred metres away. There the cemeteries were only separated by a long barbed-wire fence through which I could step into another world. On one side was the beautifully tended, tree-shaded and abundantly flowered Protestant cemetery dotted with devoted relatives peacefully tending the graves; on the other side, the Jewish cemetery was deserted and knee-deep in decades' accumulation of rotting leaves, dead grass and the rankest of weeds. There were no flowers on the graves; there was no one left to care for the graves of these masses of dead Viennese Jews ... testimony to a once huge community now numbering less than four thousand people. The graves had sunk deeply into the detritus of what had been a rich, varied and influential presence in a once great city. While the extent and negligence of the Jewish cemetery felt oppressive and tragic, it was the gravestones which affected me the most. Most of them were dated before 1939; in many cases, addenda had been engraved onto corners of the large gravestones, naming those people whose remains had blown to the winds as ashes in Poland. The Nazis had almost succeeded in making Europe *Judenrein*.

It was, however, the names on the stones themselves which penetrated my heart most sharply: names like Ilse, Lotte, Klara, Frieda, Grete and Edith, coupled with German–Jewish surnames, were like the names of familiars. They were the names my schoolmates and childhood friends might have had, if: if we had stayed; if there had not been National Socialism; if there had been no war. Their disappearance off the face of the earth has abandoned me to a life steeped in ignorance of community. I am only partially nourished by the yet shallow roots set down by my parents in Quebec, a place where the "elect" themselves proudly and exclusively refer to the depth of their somewhat deeper roots with the expression, *Québecois de souche* [Quebecers with deep roots]. For the first time in my life, I had found a semblance of community; I had also scanned a map of my loss as a tertiary survivor.

What if the "if" had happened, and I were living the life of an ageing *yeke* in Hitzing, the area of Vienna where my mother grew up, writing an essay on my identity as a Jew and a feminist in German instead of English? I would probably be writing that I was a feminist, first. However, I would be writing for an audience of Viennese Jewish feminists like myself who might nod their heads in such finely calibrated understanding that I might not have to write such an essay at all.

NOTES

1. Joan Ringelheim, "Women and the Holocaust: A Reconsideration of Research," in Carol Ritter and John K. Roth, eds., *Different Voices: Women and the Holocaust* (New York: Paragon House, 1993), 374–375.

2. All quotations of Norma Baumel Joseph stem from my notes at the time. I take full responsibility for any inaccuracies.

FORGETTING AND REMEMBERING:

FRAGMENTS OF HISTORY

❧

Yvonne Singer

Visual artist Yvonne Singer tells an unlikely but true story. Born in war-torn Budapest in 1944, the god-daughter of the Swedish diplomat and hero Raoul Wallenberg, Singer was raised a Christian. Unaware of her own Jewish heritage, she converted to Judaism as an adult and learned of her relationship to Wallenberg from a newspaper article over thirty years after her birth. For any person, this background would present a challenge; for an artist it can become both subject and stimulus for creativity. In this discourse on incorporating history and memory into one's life and work, Yvonne Singer takes us on a fascinating journey of discovery and transformation.

PRESENCE AND ABSENCE; people and places revealed and concealed. In my life and work as an artist, questions about identity and the intersections of public and private histories have always compelled me. It is my intention in this essay to understand and describe the transformations that occur in the matrix of circumstances and events that I call my life, my subjectivity and my artistic practice.

Is my personal history responsible for these interests? Are the conditions of being uprooted and alienated from my place of birth responsible for making me an artist? The painter Georgia O'Keefe was adamant that she was an artist first and foremost and that her gender was irrelevant. Do I want to be identified as a woman artist? Is my Jewishness or femaleness relevant to my art practice? Do Jewish artists make Jewish art? What does it mean to be Jewish? What does it mean to be a woman artist? Labels to define or categorize identity are limiting, ambiguous and problematic for many reasons.

I was born in Budapest, Hungary on November 4, 1944, at a particularly turbulent moment in the Second World War, in the midst of severe bombing of Budapest, when the Russians were advancing into Hungary and the Nazi government was desperate to exterminate the remaining Jews. My parents tell of my grandparents' attempt to visit me, their first grandchild. They were waiting for a tram to take them across Margaret's Bridge from Buda to Pest to bring baby clothes to my mother when the bridge was bombed. My grandparents just missed being on the tram that was crossing the bridge at the time. I was also told that I was born in a private home, not a hospital and that my father worked with the underground Resistance forces. I heard other stories about pre-war Budapest with its lively, sophisticated cafés, hot spring pools and vibrant cultural scene. I also heard stories about how a bullet came through our apartment window and nearly missed my father; about my family running to hide in underground shelters during air raids; about putting ashes on my father's beard to make him appear too old to be grabbed off the streets for a labour camp or the Germany army; about the Russians who raped the women and robbed people at gun-point for their watches. These stories and others were the backdrop to my youth and they left me with a sense of anxiety. Life is dangerous and terrible things can happen arbitrarily, without warning. My survival signified that I had to do something special with my life to justify being alive.

We emigrated to Canada in 1949. I grew up in English-speaking and Jewish neighbourhoods in Montreal, a city where schools were divided into English–Protestant and French–Catholic. I also grew up in a family that, in their zeal to assimilate and erase their own differences, had an aversion to certain labels. Therefore "Canadian" or "internationalist" were good labels; "immigrant" was a derogatory badge of identification. Assimilation is easier said than done where language signifies belonging. My parents retained their distinctive Hungarian accents, an accent which still makes my mother self-conscious and apologetic.

One of my earliest memories in Canada is learning to speak English ... calling to Charlene Tiplitsky in the neighbouring backyard from my second-floor balcony ... asking her name and giving her mine. I was six years old.

I was raised as a Protestant. Since we lived in predominantly Jewish neighbourhoods, I was a minority and experienced reverse prejudice from my peers and their parents. To others and to myself, I was the immigrant child whose difference was based in both language and religion. Learning a new language as well as learning the complex cues and signs encoded in the unfamiliar playground culture made me very self-conscious. I became the outsider ... the one they picked on in games of Hide and Seek, the one accused of "stepping on the cracks" in the sidewalk. I was left to walk to school by myself. I was the only one in our group who went to school on the Jewish holidays. As I passed by on my way to school, the other children called me names like "Hungarian puss." In high school I walked to school daily with Larry, who lived across the street. Larry finally plucked up the courage to ask me on a date, but his parents made him retract the invitation because I wasn't Jewish. The slights of childhood cast a long shadow into adulthood. This was Montreal in the 1950s. Ethnic diversity consisted of a population that was either English or French; Catholic or Protestant and Jewish. I was the only immigrant child in my grade six class.

My maternal and paternal grandparents arrived in Canada in the early 1950s. By 1954, my parents, two brothers and four grandparents and myself lived together in one large house in a suburban area of Montreal. Communication between the generations was difficult and limited since I spoke Hungarian like a three-year-old and my grandparents' English was also limited. We lived in a split-level house where my maternal and paternal grandparents each had their own bedroom and bathroom but all shared a basement kitchen and livingroom area.

My maternal grandparents were atheists and were more educated than my paternal grandparents, who had a crucifix over their doorway. Where other families on the street had "recreation" rooms, we had the four grandparents who didn't get along with each other cooking, eating, playing cards and arguing in Hungarian.

Since they were too old to work, unfamiliar with English or the city and without friends, they were dependent on my parents to mediate the world outside our house. At Christmas and Easter, they would emerge from their quarters and join the rest of us for these celebrations. Otherwise, we had little contact with one another. In retrospect, this tragi-comic predicament could be considered the stuff of situation comedies. But I must confess that for a child who was desperate to be like everyone else, these strangers living in my basement were an embarrassment. For all these reasons, I could not learn about my family's history from my grandparents; nor was I particularly interested. By the time I wanted to know more, they had died.

In 1966 a religious marriage ceremony was required according to Quebec law. My fiancé was Jewish. I decided to convert to Judaism in reaction to the alienation I felt within my Protestant environment. I was attracted to the strong sense of community in Judaism, represented by my fiancé, Ron, his family, friends and the Jewish neighbourhoods which I had known growing up. I wanted to belong and this was the community where I intuitively felt at home.

My conversion involved three months of readings and discussions about Jewish philosophy. For my "final exam," some of the elders of the Reform synagogue met with us in the rabbi's study to question me. The final question was, "What is the traditional food for Yom Kippur [the Day of Atonement]?" Although I had attended synagogue as part of the conversion process, I knew little about the rituals of the Jewish holidays. I panicked and my mind went blank. There was a pregnant silence until I answered, "Oh yes, nothing, because you fast!" Everyone breathed again as the rabbi pulled out a bottle of wine from behind his bookcase to celebrate.

Both families were uncomfortable with our forthcoming "mixed marriage." My father cited the horrible events he had witnessed during the war in his Resistance work as a reason for his concern. But I was twenty-one years old. Ron and I were flushed with excitement about our wedding. We felt defiant about flaunting convention by marrying each other.

A year later, in 1968, we left for Europe. There we met a cousin of mine. To my surprise, she mentioned that my parents had been married in a synagogue. Although the revelation was puzzling, it was unsubstantiated; so life continued and my confusion about my parents' religion hovered in the background for many years. The next fourteen years of my life were spent travelling in Europe, living in London, England, Ottawa, Stratford and Toronto, teaching, pursuing an art education and having babies.

I gave my daughters Hebrew names — Tamara, Sara, Hannah Leah Shoshanna — as a way of claiming this "adopted" identity as a Jew. I initiated Passover seders with other friends in mixed marriages For a while, we still celebrated Christmas. We never joined a synagogue; only one of my daughters wanted a bat mitzvah. The question of belonging as a Jew was only one of many aspects of identity that concerned me. I was redefining myself as a feminist, as being different from my mother. I was also juggling a burgeoning ambition to be an artist with being a wife and mother. I was in the midst of building a community of other women like myself who were exiles or expatriates for various reasons from their place of origin and were struggling with some of the same concerns.

It was on a Saturday morning in October 1979, when I was thirty-four and pregnant with my third daughter, that I noticed a front page headline in *The Toronto Star*. The article featured was about Raoul Wallenberg, a Swedish diplomat who had saved the lives of 100,000 Jews in Budapest. I read the article aloud to my husband Ron and came to a paragraph about a young couple who had come to Wallenberg's offices in search of a safe place to give birth to their first child. They had been unable to get access to a hospital. Wallenberg had offered his private apartment for the birth while he slept in the corridor. At 7:00 a.m. the next morning, he was called in to see the baby girl, who had been named Yvonne Maria Eva. Wallenberg was asked to be the child's godfather. The young couple were my parents. I was that child. I had been completely unaware of my connection to Raoul Wallenberg. The story, of course, made me even more curious and confused about my parents' background. My subsequent research led me to a cousin who had emigrated to Israel in 1949. It also led me to study the history of Hungarian Jews in the twentieth century.

To be a Hungarian and a Jew is to exist in contested private and public territory. Hungary claims that everyone born on Hungarian soil is a citizen even if they are also citizens of other countries. The Orthodox rabbis in Israel have strict definitions of who can claim to be a Jew. I learned that many Hungarian Jews were secular, assimilated and identified themselves as Hungarian first. I understood and appreciated why my parents, like many other Hungarians in their situation, were reluctant to disclose a past after their war-time experiences.

To know that my personal story participates in the larger history of the Hungarian Jews situates me historically as part of the continuum of the Hungarian Jewish diaspora. It is also to know that I participate in the conditions of being an outsider. But questions of identity and belonging are complex. Identity transforms as the choices we make to construct a viable identity continually change. I have resolved many concerns about who I am and where I belong. Nevertheless, questions about the ways we construct our identity, the role of memory and the intersection of public and private histories intrigue me and remain a driving force in my work. In the world of contemporary visual art, place, location and cultural diversity are significant subjects for discussion. Ironically, I now find myself, the "outsider," as "insider" — in the centre of these ideas and located in the company of other women artists, investigating their relationship to their particular political and social histories.

The exhibition, "In Memoriam: Forgetting and Remembering Fragments of History," investigates my position in relation to my parents' history and experience. The circumstances of my birth — the time and place, the condition of war and my connection to Raoul Wallenberg — are all accidents of history. While they are beyond my control they are events that profoundly affected my life.

The exhibit poses a variety of questions: What part of this history can I claim as mine and what belongs to my parents? Who is Raoul Wallenberg? What can I know about him? What is my obligation to this man whom I have never met but who is connected to me as my god-father? My perspective of history is constructed from fragments of other people's memories, stories from newspapers, family photographs, historical documentaries. This being the case, how can I question representations of the Holocaust and critique the official valorizations of Wallenberg and yet honour him and my family's stories? How can I translate these ideas in a material form, without being too self-referential?

In response to these questions I chose not to use photographs of Wallenberg or images of war or concentration camps. We have become desensitized to them and they too easily distance us from the images we see. Instead, I used materials such as glass, felt and steel, as well as words which are seen only in shadows as metaphors to evoke each viewer's associations and images. In The Felt Room and The Glass Room I constructed empty spaces for the viewer to inhabit with their body and experiences. What is absent or implied is as significant as what is present or stated.

Since I wanted to leave a clear field for viewers to enter the work in their own way, the catalogue doesn't identify me as Jewish or as Wallenberg's god-daughter. I was also concerned that the work would be ghettoized as speaking only to a Jewish community. All artistic work comes out of who we are, what we know and how we experience and organize the world, but is it important, initially, for the viewer to know about the artist? Can the work stand independent of the artist's biography? The debate about the intersections of art and biography is an ongoing one. As an artist, my life is my source material and my art is the means for transforming and understanding experience. However it is also my intention to engage the viewer.

"In Memoriam: Forgetting and Remembering Fragments of History" occupied two spaces at the Koffler Gallery, Toronto, in 1993. The work investigates memory and the moments where public and private histories intersect. Raoul Wallenberg arrived in Budapest in May 1944. I was born in November 1944. Wallenberg was arrested by the Russians and disappeared in January 1945. This matrix of events was my starting point.

The viewer first encounters The Felt Room, a dark, brooding structure at the entrance of the gallery. A single spotlight is focused on the entrance passage, the only exit or entrance to a dimly lit interior. The walls are made of thick, charcoal brown felt supported by a grey steel

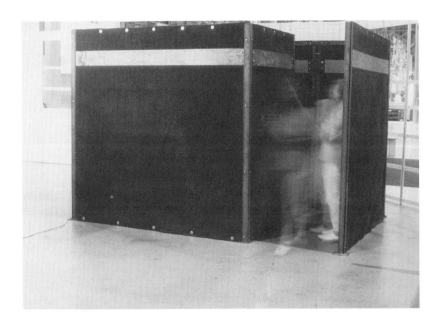

YVONNE SINGER: "The Felt Room" 1993
Steel, felt, LED board, 7'x 7'x 7'x 10'
Photo by Isaac Applebaum

frame suspended by airplane cables to the ceiling. From the outside, the structure is reminiscent of a tent, solid but precarious. At the opposite end of the small room is the electronic sign board which pulsates with words composed of red dots of light.

> Listen carefully ...
> This is ... important ...
> Look at me. Watch me ...
> Swedish diplomat ...
> saves ... 100,000 Jews in Budapest ...
> Raoul Wallenberg ... scion of a wealthy family ...
> and a ... non-Jew ...
> at great personal risk ...

single handedly saved more Jews than whole governments ...
This "angel of rescue" was kidnapped by the Red Army and never
seen again outside a Soviet prison ...
Sorry ... I ... can't ...
hear
you ... sorry ... sorry ...
I can't see you ...
Wallenberg didn't look like a hero ...
He was not the square jaw type ...
his slightly balding head made him look too young and sensitive ...
for the nightmarish job ahead ...
Classmates recall him as warm, friendly, not snobbish ...
He was not fearless by nature ...
I am telling you a story which I cannot tell ...
(I have been sworn to secrecy) ...
I am saying things I cannot say (I have been sworn to secrecy)

The voices in the text from which the above is excerpted recall
newspaper articles shouting fragments of headlines about Wallenberg as
well as whispered responses, referencing private spaces of forgetting and
remembering. Memory, like history, is selective. What is denied and
forgotten is as significant as what is remembered.

The Glass Room is situated in an adjoining space of the gallery.
There is only a large, empty space, dimly lit, with glass shelves and
shadows of words on the wall. Shelves are usually repositories and sup-
ports but these shelves are empty. They hold only the words etched on
their surfaces which we cannot see. We move closer to read the shadows
on the wall. The single shelf reads as follows:

When I was younger, I always had fantasies about what it would
be like in solitary confinement. I would imagine my restricted
cell, with a cement floor, stone walls, small grilled window, too
high to reach and I would imagine how I would pass the time.
Would I have enough resources inside my head to keep me going?
How many songs and poems could I remember? I was told that
my grandfather had a prodigious memory. He could remember all
the words to over one hundred songs and could speak several languages. I thought, he would do well in solitary confinement.

Here memory and events, real and imagined, are conflated and beg many questions. Who is the "I," the speaker of this text? The grandfather is a link to the past, but a tenuous one. The speaker in the text has only someone else's hearsay about the grandfather's prodigious memory ... a memory of a memory. The words are shadows, further evidence of the fragility of memory. If the lights are turned off, the words are gone; memory is denied.

The single words on the multiple shelves on the adjacent wall are confusing and disorienting. How are they meant to be read? horizontally? from right to left? vertically? from top to bottom? Why have they been positioned in a way that confounds meaning?

Words are grouped in verbs, negations, questions and as pronouns shifting our position as viewer from "I" to "you"; also enabling us to move in and around the text in several ways to construct different meanings. Language is unstable and shifts as we the viewer/speaker read it. This reading situation recalls how we first encounter language and the complex transaction that occurs between the reception, construction and production of meaning. The words provoke questions and do not readily reveal anything. They are a game, like those hand-held squares with letters that can only be moved horizontally or vertically, one square at a time to be made into complete words.

"In Memoriam: Forgetting and Remembering Fragments of History" is filled with absences: parts of sentences and stories, incomplete facts, shifting and fragmentary voices, empty rooms, empty shelves, no photographic images. I wanted the experience of the piece to trigger the viewer's own images.

Raoul Wallenberg's elusive presence is a metaphor for the fragility of memory and the instability of identity. What we know of him for certain is frozen at the moment of his disappearance and dependent on the testimony of witnesses, on rumour or hearsay. History happens to you because you are born or live at a particular time and place. There are many missing and ambiguous pieces of information surrounding my family's history as a result of being uprooted and exiled and as a result of the choices they made. I wonder what my life and identity might be if my family had remained in Hungary. I wonder what Wallenberg's life would be if he had not met the Russians on January 15, 1945.

Being a woman, Jewish (or Hungarian, for that matter) is not the same as exemplifying womanliness or Jewishness or Hungarianess. At the same time, there is no question that my gender, social class, religious, cultural, historical background have contributed to my perspective as an artist. However, as an artist my relationship to these factors is continually shifting; some aspects are out of my control; some I chose to avoid, others to affirm.

MEMORY MOVING:

A FRAMEWORK FOR EXPERIENCE

෴

Mimi Gellman

Visual artist Mimi Gellman describes her curation of an exhibit of mixed-media works by Jewish women which combined feminist Jewish concepts with the theme of memory. This eclectic, ground-breaking exhibition accompanied the winter 1996 Toronto conference "From Memory to Transformation: Jewish Women's Voices." The exhibit illustrated the diverse styles and genres used by Jewish women artists in their quest for personal and communal identity. Photos from the exhibit appear on pages 126–132.

INTRODUCTION

IT BEGINS as a slight tugging, a sensation that grows out of a stirring in the heart. Sometimes it is felt as a sensation on the skin like cold, wind, or burning. It free floats, hovering in the body or in the mind until, through some unknown force, it reveals itself. A memory steals itself from the archives of our past and reveals to us who we are, or were, or believe ourselves to be. The act of remembering suspends us in a zone where past, present and future seem to overlap and continue to influence each other. It is our memory, our personal history, the record of our experiences, that we grapple with daily as we work to transform them into a meaningful understanding of ourselves and our culture.[1]

In the spring of 1995, I had the opportunity to curate an exhibition of visual art by eight women artists for the conference, "From Memory To Transformation: Jewish Women's Voices." As a visual artist and educator, I was deeply committed to ensuring that opportunities were available for the exhibition and for discussion of the contemporary visual arts, specifically in the form of conceptual art, which generally is perceived as obscure and impenetrable. I was fascinated by the apparent dichotomy of the designation "Jewish feminist artist." What might this mean? And how would the artists' modes of expression contribute to the discourse on Jewish memory? What shape, context and material nature do these artists employ to make their ideas manifest? Of particular interest to me was the exploration of the work of visual artists who come from a culture based so forcefully on the word, a culture which also carries a historical prohibition on the representation of visual images. The second of the Ten Commandments prohibits the creation of "graven images," idolatrous images for worship. The prohibition was interpreted by Jewish culture as a proscription against the visual representation of the human form.

The contemporary visual arts offer a unique level of engagement and insight on issues of memory and identity. Jewish history and Jewish memory are subjects from which, as Jews, we are never very far away. We carry within us the vast chronicle of our biblical beginnings, the Jewish diaspora and, most recently, the trauma of the Holocaust. It seems essential within Jewish culture to memorialize our history and our past, to carry this collective, monolithic remembering as we relive the fundamentals of the Jewish belief system again and again through the yearly ritual repetition of stories and traditions. Metaphorically, I envision this collective memory as fixed or frozen memory, as memory encased in ice, and as the first permanent record.

As with most other cultures, the evolution of a feminist approach or identity for Jewish women has created the possibility of a different kind of history, a different remembering. Jewish feminist artists still subscribe to the need to record their experiences, their history, but in their expression, history takes decidedly altered forms. The works of these artists embody a history of the feminine, an alternate system of processing and disseminating information. The art works are informed by the artists' personal experience as women, from their traditional and non-traditional roles to issues of marginalization, loss and absence, and to their emergence as a significant political force. The combination of conceptual ideas with the visceral experience of the body has led to the creation of works containing a multiplicity of perspectives and meanings. This form of memory, and its expression, I envision as watery memory, a fluid memory which is not fixed in time or space.

From the mid-1960s on, contemporary art-making practices have gone through a shift, an internal change involving the abandonment of painting as the central form of artistic expression. Art is treated less as an object and more as a process that created the subject: art as social practice. A new formal infrastructure has been developed in response to the need to express ideas that differ radically from patriarchal notions about what art is and how it can be experienced. With these new works, we are shifted from the patriarchal notion of the gaze to an experience of the haptic realm, where we perceive the works through the sum of our senses, through our physical engagement with them as opposed to through a merely retinal experience. Art works no longer associated solely with formal ideas of beauty have found expression in the form of conceptual art installations which rely heavily on context and the juxtaposition of site and materiality.

In Arthur C. Danto's book *Embodied Meanings*, Danto refers to artists who strive to involve their audiences in a relationship that is more intimate than vision alone permits; installations which "transform the viewers onto another plane as celebrants and as metaphorical participants in a larger spiritual transaction."[2] Thus, as Danto states, "the viewer embodies the meaning the work confers."[3] It was my intention to mount an exhibition that succeeded in generating this experience for the audience. The process of selection was an amorphic one, each artist leading me to another, and to the many long and invigorating discussions that led to the final assemblage. The artists I chose worked in an eclectic mix of media and styles within the visual arts, presenting a diverse experience of Jewish feminist work.

THE ART WORKS

Curation began with an excerpt from a work by Mindy Yan Miller called "Every Word, Their Name." In this work, the name "Hannah" is presented to us written in human hair. On a solitary wall, a long dark hair is meticulously placed on each of thousands of tiny pin heads comprising the name Hannah. The methodical nature and process of building this work conjures memories of textile and needlework, which have been historically considered part of the women's domain. This beautiful and compelling work charges the viewer with a visceral memory, confirming our sense of the present. We identify with "Every Word, Their Name" through our own hair, through the shared substance of our bodies. It implores us not to forget the archetypal Hannah, symbol of our history as Jewish women. It is at once a specific and a universal signature of having been.

In many of the works, a diverse range of non-traditional art-making materials are chosen for their evocative characteristics. Nadine Norman's "Swastika, Sauvastica," a work created in ash, transformed a small light room into a swirling, vertigo-inducing cave. In four colours of ash, over a week, Norman and her minions screened swastikas and the reverse form, the Sanskrit sauvastica, like wallpaper designs onto every conceivable surface. As Norman explains,

> the fabrication process involved in the production of my work becomes an integral and visible means of revelation: a way of fusing the past with the present, the spiritual and corporeal worlds. The repeated use of ash, an element representing carbon, a basic compound for existence, also implies the finality of life. I am equally intrigued by its multiple histories (agricultural, economic, social, cultural and political): ash is used as a base of soap, to renew soil and for ritual purification.[4]

To many viewers, it was also a painful reminder of the Holocaust. The most moving aspect for me was the ever constant, ever silent build-up of fallen ash that collected in small mounds at the base of the walls, the swastikas and sauvasticas slowly deconstructing.

Art historian Lucy Lippard states that "one of art's functions is to recall that which is absent, whether it is history, or the unconscious, or form, or social justice."[5] Ruth Libermann's work profoundly addresses this absence. "Scroll #1" first appears to be an abstract drawing, fine black lines on a large field of drawing paper pinned to a wall and scrolled at both ends. As one nears the drawing one realizes that the drawn lines are in fact intricately penned writings, lines and lines of minute overlapping script. At moments these lines reveal personal journal entries and at other times they conceal their concrete meaning. The powerful message of the importance of the recording of an individual life and the subsequent necessity to preserve the privacy and dignity of that record is revealed.

Libermann explains how,

> like a refrain, memory repeats to us what we have not understood, what is ungrasped. But it easily presents itself as a finished product lacking traces of remembering. In suspending the narrative between withholding, revealing and revising, my attempt to engage the process of remembering unfurls as an ambiguity between the desire for narrative and its simultaneous censure.[6]

"Scroll #1" succeeds as a rigorous conceptual art work, as it speaks about the importance of the word, its scroll-like shape alluding to historical, and possibly sacred, documents, its graphic structure providing as well a challenging visual experience.

Andreas Huyssen refers to a recent development in art-making which he calls "memory sculpture." "In these works, the material object is never just installation or sculpture in the traditional sense, but it is worked in such a way that it articulates memory as a displacing of past into present, offering a trace of the past that can be experienced and read by the viewer."[7] Sylvia Safdie, Rochelle Rubinstein and Irene Frolic offer us works that provide an opportunity to experience this displacement of time and place.

In Sylvia Safdie's work, "*Lehav*" [Hebrew for light], a shimmering flame is magically created through the refraction of light. The flame dances solemnly above a beautifully formed transparent laboratory vessel containing water. The vessel hangs tenuously from a fine wire. Spare and reverential, this work reminds us of the eternal flame and our elemental beginnings — water, air and fire — speaking of the interrelated nature

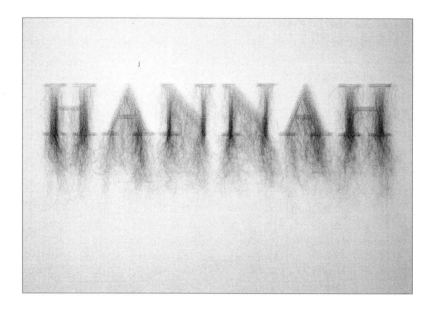

MINDY YAN MILLER: Detail of "Every Word their Name" 1993–1996
Pin-letter skeleton, human hair, straight pins, 7¼" x 50¾"
Photo by Peter McCallum

RUTH LIBERMANN: "Scroll #2" 1996
Typewriter, film, ink on paper, 60"x 240" x 6"
Photo by Simon Glass

SYLVIA SAFDIE: "Kever" 1994
Steel, stone, plaster, glass, 70 x 66 x 198 cm.
Photo by Richard Max Tremblay

ROCHELLE RUBENSTEIN: "Soul" 1996
Woodblock prints on veiling, 8' x 25'
Photo by Simon Glass

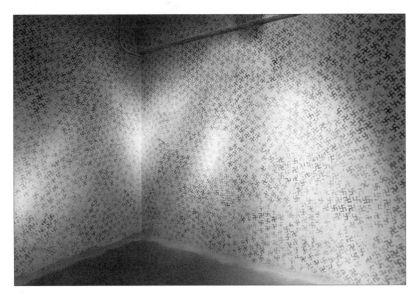

NADINE NORMAN: "Swastika/Sauvastica" 1996
Stencilled ash in room, 10' x 12'
Photo by Simon Glass

ELAINE BRODIE: From the series "Still Life" 1994
Selenium-toned silver print, multiple exposure on a single
6x6 frame of black and white film, 16" x 16"

YAEL BROTMAN: Detail of "Singers & Sewers" 1996
Silk screen, ink/acrylic transfer, 108"x50"
Photo by Simon Glass

IRENE FROLIC: Detail of installation "Healed" 1996
Cast glass with metal inclusions, 19"x10"x10"
and burnt steel wall, 9'x9'
Photo by Simon Glass

of all things. In "*Kever*" [Hebrew for grave], a sculpture in stone, steel and glass, Safdie requires us to navigate around the work, engaging it from multiple perspectives. A horizontal platform of burnished steel carries large vertical sheets of plate glass in which one sees multiple reflections of carefully placed bronzed stones and ghostly, foot-shaped forms in cast glass. The effect of these reflections is mesmerizing and somewhat disconcerting. One feels a solemnity both in the grave-like work and in the human footstep forms that have an uncanny ability to conjure the past. The large bronzed stone is evocative of the small stones that Jews leave as traces of our visits to a grave site. The power of Safdie's work is not found solely in her forms, but as a result of the profound space and sensibility that she creates for us around it.

Rochelle Rubenstein's work, "Soul," beckons the viewer to cross a threshold into the world of the spirit. Seven life-sized pieces of clothing woodblock printed on the sheerest of veiling float along a dimly lit wall, their shadows hovering like protectors. A sadness prevails over this installation, which seems haunted by the spirits conjured up through this play of transparent light and shadow. They represent the history of one woman's life, a woman's role choices as seen through her wardrobe, as well as representing her family, who perished in Auschwitz. The installation evokes memories of a life past and speaks of loss and displacement through the power of a work more substantial in its shadow than in its form.

The sculptural installations of Irene Frolic speak of public and private memory as the artist deals with her own history as a Holocaust survivor as well as her culture's collective memory of chaos and loss. Frolic began her art career at the age of forty and has produced a profound series of works metaphorically and literally layered with experience. These glass female busts are brooding classical beauties at once disturbing and serene, their expressions revealing a complexity of emotions. They challenge us to disclose the source of their haunting gazes and the origin of their heavily encrusted and scarred surfaces. Floating on metal stands in front of a wall of burnt steel, the wall can be interpreted as the context, the luminous glass busts as the spirit that survives and the scarred areas of glass, a testimony to healing.

Of the eight artists involved in the exhibition, Elaine Brodie and Yael Brotman are the only ones who have produced representational, image-based work. Through their use of collage and multiple layering techniques, they produce works of an unexpected, dreamlike quality which provide access to worlds beyond the visual.

In the black-and-white photographs of Elaine Brodie, fragments of text, transparent ghostly faces, stone monuments and nature motifs are mysteriously interwoven through multiple exposures on one plate. Brodie describes her series "as a continuation of an exploration of self beyond the physical plane, as both presence and absence. It began with the idea that we imprint our environment with both a physical and a spiritual residue. The images are about decay and renewal, endings and beginnings, and the beauty of the life cycle."[8] In "Still Life," Brodie's photographs create a tableau about the transient nature of existence, a compelling imprint of a passage through time.

In "Singers and Sewers," Yael Brotman's large-scale installation of vibrant wall-sized prints tells the tale of the immigration and struggles of the women in her family. "The images of this generation of my family are a metaphor for the huge population of Jewish mothers and daughters who left lives of powerlessness in Eastern Europe and immigrated to North America, South Africa and Palestine."[9] Imagery of ornate fabric, pianos and sewing machines are screened, overlapped and drawn onto the large surfaces. They speak of the difficult passage of her female relatives through the sweatshops as well as of their eventual success as professional singers. This biographical work carried with it a nostalgia, a loss and longing for this generation of women.

The artists in the exhibition are representative of a specific moment in art history associated with the expression of feminist principles through visual art. The specific art works were selected because of their evocative qualities and their ability to allude to ideas which do not have a material substance but which are made material in the works themselves. They reveal to us the tenuous, constantly shifting energy of memory, and pose questions regarding the place in which memory resides. These installations act as vehicles for the mediation of history as place and history as presence through their ability to create a special zone, a framework consisting of a careful juxtaposition of private and public, personal and universal, thus enabling the viewers to experience a personalized individual memory, a fluid and watery memory not fixed by ritualized social remembering. The very structures of their installations, the context in which they situate their ideas, and the materiality of the objects they produce, all create a framework for the experience of memory. They invite us to set memory wandering, and to watch carefully where it moves.

NOTES

1. Mimi Gellman, *From Memory to Transformation* (exhibition catalogue, Toronto: 1996).
2. Arthur C. Danto, *Embodied Meanings: Critical Essays and Aesthetic Meditations* (New York: The Noonday Press, 1995), x.
3. Ibid., xi.
4. Nadine Norman, in Gellman.
5. Lucy R. Lippard, *Overlay: Contemporary Art and the Art of Prehistory* (New York: Pantheon Books, 1983).
6. Ruth Libermann in Gellman.
7. Andreas Huyssen, "Sculpture, Materiality and Memory in an Age of Amnesia," in *Displacements* (exhibition catalogue, Toronto: Art Gallery of Ontario, 1998), 31.
8. Elaine Brodie in Gellman.
9. Yael Brotman in Gellman.

THE CHEQUERED STAIRCASE:

JEWISH LESBIANS AT MID-LIFE

⁙

Helena Lipstadt

Acceptance by family, the search for a spiritual community, dealing with marginality and homophobia in both the Jewish and non-Jewish world — these are all part of the struggle lesbians confront through much of their lives. In this evocative personal account, Helena Lipstadt discusses how women are challenging their "multiple oppressions" and creating full, rich and satisfying communities for themselves and their families in their middle years.

HARBSTLID [Autumn Song]

It is autumn and all that bloomed is yellowing.
And I thought that spring would last forever,
and that I could hold eternity in the palm of my hand.
O, falling leaves, O fleeting days.
How will I find my way
when autumn's haze shrouds my path?

> — Beyle Schaechter-Gottesman
> (translated from the Yiddish
> by Adrienne Cooper)

MY FRIEND SUE died of breast cancer last Friday. She was fifty-two. She had been battling cancer for seven or eight years, using only alternative methods of healing: acupuncture, homeopathy, herbs and above all, her unflagging spirit. Sue amazed us all as she pulled herself through crisis after crisis, got back on her feet, set goals for herself. She would say, "I'm buying a camper and Susan and I are going on a road trip — we'll be by your way in January," and would not stop telling and laughing uproariously over her awful jokes.

Sue was one of the cleverest, most cantankerous and willful women I've known, dauntingly, humanly courageous in facing her illness. She did not become a saint; she simply chose life, absolutely.

Nancy, a close friend and carpenter, built Sue's coffin on Saturday, clear pine panels with a Jewish star on the lid. Mochi, Sue's little dog, kept trying to crawl in, not understanding. As if we did.

Her body lies buried in the town cemetery in Swanville, Maine. The graves of Protestants, Catholics and Jews are interspersed, mingled as they lived, as neighbours in the town. Six friends carried Sue's body to the truck from her house and drove the couple of miles to the grave-yard. Six women pulled the coffin from the truck and carried it to the grave site. Dozens more gathered, said their words over her, lowered the box into the hole, shovelled in the dirt.

Sue had lived in Swanville for twenty years. She had built her house and workshop near the road, never got around to replacing her own temporary kitchen cabinets, like the cobbler's kid who wears worn-out shoes. Sue built houses and cabinets for a living, all her work done with precision, with skill, with an eye for beauty. She was buried with her hammer, like an Egyptian queen.

At the graveside, Sue's partner of nine years, Susan, stood quietly behind Sue's parents. Susan had unflaggingly cared for and supported Sue through the years of her illness. Sue's parents had come up from New York to spend Sue's last week with her. Sue's father, a *shul*-going Jew who knew how to conduct a service, dominated and Sue's community of women deferred to him. Not one of them felt like she had the skill — or maybe the chutzpah — to lead the *davening* [praying]. There was no Jewish lesbian rabbi among them.

Sue's father did not mention that Sue left a dedicated partner. He did not mention that the lesbian community lost a vital member. Sue had lived as a vocal Jewish woman in the centre of her lesbian community, at the edge of the country, on the fringe of the mainstream. However, at her funeral, at that moment of the summing up of her life, Sue, the Jewish lesbian feminist, was invisible.

Sue's story contains many elements I would like to explore further in the following pages, through the examples of other mid-life Jewish lesbians. Some are stories of building community, some of affirming ourselves in our biological families of birth. Some of the stories show where Jewish lesbians seek spiritual connection, how we, as older women, deal with raising children in a homophobic world, or decide not to have children at all. These are stories of marginality and links, how we seek out and connect with each other as Jewish lesbians within our community, how we stretch beyond that to the broader Jewish feminist community, to others struggling for justice and peace, as Sue did in her community in Swanville, Maine. These are stories of breaking isolation.

But first I have to locate my subjects. I find myself asking lately, where are the middle-aged lesbians? I cannot find middle-aged lesbians with the ease I once found younger lesbians at the usual haunts, the concerts, readings, rallies. Where are we? Is everyone home, exhausted from trying to make a living? Has our slowly growing social acceptance, like Jewish assimilation, robbed us of the vibrancy, the urgency we once had? Or is it that we are harder to spot?

Walking in town the other afternoon, my partner Elana commented that she notices young girls on the street, their quick bodies, their intense giggling teenage huddles, and she notices old women, bridges from the past and omen of her future, but she doesn't see middle-aged women. I have the same blindness. When I'm in groups I look for my contemporaries in the wrong decade. I look for peers in women in their thirties and forties, as if I were not fifty years old.

Middle-aged women are hard to see, almost invisible. Lesbians are also hard to see. Then who is that woman in the mirror? That middle-aged woman? That middle-aged Jewish dyke? Wearing my mother's face?

I came out as a lesbian in the seventies, attracted to the music, writing, political decisiveness that my lesbian friends were fired by. My friends, already out, stood arms akimbo, tapping their feet, wondering what took me so long. The spirit within lesbian culture was enormous.

I remember sitting on a blanket under the stars among 10,000 women at the Michigan Women's Music Festival, listening to Alix Dobkin sing "*Dortn, Dortn.*" I swooned with delight and for the duration of the song, two of my worlds, lesbian and Jewish, came together.

I came of age in the political movements of the 1960s and 1970s. Now those of us forged in the fire of radical politics face the challenge of ageing well, creating new images of what it's like to be middle-aged, Jewish and lesbian. It is a revolutionary act to claim proud ownership of any or all of these identities, to fight the pressure to go quietly into the twilight, to make ourselves visible. How do we do this? One way is by literally building community.

I recently met a woman, Lisa, who spent the last four years in Israel working for an American computer firm. Fifty-five years old, she has no kids. Her relationship with her parents in the USA is not close and her sister, a Pittsburgh banker, feels Lisa is a "bad influence" on her nieces. Lisa has been a lesbian since the early 1970s and considers the lesbian community her true family.

Lisa has a plan. She wants to come back to North America and buy land and build that venerable lesbian myth, the lesbian old age home. Her image is communal on the lines of the Israeli *moshav*, the collective community, with shared ownership and care-taking. Lisa wants to include lesbians of all ages with the understanding that older lesbians receive both respect and priority for their needs, and she feels it couldn't hurt to have young strong lesbians around to read the fine print when creaky middle-aged gals misplace their glasses, and to help tote those heavy bunches of grapes in from the vineyard.

Lisa wants to make room in the land collective for all the varieties of spiritual expression (from scrupulously crafted feminist liturgy, to Orthodykes to Goddess worshipping lovers of the moon, to the woman who feels most connected when she sings labour songs around the campfire), as well as for the devotedly secular. Her image, honed by many years of consensus decision making, is spacious and progressive.

A place for Jewish lesbians to grow old in community, not shuffled by default back to the isolation and erasure of their biological families. On the lesbian *moshav*, women could age with their values alive around them, their surroundings every day reflecting their lifelong and dearly held choices.

For many women, fashioning a new life in a rural community is not the answer. In fact for many of us, growing older means looking back. We find ourselves more interested in our blood families and places of origin than we have been in years. We look for connection in the Jewish community and find it in two distinct places: the Yiddish revival and religious observance.

When I first went to Klezcamp (an annual week-long klezmer music and Yiddish culture event) in the mid-1980s, two things struck me: how much fun I was having learning Yiddish songs and dancing to spiralling clarinet and violin rich klezmer bands till three in the morning, and how many lesbians were there. Why were there so many lesbians there? In our search for home, rejected by the dry congregations we suffered through Hebrew school but still determined to find our way "back home," we found it in the generations that came before our parents, for those of us who are Ashkenazic, in the shtetls [villages] of Eastern Europe. Lesbians are legion at Klezcamp, at YIVO's summer Yiddish Language Institute, at the National Yiddish Book Centre; from "baby dykes" to salt-and-pepper veterans, we fill the meeting rooms and dance hall. Free from the rules and regulations of the religious community, comfortable in the Catskills (the area itself a relic of the 1930s heyday of secular Jewish culture), we find a *heymishkeyt*, a warm embracing familiarity in the music, reminiscent of the celebratory communities of our grandparents in Europe. And *meydl* [girl], is it fun!

Sometimes, however, it is the intractable places that draw us. The rabbinate, for example. Could there be a heavier door for Jewish lesbians, for Jewish women to push open? The creaks and groanings of that push are loudly reverberating as lesbians graduate from the Reform, Reconstructionist and Conservative rabbinical schools, receiving a range of welcome. The institutions are more ready to admit lesbians than the congregations are to accept them as their spiritual leaders. They most often find work as congregational rabbis in progressive and gay/lesbian communities, as chaplains, teachers, administrators, where the older graduates with more life/work experience have an advantage.

Lesbians are eager to change the image of rabbi. What's the draw? Again, we look back. We want a Jewish context with spiritual dimensions. We want to study the vast body of rabbinical teachings and add our voices to the lists of opinions. "Rav Devorah says ..." We want to wear a *tallit* [prayer shawl] and yarmulke [skullcap, head covering] and lead our congregations in prayer. There is the misogyny to deal with. Along with inspired, ethical teachings come layers of woman hating. Most of the lesbian rabbis I know feel the struggle is worth the effort. They feel they are making a difference, especially in the next generation. A woman rabbi I know in Bangor, Maine, fifty-two years old with a rich contralto voice, called one of her congregants on the phone. The congregant's young son, a student at the Hebrew school, answered the phone. After the rabbi identified herself to the boy she heard him shout to his mother, "Ma, God's on the phone!" *Yidishkeyt* [Yiddish culture], both secular and religious, is our cultural heritage, an endless mine. For some of us, however, the premier battleground for visibility remains within the arc of our biological families. I find I still struggle in this arena, even after being out for twenty years.

Two years after my mother died my brother and I went to New Haven to clear out our parents' house. It had been rented fully furnished, and was growing increasingly worn and neglected. Neither my brother, my father, nor I had the energy to deal with the house and its attendant memories and I encouraged my father to sell. I hoped my father would eventually be relieved by its sale and could then turn to the present-day pleasures of his life.

The house sat on the market for months, still holding family spatulas and colanders in the kitchen cupboards, wine glasses in the dining room breakfront. My brother and I made a plan to meet in New Haven with our father to clear out all of the remaining *tshatshkes* [knickknacks] and furniture.

Packed away in the cellar we found shoe boxes full of old letters, photos of tap dance recitals and Hebrew school classes. Upstairs, a favourite desk, the hand-made holiday tablecloth, stained, but usable.

"Do you want the desk?" my father asked my brother. "How about the dining room table?"

"Wait a second, Dad; I want the dining room table," I said.

"But you're not married, Helena. Aaron has a family."

"I may not be married, Dad, but I have a home, and a family."

As lesbians, many of us have had to struggle for context in a way our straight sisters know nothing about. We have had to fight for acceptance in our families, for ourselves and for our love relationships.

We have had to fight for the security of our jobs, for housing, for the right to parent. There are assumptions about our childlessness — which is rapidly being belied by the Jewish lesbian baby boom — and questions about who will care for us if we have no children and become infirm.

While childlessness was quite common in the Jewish lesbian community of the 1970s, this has changed in the 1990s. There is an active Jewish lesbian baby boom, through adoption, donors, co-parenting. Not even menopause stops the tide as friends adopt well into menopausal years and join *shuls* so they can send their boys and girls to Hebrew school. In doing so they change the face of the Jewish community.

Joanie, at age forty, has just adopted Alex, a bright-eyed one year old from Guatemala. He is her fourth child. Sarah, ten, Robbie eight and Kate, six, all have donor-dads. Joanie teaches a Hebrew school class at the Germantown Jewish Centre. One day, Sarah came home from Hebrew school with an assignment: to make a family tree. A handy, oh so traditional, chart was provided with spaces for mother, father, grandparents on both sides. Sarah, unusually resourceful and unabashed, traced her lineage in all its uniqueness, acknowledging her donor-dad, but Joanie saw the work that had to be done. Joining forces with another Hebrew school parent, the straight father of an adopted Korean child, she created a school-wide staff and parent workshop on alternative families within the Jewish community. Joanie seized the opportunity to underline her daughter's wholesome pride in her family.

We fight for the simple fact of visibility, fight erasure, in both the women's community, where we have sometimes been silenced by anti-Semitism, and in the Jewish community. All this fighting serves to sensitize and strengthen us, if it doesn't break us, and commonly we go through many cycles of empathy, strength and despair. Our Jewish survival skills, tempered through centuries of maintaining identity in hostile surroundings, help us cope.

One Jewish survival tactic, the biblically commanded "be fruitful and multiply," sticks in the craw of those of us who decide not to have children.

The summer I was thirty-five I breezed down a winding Maine road in a car with my mother and father and brother.

My father, never one to mince words, asked, "So, is this the end of the Lipstadt line? Neither you or Aaron are going to have children?

And the family line stops here?"

Aaron and I rolled eyes at each other and squared our shoulders for the plain truth: maybe so.

Was this sacrilege? After the Holocaust, wasn't I required to have a child?

Two years later, my brother did have a son, my beloved nephew Isaac. I felt great relief. It would not be the end of the Lipstadt line, and I was off the hook, the big Jewish procreation hook, outlined in *halakhah* [Jewish law], in social custom, in the car with my father.

I didn't want to have a child then, and as I wake up at three in the morning in peri-menopausal wakefulness, do not regret my decision. I don't know how I would feel if I didn't have a nephew. My nephew provides me with a sense of genetic continuity, but who is my spiritual heir? Isaac, as much as I love him, is not. I can get wet-eyed over the daughter I never had, the one who would carry on my values and my shticks, but really. A child is like a kite, sent out into her own currents of air. This mythical daughter I never had comes with no guarantees of rapport, of spiritual recognition, of continuity beyond the gene. Would she sing the songs I love, tell my stories? Would I bequeath my house to her, just because she is my mythical daughter? Or would I rather bequeath it to Karin, my close friend of twenty years, or as a writers' retreat, to further another Jewish lesbian's work?

Who will take care of me when I'm too old to take care of myself? I don't know. My mythical daughter might not have the resources, or want to. I will have to live right, have a *bisl mazl* [bit of luck], and die of old age in my bed — perhaps on the lesbian *moshav*.

None of us do our work in the world alone. Sue and Lisa and Joanie show, by the examples of their lives, a world made rich by dreaming of, and working for, just community. We, mid-life Jewish lesbians, along with our straight sisters, gather to fight the forces that would erase us actively through homophobia and passively by denying our existence. We gather to make community, without which these passages would be less comprehensible, more lonely. We gather to affirm our perceptions. We gather, having learned the power of the community to support and enlighten us as we create new paradigms. We listen to the stories of each others' lives so far and to the questions of the moment. How do we want to spend the rest of our lives? Can we help each other live them better? If we have dreams still unfulfilled, these are the days to create them.

> We'll dream of a longer summer
> but this is the one we have:
> I lay my sunburnt hand
> on your table: this is the time we have.
>
> — Adrienne Rich

SELECTED BIBLIOGRAPHY

Adelman, Marcy, ed. *Long Time Passing: Lives of Older Lesbians.* Boston: Alyson Publications, 1986.

Beck, Evelyn, ed. *Nice Jewish Girls: A Lesbian Anthology.* Boston: Beacon, 1989.

Greer, Germaine. *The Change: Women, Aging and the Menopause.* New York: Ballantine Books, 1991.

Jay, Karla, ed. *Dyke Life: From Growing Up to Growing Old.* New York: HarperCollins Publishers, 1995.

Kehoe, Monika, ed. *Lesbians Over Sixty Speak for Themselves.* New York: Harrington Park Press, 1989.

Levitt, Laura. *Jews and Feminism: The Ambivalent Search for Home.* New York: Routledge, 1997.

Lynch, Lee and Akia Woods, eds. *Lesbians Off the Rag.* Norwich, VT: New Victoria Publishers, forthcoming.

Old Lesbians/Dykes, *Sinister Wisdom* 53 (1994).

Orenstein, Rabbi Debra, ed. *Lifecycles: Jewish Women on Life Passages and Personal Milestones.* Vol. 1. Woodstock, VT: Jewish Lights Publications, 1994.

Rich, Adrienne. *Your Native Land, Your Life.* New York: W. W. Norton, 1986.

Sang, Barbara, Adrienne J. Smith and Joyce Warshow. *Lesbians at Mid-life: The Creative Transition.* San Francisco: Spinsters Book Company, 1991.

Sumrall, Amber Coverdale and Dena Taylor. *Women of the 14th Moon: Writings on Menopause.* Freedom, CA: Crossing Press, 1991.

Weed, Susun S. *Menopausal Years: The Wise Woman Way, Alternative Approaches for Women 30–90.* Woodstock, NY: Ashtree Publishing, 1992.

TRANSCENDING
DIFFERENCES

༄

Faigel Brown

When Shirley Met Florence *is a highly successful documentary made in 1994 by film maker Ronit Bezalel for the National Film Board (Canada) about two Jewish women, one straight, the other lesbian, whose friendship spans more than five decades. Faigel Brown, the Florence of the film, tells us about how their friendship transformed their lives. In their seventies today, these two women, with their strong senses of identity and humour, serve as meaningful role models for a younger generation of women, both straight and lesbian. Their lifelong friendship is a vibrant precedent for our own concept of sisterhood.*

WHAT MAKES *our* friendship unique? Shirley and I have helped each other grow and develop as individuals during our six decades of being together. Ronit Bezalel, who chose to portray us in the NFB (National Film Board) film, has emphasized that we are ordinary women who did *extraordinary* things. After receiving acknowledgement through the mail, the media, the grapevine and by word of mouth that our film — which has been shown in various parts of the world — has brought comfort and support to women, lesbians and people in general, the two of us have begun to believe it, and to feel gratified.

Shirley and I never deliberately set out to act as role models. The very concept was unknown to us when we were younger. However, whenever possible, if we encountered someone who exhibited talent or just needed direction, we always made an effort to guide that person along a productive path. It is probably more accurate to say that, just by being ourselves — with courage, dedication, obstinacy and of course a little humour — we've influenced more people than we know. Let me start at the beginning.

Shirley and I met in 1936. Fortunately we lived a half block away from one another. We both attended Bancroft Elementary School in Montreal where we were lucky to be exposed to the most wonderful music teacher, Goldie Schlosberg. Our mutual respect for this creative woman definitely reinforced our friendship. Our relationship began when I boldly climbed through Shirley's window, drawn to a Tarantella emanating from her house. (Shirley has a different version of our meeting.) It was, however, sustained by this fantastic musical influence.

Goldie was like a surrogate mother. Shirley and I too soon grew to love each other. Even at so young an age — I, nine years old and she, two and a half years older — we were sensitive to each other's emotions and basic needs. This was providential for we each harboured a secret, which — if we hadn't found a confidant in one another — might have overwhelmed us.

As time went on and as we began to rely on each other, Shirley and I felt free to confide in each other. Shirley no longer tried to hide the fact that her mother was "mentally unstable." (She eventually was institutionalized.) Her mother liked me and was not agitated by my presence as she was by others'. I was more saddened than judgemental about Shirley's mother's ill health.

I'd sit with Shirley for hours with suppressed tears, listening to stories about how her father had left Poland at the beginning of 1935 to pave the way for the rest of the family to come to the USA. In the city of Lemberg — where Shirley and the rest of her family remained — daily pogroms were going on. And *they* knew the horrors of these pogroms: many a time her father had come home all bloodied, his body lacerated by broken glass from the front door of his furrier shop as he tried to prevent Polish hoodlums from entering.

To augment their fears, the family had an even greater penetrating anxiety — that of starvation. When the money from Canada didn't arrive on time and their cupboards were bare, Shirley's family often went to bed hungry. Being isolated as they were — cut off from the rest of the immediate family in Poland; distrusting the neighbours; no word from abroad — took its toll. It's not surprising that, after arriving in Montreal, Shirley's mother began to horde food anywhere and everywhere.

The first time that Shirley's mother had exhibited signs of her impending illness was several months after her father had left Poland. Though the mail had oftentimes been erratic, it had never been so late. The Polish president, General Pilsudski, had died, and all public services came to a halt, including the mail. The fact that Shirley's family suffered hunger and despair simply didn't reckon in the Polish government's scheme of things.

When the mail finally arrived, there was a letter edged in black. Shirley's mother — immediately jumping to conclusions — presumed her husband was dead. Not realizing that the black border was nothing more than a formality to honour General Pilsudski, Shirley's mother broke down. When the documents and tickets eventually arrived for their emigration to Canada, she did recover enough to gather her children and some of their things together for the voyage. Nevertheless, Shirley's mother was never the same again. As I listened to my friend recounting such stories, I ultimately understood her mother's behaviour.

Then the roles would reverse and I was happy to share my problems with Shirley. The most pressing one was how to tell her I was a lesbian — even though I didn't know the word at that time. All I had heard was "pervert," "queer, "homo," which conjured up terrible emotions. No surprise that I had an aversion to homogenized milk long after I understood that "homo" meant "the same." It has only been in the past twenty years that the word "lesbian" began to roll easily off my tongue; only because such words — which had had terrible connotations — were being defused. Before then I'd use the clinical term, "homosexual."

The fear I had felt about revealing my secret to Shirley was unwarranted. She did everything to allay my doubts, beginning by reading the story of Waslaw Nijinsky — the famous dancer who'd been involved with Sergei Diaghilev of the Ballet Russe — to me. This opened up the world of classical dance for me. Shirley then recommended that I read the biographies of Michelangelo, da Vinci, Tchaikovsky, Schubert — all apparently homosexual — which introduced me to the world of art and music. She had me hobnobbing with all these giants. If there were no woman among these titans, it was only because in the late 1930s and early 1940s, few women writers — or biographies of famous women — had been published. In time, however, I did discover Radclyffe Hall's *The Well of Loneliness*, Sappho and Gertrude Stein, amongst others. Nevertheless, even though I was convinced that I was in good company, the anxiety that I felt about being exposed as a "pervert" was not alleviated.

Not everyone was like Shirley. We were living then in an ultra-homophobic and narrow-minded society, where people were repulsed by the mere mention of homosexuality. I was delighted that I could come to Shirley with my tales of woe or happiness whenever I had a crush on someone.

There was also the music we shared, the language which transcends distinction and differences. Though we never had difficulty understanding each other using ordinary English and Yiddish, we'd communicate best when she'd accompany me on the piano or mandolin while I sang folksongs or lieder by Schubert, Beethoven, Handel and Purcell. Music solidified our relationship. While I enjoyed playing baseball, football, hockey and soccer with the boys on the street or in lanes — games which were their sole domain — and Shirley loved to read or just enjoy her solitude, we couldn't wait to get together and make music.

We shared our music with mutual friends and relatives, playing and singing at parties or at any occasion, and having the others join in. Before long, we had our first "professional" performance, in 1938. We were each given a dollar for coming first in an amateur hour at the Belmont Theatre. While singing with another girlfriend in three-part harmony, Shirley accompanied us on the mandolin or filled in with the harmonica.

As our friendship blossomed during our teens and the two of us began to mature, Shirley found herself being courted more and more by young boys. I, meanwhile, had a succession of crushes on young girls. I must admit I didn't appreciate all the male attention Shirley received, as I didn't want anything to threaten our relationship. And I showed it at times! And, if I babbled on about my futile love for this one and that one — oblivious of her feelings for me — it was not out of callousness; I knew that no one would ever usurp her position in my heart. So, if at times we inadvertently hurt one another, it meant nothing; our friendship was basically sound.

We were growing into young women and our lives were taking different courses. Nonetheless, we were still chumming around and performing as a team. Shirley had met my brother Moses and was betrothed to him in May 1945. I may have been a little jealous, but I certainly kept it under wraps. If Moses resented our relationship, he never mentioned it. He took it for granted; after all, Shirley and I had been friends for nine years when he came on the scene. Shirley was obviously happy. We'd now be *mekhutonim* [in-laws]. She had always felt that she had a foot in the Brown's house, but now she'd have both feet securely planted.

In early 1946, when I was living in New York and studying music at the David Mannes Music School, I first learned that Shirley was pregnant. I was determined to go home for the auspicious occasion. In the meantime, I was sending her twenty page letters describing my activities and philosophy in detail, especially after I'd attended a concert, a play or a museum. While I enjoyed these events by myself, I always considered how much more enjoyable they would have been if Shirley had been there to share it. Shirley never complained about my lengthy letters; her only complaint was that they were too short and that I seldom finished my sentences but ran one idea into the other. Although Shirley wasn't as conscientious, when I did receive a letter from her it was as if I were in her presence.

After the birth of my niece, I resumed my studies in New York for a period of two years. And, while I was involved with my life and immediate routine there, and Shirley was busy with hers in Montreal, we were, nevertheless, perpetually on the same wavelength. When I returned to Montreal, the two of us picked up where we'd left off. Our friendship didn't infringe upon anyone else. While Shirley shared

certain interests and domestic activities with Moses, she and I participated in all sorts of other activities.

At the same time, there were activities in which I participated but
which didn't include Shirley. A rebel and idealist, I had aligned myself
with the left-wing movement. I didn't like American or, for that matter,
Canadian politics. How could I condone anti-Semitism? Rabbis were
being burnt in effigy; there was a maximum quota for Jewish students
at universities; Jews fleeing from Europe — before, during and after the
Second World War — were refused entry. How could I justify the
lynching of Blacks, the beating up of striking workers or the persecution of gays and lesbians? With such a record, no wonder I thought
that the "other side" was greener. While Shirley was raising her family, I
was raising my consciousness.

After an aborted marriage — at the age of twenty-four — I met the
person with whom I would share my life for twenty-five years. Sophie
was a psychiatric social worker. It was to Shirley that I first brought
Sophie. I believed that, if Shirley liked her, so would my family. So
when Shirley embraced my lover with alacrity, I knew that I'd chosen
well. Although my parents and their peers never thought to speak
about "it" aloud, they certainly acknowledged my relationship with
Sophie in many subtle loving ways. We were treated as a couple. There
were countless times during our years together when Sophie was referred to as a daughter by my mother and father and a niece by my
aunts and uncles. She was loved by all. However, what thrilled me most
was when my nieces and nephews adopted her as their aunt. So,
whereas I once felt like an outcast, excluded, I now felt included.

My life had fallen into place. Never again did my father call me
"*aza modne mentsh*," such a peculiar person. Since he respected and admired Sophie, he now respected me by association. Besides, what mat-
tered was how I felt about myself. And I liked me! This gave me the
impetus to create and live a constructive life.

By the time I was in my mid-thirties, I was a professional
folksinger/guitarist and a singer of classical songs. To earn a consistent
living, I had decided also to teach the classical guitar. Although I had
been offered a three year contract to perform at various places in the
USA — after singing at Carnegie Recital Hall in New York — I could
not see myself living away from the two most important people in my

life, Sophie and Shirley. I settled for singing at local Bar Mitzvahs, weddings, Zionist functions, TV programmes, radio shows and concerts. Whenever possible, Shirley would join me in these productions.

Since Shirley was compelled to stay close to home because of her children, I suggested she teach the mandolin and the guitar so that she and I would have the same schedule. Though we kept our noses to the grindstone, every now and then we'd go out on a shopping spree. Shirley enjoyed these outings because she liked my taste. She couldn't wait for me to gain weight so she'd inherit my castoffs. I became, and still am, her scout. Whenever I see something I think will suit her, the odds are that she'll buy it.

Then there came a terrible time in my life. Sophie was diagnosed with Amyotrophic Lateral Sclerosis, Lou Gehrig's disease. Shirley was constantly at my side. Little was known of this affliction twenty years ago. The doctors, in their frustration, were cruel; at least the doctor who looked after Sophie made our lives miserable. It was Shirley who frequently accompanied us to the hospital before the prognosis was known; who helped us at home when Sophie was a shut-in for two years; and who subsequently visited the incurable hospital with me where Sophie remained for almost two years until her death in 1977. Thanks to Shirley I was able to cope. Shirley helped me turn this nightmare into a tolerable, sometimes even a warm, experience. Instead of agonizing, we performed music of various lands for Sophie and the other patients — bringing joy to the attendants and to those poor people who were being attended. This allowed me to take one day at a time until Sophie died.

After that horrendous experience — during which time we both put our lives on hold — Shirley decided to go back to school. She was a grandmother and about to turn fifty-three. As she put it, "I am now the focus of my own attention." Shirley chose to major in literature and Jewish studies; she was determined that nothing would stand in her way. She meant to claim her right to participate in any and all activities. Despite the comments — "What does she need more education for? She's raised her children and she already knows how to diaper her grandchildren." — Shirley stood fast. And despite the long hiatus since her studies in her youth, and the opposition, she was adamant about returning to school.

When, during her studies, Shirley expressed her thoughts, we allowed our views to intermingle. This blend of ideas inspired her to write provocative and interesting papers and essays. No matter what time of day, early or late, our hotline was open and active. Now it was my turn to listen; and I listened, and heard.

When Shirley began to sound like a *rebetsn* [literally, rabbi's wife, learned woman], and quoted from the Torah, I suggested that she go into Jewish Women's studies. She offered no resistance! Nor did she hesitate when, while scanning her syllabus, I urged her to take a course which had never before been given in any university entitled Jewish Lesbian Feminists. The die was cast; Shirley enrolled, and I was backstage waiting to hear all about it.

I was delighted when Shirley got permission for me from her teacher to audit a class. As a lesbian — and, fifty-five years after the fact — I was curious to learn how such a *specialty* would be taught. Very interestingly! And, when I was allowed to contribute my two cents worth, I didn't hesitate. Some of the young women valued my participation and we subsequently became friends. Their youthful enthusiasm and dedication to female concerns inspired Shirley and me, and gave us new direction. This was a beautiful example of how women of all ages can work together for a common cause.

It was at this time, through Shirley's participation in a film documenting the Jewish Lesbian Feminist course she'd just completed, that we came to the attention of Ronit Bezalel. We were asked to star in a documentary for the National Film Board based on our friendship. For two years we were followed around by camera and sound people.

Shirley and I were literally thrown into the past. Together we explored every street and byway, returning to our former houses and schools. While we delved into the past and wandered down backyards and lanes we had shared years ago, spirits and shadows loomed large. We relived our joys and sorrows daily, laughing and crying as we reminisced and remembered. As we visited familiar places and the place we have yet to share, Shirley and I once again recognized that our friendship was unique; because, at the cemetery, where our loved ones lie, we were aware that, even in death, we'd be close to each other.

Although we are no strangers to death, having lost family in the Holocaust, our parents and our friend Sophie, we, nonetheless, are not preoccupied with dying. When we walk amid the tombstones, visiting the graves of family and extended family, friends and lover, instead of being overcome with grief and unhappiness, we're comforted and energized by the memory of those who have gone before us. Shirley and I are grateful that — at the threshold of our eighth decade — we still have a lust for life.

DENIAL OF THE
FITTEST

☙

Written and conceived by

Judith Sloan with Warren Lehrer

Judith Sloan is a superb performance artist who makes the personal into the political. She takes the nuances of personal everyday life experiences and combines them with larger current world issues, plays with them and entices her audience with biting insights and poignant realities. In her performance piece Denial of the Fittest, *her protagonist must deal with the deceptions and secrets of her family and her own inner past before she can find her authentic identity.*

Play starts in a blackout.

JUDITH: I always felt like I've been saying the right thing at the wrong time; or the wrong thing at the right time or the right thing at the right time in the wrong place. I always felt like I've been running around screaming, "the sky is falling, the sky is falling," and most people would say, "don't be such an alarmist!" Now I run around saying, "the sky is falling, the sky is falling," and most people say, "yeah ... so what else is new?"

Judith in a complete blackout, manipulating glow-in-the-dark balls.

There's a big hole in the ozone layer. Actually ... there are two big holes. One over the South Pole and one over the North Pole; and now the National Aeronautics and Space Administration (NASA), along with scientists from several other credible, mainstream, certified, Ivy League, neo-military institutions discovered record-high concentrations of chlorine monoxide, a by-product of chlora-flora carbons, in the northern skies. Tell-tale signs of a third gigundo hole over Russia, Scandinavia, Germany, Britain, Canada and New England ... *is anybody doing anything about this?!*

There was a group of scientists in Los Angeles who thought they could take the ozone that's trapped in the smog of downtown LA, put it in a rocket, shoot it up through the stratosphere and spray it into the hole ... *voila!* But then they discovered that the energy it would take to get it up would make a bigger hole. In fact, each time a space shuttle takes off, it makes a hole in the ozone layer, then it orbits around the earth so it can take a picture of the hole in the ozone.

Glow-in-the-dark balls disappear.

All of this I take very, very personally. Because everything in my own life would be just fine, if it wasn't for the fact that the whole world is turning into *a festering, post-modern, neo-fascist garbage dump. I would be fine, I would be just fine!*

Lights up.

I didn't even know what the ozone layer was until I first learned that hair-spray in aerosol cans contributed to the hole in it. I was nineteen years old in hairdressing school. I tried to convince everyone else at the Wilfred Academy of Beauty Culture not to use hair-spray in aerosol cans. They said, "What are you, crazy? How could we even function in here without hair-spray?! How else can we get that *up*-do to stay right?" I don't know, what about Dippity-Do, or hair-spray in the pump bottle? "No, we need the hair-spray in the can." I hated the hair-spray and all the chemicals because I was a vegetarian, although I was smoking cigarettes and drinking a lot of whiskey at the time. The socially acceptable way of committing suicide.

When I was a little girl, my mother, my father, my brother, my sister, my grandmother, the dog and I moved to a new house. When I was nine, my grandmother died. When I was twelve, my father died. When I was fifteen, we had a big fire. I discovered Frank Zappa records do melt. All and all, I had a very happy childhood. I did. Really. I did.

Blackout. Changes into a young girl. Lights up.

JENNIFER (little girl): I really like the springtime. It's my favourite season, I get to do stuff like go walking in the woods with my father. Once, my dad walked right up to a tree and he hugged it. I said, "Dad what are you doing? You look ridiculous hugging a tree." He said, "If you see an old tree, it just looks still. But if you walk up to it and hug it and put your ear next to it, then you hear all kinds of stuff moving around inside it. That's how you know it's alive." I think my dad thinks he's a tree 'cuz you got to walk up to him and hug him and put your ear next to him. Then you hear all kinds of stuff moving around inside him. That's how you know he's alive. He said I was like a young tree, 'cuz you could see my stuff moving around on the outside. I don't know what he meant, but I believed him.

Blackout. Lights up. Judith is juggling while talking; first with one ball, then two, then three, never looking at the balls.

JUDITH: I wish I was able to think about one thing at a time. I wish I was able to *do* one thing at a time. I used to think I wanted to save the world. Now I'm happy if I have time enough to do my laundry. I'd be happy if I could just spend a little time cleaning up my apartment, putting things into their proper place. Creating proper places to put things into.

Almost everyone I know is doing more than one thing at a time. Two things at a time are not so bad. I can handle thinking about two things at a time, like thinking about making a left turn and thinking about going back to public school so I can learn how to pray. After all that might be the health care policy for the next century ... PRAY THAT YOU DON'T GET SICK. I can handle doing two things at once, like eating breakfast and reading the paper. I can handle that. But the fact is, I'm doing too many things at once ... [*Starts juggling three.*] ... I'm on the phone to my congressman, my senator, everyday. If it's not one thing, it's another. I'm taking a vitamin C with my second cup of coffee and at the same time I'm listening to a radio programme on natural health. I'm calling the man who told me to send him a video on Monday, who told me to call him back on Friday. I'm on hold, I'm on hold, I'm on hold. [*Balls are suspended under chin.*]

I jump on the subway to go to the gym to sit on a stationary bike. No wonder I feel like I'm not getting anywhere ... this is what it's like. [*Juggling pattern is continuing in front of her body; looks like the balls are moving on their own.*] It's like my life is out there rolling along with a mind of its own, out there in front of me and it just goes on and on. [*Aside to audience.*] Please don't get the impression that I like this activity, juggling. I hate it. I don't want you to go away thinking I'm a juggler. I'm not. I just want to talk to you and I don't know what to do with my hands. I'm not into Denial. Not me. From the time I was a young girl, I learned that as a woman that I was supposed to keep things nice and smooth ... like this ... [*Referring to juggling.*] And smile. Everything is okay. I'm *fine*. Just lost my job, but I'm *fine*. Hole in the ozone; doesn't bother me, I'm *fine*. Keep it nice and smooth. And if anything gets out of hand, don't let it show! I read in the I-Ching the symbol for crisis was danger and opportunity. Sounds like something a therapist would say, "It's another wonderful opportunity for growth." One time I was going through a whole series of dangerous opportunities all at once. Everything got out of hand. [*Juggling backwards.*] I started doing everything backwards. The scary part is that nobody noticed.

Blackout. Lights up — balls are gone.

I always thought I was going to die young. I don't know why, but I never thought I would make it to thirty. Maybe because I was *miserable* in my twenties. I always use the word "die" in the normal course of living. I think a lot of people do. Common sayings like, *sweetheart, it's to die for*, or *I died laughing*. Comedians use death imagery all the time, *I went out there and I killed!* Actors use violent language ... *Go out there and break a leg ... We bombed in New Haven ... It was a smash hit!* You'd think the theatre was some kind of a battlefield. Certainly the battlefield is made out to be some kind of theatre.

One ball is tossed and balanced around her body.

life	death
sport	death
illusion	death
love	death
power	death

Theatre embodies all of these things. That had something to do with why I left home when I was seventeen and joined a theatre company. I always thought Jews were supposed to talk about everything. Well, that's just it, that's the confusion right there. My family did talk about lots of things: politics, books, movies, films. (You know those are two different things, movies and films.) We just didn't talk about certain things ... like ourselves for instance. My mother talked about her pain every day for five years after my father died.

She marks off space on the stage in the shape of huge square.

There was a certain ... amount ... of space ... in the house for pain ... and she took up all of it. If anyone else felt pain or any other emotion, you couldn't get in! So when I was seventeen, I moved out. I was so sick of hearing about my father being dead. I didn't even want to *think* about it!

Crosses to centre.

In the theatre, I could turn myself into anybody. I learned how to speak like this ... [*Speaks with perfect diction.*] Like I don't come from anywhere.

Have you noticed that about actors? They sound like they don't come from anywhere. How can you trust anybody who doesn't come from anywhere? All my friends kept saying, "Would you stop tawkin' like that you sound like you don't come from anywhere? How can we trust you when you keep tawkin' like that?" I liked not coming from anywhere. No one in my family understood my new life as an actor. *What are you doing that for? Where's it going to get you?* My uncle used to say to me, "Sweetheart, why don't you get a real job?" As if a job was more real than what I was doing. I was having the time of my life, and all my family could say is what kind of living is that? *Living!* When I was acting it was the only time I felt alive. *You're fulfilling yourself but what kind of a* livelihood *is that?*

After being in a theatre company for two years I realized my family was right. I needed something more secure to support my theatre habit. I found out that because my father died when I was twelve, I could collect Social Security until I was twenty-two, as long as I was in school. Back then I was nineteen and I was eligible. I came across this brochure for beautician school and, growing up in New Haven, Connecticut, I had always been surrounded by a small college. Yale University. So I had to decide should I go to: beautician school ... or Yale, beautician school ... or Yale, beautician school ... or Yale. I went to the Wilfred Academy of Beauty Culture. What a good choice. My mother was furious! "Judith, what kind of thing is that for a Jewish girl to do?" I really got into it. I loved it. I entered a hair-cutting competition. And I won! First prize. *[Shows trophy.]* I schlep this around with me from apartment to apartment. It has a little scissors and a little comb on it, 100 per cent plastic. This is priceless. After I won, everyone had a new respect for me. Even my mother. "Judith, you think you could do a little something with my hair?"

For the next six years I was very busy. I had two careers. I had forty regular haircutting customers. I performed in over four hundred shows with a theatre company. I wrote four solo scripts. When I was twenty-two years old I created this character: Sophie. She was like an alter ego. Whenever I wanted to say something that I was too scared to say as myself, instead I would say it as her. That's how healthy I was.

Blackout. Changes into Sophie; an old Jewish immigrant with a hat and veil, a shawl and a thick accent. Lights up.

SOPHIE: I have a grandson. He moved vay far avay to the country. Vent back to the land and stayed there. So primitive the vay he lives, no plumbing. He says to me, "Vhat do you think, Bube, you like the vay I live?" I say to him, "To tell you the truth, the vay you live reminds me of the old country." In the old country, ve used to eat inside the house and go outside to take a crap. In this country, you crap in the house and go out to eat. Every place is different. So many grandchildren. I have a granddaughter, she comes to me all the time. Von time she came to me, she vas so upset. I could see by her face she vas troubled. I said to her, tell me vhat is on your heart. She looked at me, "Bube, I vant to die." This from a young goil. I said, talk to me. She said, "I'm afraid to live, I'm afraid to die." I tell her I think everybody is a little bit afraid to live a little bit afraid to die. I tell her a story. She never met my Morris. He vas gone by the time she vas here. I don't know how it happens, but vhen she came out, she looked the image of mine Morris. How does it happen? So, I have for her, a special feeling. I tell her, she has inside her Morris's soul, yeah. He didn't have a lot of money, but he had a heart as big as the sky. When Morris took sick (and the rest of his family perished on the other side) he looked at me and said, "Sophie, I'm not afraid to die, I just don't vant my life should be *fargesn*." I told him, by me you vill never be forgotten. When you loose somebody you love you keep a piece vith you. In your heart. That's how you know it vas real. Vhen I lost my Morris I vas afraid to live. I vasn't proud of it, but I vent inside like a turtle. Mine heart vas begging to talk to him. So I tell mine granddaughter she's not the only von. Vhen you feel bad, you have to have a hope. You have to have inside you a dream, a desire. "Vhat is it to hope?" she asks me. I tell her, von day you feel bad, two days, a year. You have to remember von day you felt good. That is vhy I say hope is a memory of vhat is yet to become. Oy! *Ikh bin farblondzht* [I'm lost]. You'll come visit me another day. I'll make a plate. Special for you. Next time, I'll tell you a different story. Yeah, sure.

Blackout. Then lights up on Judith.

JUDITH: Everyone always thought I was doing my grandmother when I was doing Sophie. I thought I was doing my father. Actually, when I was twenty-three I began an oral history project with all these older European Jews. A lot of my friends kept saying, "What are you doing that for? You're hanging out with old people all the time. Where's it gonna get you?" I remember this one older actress told me, "if you keep doing this Jewish lady you won't get anywhere." I told her I had never really been anywhere, so anywhere I got was farther than where I'd been, so it was somewhere. I liked listening to older people. I understood them. I heard all kinds of stories. About the Russian Revolution, the Triangle Shirt Waist Factory fire. But mostly personal stories. When people would ask me to turn the tape recorder off that's when I'd hear about death, life, the suicides, the affairs, the secrets. I remember one woman, Mrs. Greenberg. I was on my second interview, my fifth poppy seed cookie. She asked me to turn the tape recorder off. "You know, Judith, I am an unlovable person." I asked her what she meant by unlovable and she said, "I could never tell other people that I loved them." Then I remembered in an earlier interview she told me that right before her own mother died, her mother told her that her one regret her whole life was that she couldn't tell her children that she loved them. I thought I was getting really good at unravelling other people's stories. I thought, gee, why do I spend so much time listening to all these old people and I never talk to my own grandmother? Then I remembered she was dead ...

In those six years, I made two documentary videos, performed in four different countries, fifty-seven cities, seventeen festivals, slept in sixty-seven hotel rooms, one hundred two couches, cots and guest rooms. I had two on-and-off long-term no-term relationships, fell madly in love with fifty-three different people, went on twenty-seven-and-a-half superficial dates. I had a vibrator, a mirror and a vivid imagination.

I flew on a hundred forty-six planes, read two hundred seventeen books, subscribed to twenty-two feminist and left wing publications, and *The New York Times, New Haven Register, The Washington Post*. I belonged to seven organizations, I had a lot of friends in a lot of cities, hundreds of compatriots, scores of acquaintances and dozens of intimate friends. I was very good at having intimate conversations with *five* hundred people at once! *And* I was all *alone* because I was completely self-sufficient! I didn't need anybody, I didn't need anything, I was *happy, I was perfectly fine!!!*

A friend of mine gave me a suicide prevention number. The lady asked me why I called. I said, "I don't really know." She said, "Is it an emergency?" I said, "I don't think so. Could I come down in twenty minutes?" They referred me to this therapist who would see me for free.

Moves to chair, down right. Moves chair with each new therapist.

The therapist said she thought I was in a rage. Then she said, "You think you're angry now, wait till you get in touch with your feelings."

So I went to another therapist for a free consultation. I said, "I think I want to die." Turns out she knew who I was. She said, "What are you crazy? You just had a review in *The Washington Post*, a piece in *The New York Times*, a big show coming up; people would kill for that kind of exposure. You have everything to live for."

My next free consultation was with a therapist who said, "Look, look at your life, you're talented, you're funny, you're young, you're pretty. What have you got to be worried about?"

I told the next therapist, "I can't sleep, I keep dreaming that I'm consumed by fire. I'm having nightmares in the middle of the day. I sit at my typewriter and for the first time nothing is coming out — my mind is flooded with noise. I keep thinking about suicide but I can't kill myself, because six hundred people are coming to a show in two weeks and what will they think?" He said, "You're going through a typical traumatic transition; a T.T.T." Then he took out his sliding scale, asked me if I would come again the day after tomorrow, and wrote me out a prescription for Valium.

I gave up on shrinks, went to the library and took out half a dozen psychology books. It turned out, according to the books, I was exhibiting all the symptoms of survivors of childhood trauma! Which didn't make any sense to me, because I had a perfectly happy childhood. I did. Really, I did. So I concluded, naturally, that I was simply out of my mind!

I took the stack of books, a copy of my press packet, and walked into the Connecticut State Mental Health Centre. I showed the lady my brochure and said, "*You see, you see? I turn myself into all these different people for a living. I think I want to die.*" Fortunately instead of putting me in a straight-jacket, giving me a shot of Thorazine and locking me up in isolation, she referred me to Mary.

Sits back down in same chair. Talks faster and faster.

I told Mary, Really strange things are happening. I have this watch that my mother gave me. It started going faster and faster. First five minutes, then ten, then a half hour fast, and I am showing up fifteen minutes early to everything, which is really strange because I'm usually late. Then one day I was looking at the watch and the hands started moving backwards and I felt like time was going backwards and my mind was unravelling, and then the watch broke. I think that is really significant. I told her, I haven't slept in months. I think there's something wrong with all the pictures in my head. I think I want to die. You see this lover I was living with for four years fell in love with one of my best friends on the anniversary of my father's death. Ach! And then I jumped into bed with this man I met at volleyball. I don't know why I did it I hardly knew him. And then I started getting all these really crazy letters from my mother, *zbsjuftr, blutha blutha blutha blutha and then blutha blutha blutha blutha and blutha blutha blutha blutha blutha blutha blutha, and then I don't even do any drugs bulthagll blutha blu-lutha and then my car, you know how machinery blutha blutha blutha bla you wanna see the books? chwsicowickowh skjdf wiydhsoiehj blgiba.!!@#!@#!@ bjudgk wokwhwy sdjdkowa!*"

She freezes, standing up on the chair, does a double-take and quickly sits down.

She waited till I was through, looked me straight in the eye and said, "I think somewhere along the line you got the message that you should be dead. Let's find out how."

Blackout. Changes to little girl, crosses down centre. Lights come up centre.

JENNIFER: He told me he knew that mountain like the back of his hands, but I shouldn't have believed him 'cuz we got lost. Finally, we got down, and were walking real quiet at the bottom, and you could hear the crunch crunch crunch of the leaves under our feet. And all of a sudden he turned around, he looked at me and said, "It's amazing how some people could get so busy, they don't even hear the sound of their own footsteps." I don't know what he meant but I believed him.

Lights up down-stage left at stairs. Judith is standing at top of stairs in window light.

JUDITH: When I was twenty-two years old, I had a dream about my father. I was in my room in an apartment I lived in with four other women. My bedroom was on the third floor and in my dream, my father was walking by the window of the third floor. I wondered what he was standing on. How did he get up there? Why did he leave me in the first place? In my dream, I found out that he wasn't really dead. He had just gone away for ten years somewhere secret because he was on assignment with the CIA or the FBI. I watched too much TV when I was a kid, James Bond, *Get Smart*, all of that. Plus, my father looked just like an actor, Ross Martin, who shows up on reruns of *The Twilight Zone*. So you see how a child could get confused.

In the dream, my dad was talking to me, and all of a sudden, we were transported to the old house I grew up in. You know how that can happen in a dream. We were standing on these stairs, the ones that went down to where my grandmother had an apartment in the basement. And I asked him why he left and he said, "I just couldn't do it any more." Then he disappeared again and left me standing on those stairs. When I woke I thought he was still alive.

I loved my father a lot. He taught me how to play ball, how to add and subtract, and how to change the gears on the stick shift from the passenger seat of his VW bus ... and he was funny. One Saturday in December when I was just twelve years old, we went to synagogue as we usually did and then we came home, changed our clothes, and then we went jogging around this field, like we usually did, and then we came home again and then boom. All of a sudden we both came down with the Hong Kong flu. I didn't know how we got the Hong Kong flu in Connecticut. I remember watching TV for a few days. Just me and my Dad. It was great. I had him all to myself. Dirty tissues were piling up. Then I got better, but my father got sicker and went to the hospital. And three days later he died ... I got better and he died ... He was forty-eight years old ...

After he died I went into a closet upstairs and found a big box with pictures of people in Russia, and pictures of my dad as a little boy and pictures of my grandmother. Old brown pictures that no one ever talked about. Pictures of my grandmother's brothers and sisters in Riga. Before the war.

I used to imitate my grandmother. She lived in a slum when I was a little girl, and she fed me [*imitating grandmother*] "strawberry jam on Saltine crackers." Her apartment smelled, but I loved it. She taught me how to speak English in a Yiddish accent. She would say, "Judelah, dus is a vinda," and I used to walk around saying, "vinda." My mother told me one day she walked into my room when I was three and I said, "Maman, give me mine pink petticoit." She thought it was cute. When my grandmother moved into our house I used to brush her hair with olive oil. She had long thick hair down to her waist. Although I have no conscious memory of it, she must have told me stories. Now, years later, I imagine I was brushing her secrets into my soul.

Then I would braid her hair and put it up in a bun. She had these pins. They weren't bobby pins, they were hair-pins. For the bun. I never saw pins like that again till I went to hairdressing school. I thought that was really significant.

I keep thinking about the things you're not supposed to say. In my family I call them the "not-supposed-to-tell stories." You know, the stories that everyone knows, but no one talks about, which is why they end up not being told, and that's how they end up being the not-supposed-to-tell stories, even though everyone knows them.

She is interrupted by loud music and bright glaring lights.

Oh my god! There are gays in the military! GAYS IN THE MILITARY!!! Everyone knows there are gays in the military. If you're gay in the military and you don't deny who you are then you're not fit to serve. If you do deny who you are then you are fit and you can serve. Don't you see? It's all the "denial of the fittest."

She catches herself, embarrassed that she is not sticking to one thing at a time.

Oh ... Oh. My grandmother. My grandmother moved into the downstairs apartment of my parents' house when I was eight. She died, they said of a stroke, when I was nine. At the funeral everyone was wailing. I remember my aunt walked up to the casket to look in, but Uncle Lou, her husband, my father's brother, kept screaming, "No, no ... no Jean ... don't look, don't look!" I had no idea why he was so upset. Why she couldn't look. Why she'd want to look.

Crosses to the chair down right.

I used to think the world was going to blow up in a nuclear war. Or an accident. Then I stopped worrying. I started worrying again, now that India and Pakistan have started blowing up nuclear bombs. Up until recently I had a recurring dream that I was standing by a lake and all of a sudden the sky turned lime green and from far off on the horizon I saw a missile shooting up across the sky and I thought, this is it! Oh my god who am I going to talk to? Who am I going to talk to? That was my biggest fear. Now I worry about garbage. The other night, I had a dream that I was walking down the street in the town I grew up in. Way off in the horizon I saw these big gigantic cumulus clouds and they were rolling through the sky with great speed. There was a highway packed with cars, packed with people driving the cars, and the clouds were chasing the cars. As the clouds got closer I realized they were right down to the ground filling up the sky. Covering up a clear blue sky, and covering up the cars as they approached. As the clouds got closer I saw they were solid, and they were filled with Snickers wrappers and Carefree sugarless gum wrappers and McDonald's Styrofoam cups. I started running and running and running away from the clouds towards the clear blue sky. I don't know if I had that dream because each year more medical waste gets washed up on the beach, somewhere, and they have to close the beaches. Last year more hospital medical waste washed up on the beach and included in the waste, according to the newspaper, were four hundred hospital meals. The really scary part is that in the hospital they call it a meal! One very hot day last summer, I was walking down Second Avenue in New York City, and I saw this truck. It said "Medical Waste Disposal Company" on the side. I walked up to the driver. I said, "Excuse me can you give me a lift? I think you're going my way. I'm going to the beach."

Blackout. Lights up. Wedding music begins to play. Judith dances through this next monologue.

Seventeen years after my grandmother died, I'm at my brother's wedding, as dressed up as I could get at the time. Talking to my Uncle Lou. My sweet Uncle Lou. You know how those family gatherings are. Everyone asks you how you are. What are you doing? How's your career? So, with Uncle Lou, I decided to tell him the truth. "I'm going through some hard times. All my relationships are a mess, and the problem is me! I don't know why, but I'm obsessed with this oral history project." He knew about my project because he read the review in *The Washington Post* and the article in *The New York Times*. And he was truly very proud of me. I was in the news. And that was a solid thing. A real thing. A comfortable thing to talk about. I asked him if he knew how my family changed their name to Sloan from Shalomovitz, and who did it first and why, because there was only my father, my grandmother and my uncle. I wondered what kind of career I would have as Judith Shalomovitz. Probably a director! Probably film. So we were talking about this and, I said, "Well, before Bubu (that's what I called my grand-mother) died of a stroke did she ..." And he interrupted me and said,

Music stops. She talks in Uncle Lou's voice.

"Oh no, sweetheart, she didn't die of a stroke. Who told you that? She took her own life."

A piece of the truth fell out of the mouth of my Uncle Lou and landed inside my heart. My brother and his bride, all the people in fancy clothes, the food, the tables, the shining forks and knives, the sparkling green grass. It all disappeared. For a moment. An eternity. I stood there like a rock, and I knew it was true. What he said. I knew it was true ...

After seventeen years I finally started asking everyone in my immediate family, *why?* Why didn't anyone ever talk about my grandmother? I asked my mother, *why?* She said it was too hard. I mean we didn't really talk much after my father died, not with words, mostly it was just ... ARRGGHHH! I mean she was a woman alone with three kids and the house and the bills in a culture that distrusts a widow with three kids and a house and the bills. I asked my sister and brother, *why* didn't any-one talk about our grandmother? They said, no one ever asked. We never talked about it. Because you're not supposed to say. Don't tell your friends. Don't tell other people. Tell them she had a stroke, she had a heart attack ... just don't tell ... them ...

One day, I asked my Uncle Lou, "How do you know for sure Bubu killed herself? How do you know it wasn't just an accident?"

"Because she lit herself on fire, sweetheart."

"But how do you know?"

"Because your father found the rags and the lighting fluid next to the bed."

I said, "It wasn't the bed. It was a chair in the middle of the room. I was there." But I could barely remember anything about it. I could barely remember my grandmother. Meanwhile, I was running around the country performing this old lady, Sophie ... I couldn't tell if I was doing my grandmother, my father, or me.

SOPHIE'S VOICE: You sit still; listen to your heart, the voice that talks to you in your heart vill tell you vhat is real. The voice that talks to you in your heart vill tell you vhat to do.

JUDITH: I called my brother. I asked him, Can you help me out? I'm remembering things for the first time in my life, and you were older than I was. Do you remember that day? "Yeah," he said, "I remember everyone screaming Bubu's burning, Bubu's burning." I called my older sister. I said, I'm remembering things for the first time in my life. Do you remember? "I remember," she said. "I remember the stairs." I said, I remember going down the stairs, following Daddy as he ran down the stairs with a blanket to put out Bubu. She said, "I think I followed him too. I ran down the stairs." We ran down the stairs together. She said, "You know, I remember turning the corner of the stairs." Yes, I said, I remember turning the corner of the stairs, Bubu was in a chair at the end of the room and then I go blank. My sister said, "Me too."

We have the exact same memory and the exact same memory blocks.

My sister is my corroborating witness. I understand why you have to have a corroborating witness. Because with the testimony of a corroborating witness, a memory, a series of images, a story becomes real. A life becomes validated. The details. It's the details that you remember when you remember. I never will really know *why* my grandmother did it. I settle for *how*. I couldn't save her life. All my projects. All my interviews. I just couldn't save her.

Too bad foresight doesn't have twenty-twenty vision.

Judith moves to up-stage light. In coloured light, she begins moving backwards from up-stage to down-stage with her back to the audience in various deep coloured light. There is a large shadow cast on the back of the stage, as if the shadow is speaking to the audience.

A grandmother sets herself on fire. All her brothers and sisters are shot and dumped in a ditch thirty years earlier by the Nazis in Riga so they could build their concentration camp in Russian territory. So the Nazis could burn the aunts and uncles and nieces and nephews. So organized, so methodical, so much attention to detail: *These are the things you just don't talk about.*

The shadow gets smaller and smaller as she continues.

A father dies from the flu in a hospital, a very good hospital ...

MALE VOICE (off-stage as she continues to move): We did everything we could to save his life.

JUDITH: *These are the things ...*

Judith continues to move backwards from up-stage centre to down-stage centre. The shadow is huge.

Plutonium leaks invisibly into neighbouring communities.

MALE VOICE (off-stage as she continues to move): We did everything we could. We informed the public as soon as we knew, and anyway there's no empirical proof that there is any leakage and if there are any deaths they are not a result of the leakage.

Judith turns to deliver the next line. Pinpoint light in centre isolates her in a box.

JUDITH: *These are things ...* that you just don't talk about.

Because ... it's just too much. Because if you were to really think about these things you just might ... you just might ...

[*She mouths the following words as she boxes herself in with her hands.*]

... set ... yourself ... on ... fire ... or ... or you just might go out on the street screaming ...

JENNIFER: ... the sky is falling the sky is falling ...

JUDITH: ... and then you might get locked up for disturbing the peace, or even worse, you just might be ignored.

SOPHIE: Remember, if you rock the boat it might *tip over* ...

And you, my darling, how are you feeling?

JUDITH: Me? Me? What about Me? Oh, I'm fine, just fine. So I wasted seventeen precious years of my life thinking I was making up my nightmares and now I'm fine, right? What happens? I unsolved my mystery and *I'm still saying the wrong things at the right time in the wrong place.* What was I thinking? That I'd work out my personal grief, and all of a sudden I'd win a prize?! That I'd get credit? A diploma? A PhD in pain? That people on the street would congratulate me? That I'd become a new person like all those New Age spiritualists promised? All of a sudden I'd become a tall blonde *shikse* on skis? No ... that's not what happens! I wanted to walk out on the street, and have someone come up to me and say, congratulations Ms. Sloan, you get the car *and* what's behind the curtain!

She is out of control.

MALE VOICE (interrupts from off-stage): Uh ... uh ... uh ... Ms. Sloan ... Ms. Sloan.

JUDITH: Oh. I'm sorry. I am so sorry, ha ha ha hha hhha ha ha ha ha. Your friend told you I was a comedienne. Heh heh. Well, uh, I am. Really. Cause I'm just kidding with all of this. Don't worry about it. It's just a play ... *Denial of the Fittest.*

Blackout.

☙❧

PERFORMED BY JUDITH SLOAN.

This version of *Denial of the Fittest* has been edited and adapted for inclusion in this anthology. The full production includes several characters who are not represented in this adaptation. *Denial of the Fittest* was developed at La Mama Experimental Theater in New York City. The work received critical acclaim at the Edinburgh Fringe Festival, has been produced in theatres, universities, at festivals and conferences throughout the USA and in Canada.

PART THREE

RELIGION

AND

RITUAL

ZAKHOR:

MEMORY, RITUAL

AND GENDER

❦

Norma Baumel Joseph

In traditional Judaism, women are matriarchs of the household and transmitters of Jewish culture. Yet when it comes to religion and ritual women have almost no role. Traditionally, women are excluded from the honour of reading from the Torah; they are not counted as part of the minyan [quorum]; they are prohibited from reciting Kaddish, the prayer for the dead; nor can they initiate their own divorce. Today these and other restrictions are being questioned and altered as observant Jewish women demand more religious and personal equality. Scholar Norma Joseph has been a forerunner in advocating that women need not abandon Judaism to break free from its constraints. Instead they can seek new understandings and interpretations of original Jewish sources and use these in their arguments for equality. In the following essay, she uses traditional sources to substantiate her argument: that Zakhor, the Jewish requirement to remember, must be inclusive of women's history and women's experience.[1]

ZAKHOR, the biblical commandment to remember, has been a fundamental responsibility of the Jewish people throughout history. It is enshrined in the Ten Commandments by association with the Sabbath (Exodus 20:8) and liturgically elevated through the *yizkor* memorial prayer for the dead. Jewish tradition recognizes the power of memory and finds unique ways to ritualize and concretize that faculty. Memory plays a major part in our understanding and conception of Judaism and Jewish community life. Presumably, it has been one of the keys to Jewish survival. Yet I find it one of the most enigmatic and paradoxical concepts to understand.

Beginning with Passover, the yearly cycle of holiday celebrations constantly reverberates with commemoration. From remembering one's ancestors to recalling one's enemies, there is a flow to the year that rests on an assumption of a consistent, continuous and common collective memory.

That is a lot of remembrance. Difficult and time consuming, presumptuous even, but what is so paradoxical and why am I so troubled?

There are two parts to the enigma of Jewish memory that I would like to explore. First of all, what do we really mean when we say "Remember!"? How do we accomplish that mandate: how do we live it? And secondly, whom do we remember: whose story do we tell and how do we tell it? The memories of women, like their voices, have been neglected and silenced. In the vast compendium of our heritage there is a rich field of women's memories that awaits our transformative inclusion.

WHAT DOES IT MEAN TO REMEMBER?

In the introduction to his insightful book *Zakhor*, Yosef Hayim Yerushalmi poses some interesting historiographic questions.

> We should at least want to know what kind of history the Jews have valued, what out of their past, they chose to remember, and how they preserved, transmitted and revitalized that which was recalled.[2]

Yerushalmi is reminding us that memory involves choice and some form of action. For both the historian and the participant, not everything is worthy of recognition, retention and celebration. Yet, that which is chosen is exceptionally influential. Judith Plaskow maintains that it is in the retelling of our past stories "that we learn who we truly are in the present."[3]

Moreover, as noted above, Judaism embraces memory as a religious obligation. Memory may seem elusive and fleeting to us, yet the Bible has no difficulty in commanding memory. The verb *zakhor* and its variations occur in the Hebrew Bible 229 times. As a noun it is found forty-seven times.[4] Unconditional and pivotal, memory is an obligation upon both God and the people of Israel. It is the foundation of the covenant that binds the two. We must remember; we are forbidden to forget. And we call upon God to remember. Moses brings the message of God to the slaves in Egypt not in the name of "The Creator of Heaven and Earth" but as the God of their ancestors, the One Who Remembers (Exodus 3:16 and 4:31). Additionally, the decalogue (Ten Commandments) introduces God as the One who acts in history.

Thus, Jews have survived as a people with a clear sense of a collective memory. It is, of course, not anything genetic or physiological but rather a social reality, transmitted and sustained through the conscious efforts and institutions of the group. For Jews memory is not merely the subject of history. It does not belong to the historians. It is more than a mere recording of acts and facts. Rather, memory is perceived and received as an integral, pivotal aspect of communal religious life. God is found in history, but it is a very special kind of story. As Jonathan Boyarin notes, Judaism manages to use story to extend divine authority into historical time and locate the people Israel in God's time as well.[5]

HOW DO WE REMEMBER?

There are many ways that a community can use memory to establish itself. Most frequently the retelling of story reinforces a collective experience. For Jews that retelling has many facets, three of which expose the paradox that intrigues me.

The first instance has to do with the holiday of Purim. One week before Purim, the biblical portion that is read in synagogues is known as *Zakhor*:

> Remember what Amalek did to you on your journey after you left
> Egypt — how undeterred by fear of God he surprised you on the

march when you were famished and weary and cut down all strag-
glers in your rear. Therefore, when God grants you safety from all
your enemies around you in the land that your lord God is giving
you as a hereditary portion, you shall blot out the memory of
Amalek from under Heaven. Do not forget! (Deuteronomy
25:17–19)[6]

Israelites are commanded to remember this particular enemy and eradicate its name. There we have it — the contradiction in all its heavenly
power. Remember! Do not forget! But also, blot out the memory! How
on earth can a people accomplish both tasks?

The ritual of story-telling on Purim offers a further illustration of
this disparity. On the holiday of Purim Jews insist on telling the full
story of peril and survival experienced thousands of years ago in Persia.
Part of the ritualized story includes repeating Haman, the villain's
name, frequently. Haman is supposed to be Amalek's descendant, from
the tribe of those who are to be remembered and erased. However, he is
not called the "unnamed one." His name is pronounced quite clearly
and frequently. Jews name him and then make a great deal of noise to
drown out the sound of his name. What a charade, what pretence, how
effective! The ritual ensures that his name is repeated as it is concealed,
hidden in the waves of sound. Is this not exactly how to remember and
blot out?

Moreover, tradition links not just Haman, but all persecutors, with
the evil of Amalek. Even Hitler is called by some "an Amalekite." Thus,
Jews continue the ritual tradition even with an historical figure like
Hitler. After mentioning his name, many will say, *yemakh shemo*, may
his name be erased, eradicated. Yet, we refuse to forget; we will not
allow his name to be wiped out. We stand vigilant that history books
tell the story accurately. We remember so that "never again." We fight
the evil of Amalek with our memory, but it is a memory that refuses to
become nostalgia or squandered and so we retain the noise for Haman
and *yemakh shemo* for Hitler. What a successful contradiction.

The second example of ritualized story-telling comes from the
holiday of Passover during which Jews turn memory into performance
theatre. On Passover, Jews commemorate and celebrate with *pesakh*,
matzah [unleavened bread], and *maror*. *Pesakh* refers to the paschal

lamb sacrifice that is remembered with a little piece of roasted meat, the uneaten ceremonial *zeroah* [the shank bone, symbolic of the lamb]. In fact, the critical ritual act of Passover for our ancestors was the offering and eating of the lamb in the Temple. All Jews had to partake of this meal. We can no longer keep Passover the way our ancestors kept it. So we ritualize the memory of it, but our memory takes quite different turns. Ashkenazim [Jews of European extraction] remember through avoidance. They do not use lamb at all for the ritual meal. In fact, they do not eat roasted meat at all that night. On the other hand, some Sephardim [Jews of Spanish or Middle Eastern descent] specifically use lamb for the meal and for the *zeroah*. Avoidance or imitation, two styles both equally operative in Jewish ritual life that establish a pattern for memory.

The ritual process proceeds with story-telling that involves eating matzah and *maror* and dipping in salt water or lemon juice. This is either theatre of the absurd or human faith in action. Does dipping a vegetable in salt water remind us of tears? Does eating matzah make us hurry or feel poor? Does one second of eating a bitter vegetable [*maror*] equate in any way with the bitterness of slavery? Paradoxically, it does.

My third and final example is from the story-telling style of the Passover liturgy. Absurdly, the Passover story of deliverance is frequently told in the first person "I":

> In every generation it is one's duty to regard himself as though he personally had gone out of Egypt, as it is written: You shall tell your son on that day: "It was because of this that *ha-Shem* [literally, the name; God] did for 'me' when I went out of Egypt." It was not only our fathers whom the Holy One redeemed from slavery; we too were redeemed with them, as it is written: *He* brought "us" out from there so that *He* might take us to the land which *He* had promised to our Fathers. (Exodus 13:8, Deuteronomy 6:23)[7]

There are certain problems with this rendition of the Hebrew that will be addressed in the next section. But first, on the general theme of memory, the third part of the puzzle is highlighted. For in this incredible chapter, we have an embedded theology of Jewish history and purpose. "I" am supposed to experience this ritual as if I had been there. Me and not my ancestors. In this ritual story-telling, the space–time continuum ceases to exist. The key events that formed the nation are remembered not as some long ago happening. The matzah and bitter herbs are to stimulate the individual's personal memory of oppression and slavery. Discussing freedom as a philosophical idea or political commitment is not sufficient. The ritualized commemoration insists upon an immediate, embodied experience and celebration. And in that moment of personalizing history, of making it my own story, it becomes the source of a profound pledge to respond and be responsible.

Jewish tradition builds on this personal sense of involvement to make the claim that Jews must eradicate the memory of slavery for ourselves and others. We must liberate the world, as we once experienced bondage and freedom. We must remember the evil of Amalek, so that we can continue to wipe it out. Our ancestors lived through these experiences and so must we. In the language of the Bible, the covenant is made with those who stood at Sinai "and also with those who are not here this day" (Deuteronomy 29:14). Whether one accepts divine authority or the power of community or both, this outrageous claim is lived out in the ritual performance of Judaic celebrations.

Thus, paradoxically, through ritual and recitation, memory is called upon to actually shatter historical time, to make present the past, and to make available a mode of experience that enriches and revitalizes a communal heritage.

WHOSE STORY; WHOSE HERITAGE?

Zakhor, remember! But whose story have we remembered, and who has been silenced? If memory is so important, if it forms the basis of identity and commitment and responsiveness, then which pieces of history have not been remembered, which have we neglected to commemorate with ritual, with celebration? Who has been left out?

Let us go back to that informative yet problematic paragraph from the Passover ritual: "In every generation ..." There are two ways to read it. One way is with all the masculine pronouns and nouns in place. In every generation a man — the Hebrew says Adam — must see himself as if he went out of Egypt, [...] he must teach it to his sons [...] for God promised the land to his Fathers. Well, surely women went out too. Are daughters not included in the command to tell the story? They don't mean just the men — or do they? And who is "they"? The English translation stands, representing a tradition full of exclusively masculine terms, perpetuating the patriarchal vortex. What do our daughters and sisters think? Does this let them out of the loop of the obligation to re-member and be re-membered? I hope not.

In order to fulfill the commandment to remember, the community of Jews must recognize and recall their female ancestors. Feminist Jews can successfully follow that traditional pattern of *zakhor*, through personalizing the story, concretizing in symbolic ritual, and remembering the past sins of patriarchy while eliminating them.

DO NOT FORGET; BLOT OUT THE MEMORY

I take it that it is our task to destabilize the privileged reading of that text. Passover is a story of redemption that is meant for women, too. The Hebrew can imply or include women. We can read "ancestors" instead of "Fathers" as the word means both. We can read "children" and not "sons," for the word means both. And "Adam" in Genesis 1 does mean person or human and not necessarily a man whose name is Adam. So it is not a history that is limited to *his* story. *Her* story is also embedded in it, and those who know the literature know that the rabbis claim it was because of the righteousness of the women that Israel was redeemed.[8]

Our challenge today is to name and proclaim the women while not implying that our ancestors were egalitarian. We cannot and should not erase the androcentrism; but we can read the ambiguities and expose the ruptures in the text. Women were a part of our history. We need to find a way to name them and tell their story in ritual format. And while doing that we must avoid both victimization and aggrandizement.

CONCRETIZE IN RITUAL

Ritual provides us with a map of religion in action. It enables individuals and communities to establish and maintain a relationship with that which they consider sacred. Religious ritual creates the arena in which the individual expresses solidarity with the group and the group manages to incorporate the individual. Feminist Jews today are exploring venues for ritual participation.

The univocality of the text can be overruled in story and ritual. Women are Jews linked in the cycle of memory and life that binds us all. But they have been left out of the specifics of story-telling and celebration. In the Purim story, how do we remember Esther's great courage in facing foolish Ahasuerus and evil Haman? How do we teach our daughters to celebrate her victory on behalf of our people? Is the popular focus on Mordecai the wise and Esther the beautiful appropriate? Are all her accomplishments linked to winning a beauty contest? Moreover, do we as feminists consecrate rebellion only by acclaiming Vashti while denigrating Esther? In the opening segment of the story, Vashti is eliminated because of her forceful (just say no!) refusal to appear before the king's — her husband's — male guests. But Esther too finds her cause and risks her life in defiance of male persecution. Is there only one voice to the text? Why not honour the talent of Esther who destabilizes the balance of power in that ancient kingdom? Why not commemorate her courage and insight as well as celebrating that of Vashti?

In many ways the texts are incomplete, awaiting our telling and dancing. Feminist Jews have already begun to explore and exhibit great creativity in ritual. We all need to join in the task of proclaiming and celebrating the memory of our female ancestors. When we remember redemption, Miriam's dance should be repeated (Exodus 15:20). Miriam, sister to Moses, was one of the principal players in the chapter of our history known as the Exodus. When the Israelites escaped slavery, she led the women in dance and praise of God. Where are our dancer/leaders?

PERSONALIZE THE STORY

The final paradox of ritualized memory is the ability to personalize the event and in so doing to render the experience timeless.[9] It is a very difficult task. We hear the women's voices so seldom and they speak from a reality that is so far removed from ours. Identifying with them, saying, "that could be me," becomes a major challenge.

The cumulative effect of the exclusion of women from history and from the public performance of ritual has left them invisible and has left us with the erroneous impression that they were not ritually active. There are numerous examples of women's rich participatory ritual life;

of women as ritual experts, confident in their skill, authoritative in their position. It is our task to excavate the record, extract women's different ritual experience and find the means of personal identification.

Feminist scholars have been hard at work uncovering these records. For example, previously, the world of women's prayers had been neglected and even denigrated. Chava Weissler undertook to reveal the religious significance of these personal petitions.[10] The *tkhines*, liturgical poems, proved to be a rich if difficult resource. Weissler's essays help us to see that, though women may not have been prayer leaders in the main synagogues, that is not the same as saying that they did not pray, create prayers or lead other women in prayer. Women had no institutional formal role. They did have a religious life that was prayer-based, over which they had control, and which frequently led them to a female-centred form of worship. Their concerns were placed front and centre. Whether in the home or the synagogue women's section, they stood with God in the intimate circle of devotee.

Unlike the traditional liturgy, *tkhines* are personalized and voluntary. They reveal great piety, knowledge of Jewish sources and a striking intimacy with God. And it is that sense of personal intimacy that I believe we must recapture.

There is one particular *tkhine* that I find incredibly instructive. It was said by the woman as she put the Sabbath bread, the challah, into the oven. It is ritual in its simplest form. A straightforward plea to God about a most mundane matter. No special locus, movement or articulation. No paraphernalia or qualifications. Just the woman, the bread, the oven and God:

> Lord of all the world, in your hand is all blessing. I come now to revere your holiness, and I pray you to bestow your blessing on the baked goods. Send an angel to guard the baking, so that all will be well baked, will rise nicely, and will not burn, to honour the holy Sabbath (which you have chosen so that Israel your children may rest thereon) and over which one recites the holy blessing — as you blessed the dough of Sarah and Rebecca our mothers. My Lord God, listen to my voice; you are the God who hears the voices of those who call to you with the whole heart. May you be praised to eternity.[11]

This woman needs no intermediary or special *terra sancta*. Her kitchen is as worthy as any synagogue. More importantly, she is as worthy as any individual. She calls upon God as she needs. And her needs — as ordinary as baking — need no apology.

Looking carefully at the text, we can feel her presence. She is an ordinary woman occupied with Sabbath preparations who expects God to participate in the enterprise.[12] Her confidence is unmistakable; she has done her part and now God must work too. In fact, God is called upon to send his angel — who has nothing better to do — to watch over the ovens. Her time is too precious. So, having prepared the dough and placed it in the oven, she is no longer responsible. If it is burnt or does not rise properly, God or the angel are to blame. And all this in order to fulfill God's own commandment to honour the Sabbath. She stands firmly and directly in a covenantal relationship with God, who is involved with her world and her concerns. Accordingly, she implicates God in the kitchen aspect of Judaism. She privatizes and personalizes her communication with the sacred. She also does so in the name of Sarah and Rebecca. Her ritualized memory embraces female ancestors. Finally, and significantly, she tells God to listen to her voice! It is ironic to recall that God tells Abraham to listen to the voice of Sarah (Genesis 21:12), while the Talmud proclaims that the voice of a woman is seductive (Berakhot 24a; Kiddushin 70a).

It is obligatory for us to tell her story and to tell it as though we were there.

For this generation, perhaps more than any other before, we need to tell the story of women too. We need to be specific; we need to do more than assume or imply. We must make sure that our children know more than just about Deborah and Golda. We must proclaim and we must celebrate. Women have a song to sing, a story to tell, a dance to perform. *Zakhor*, remember the women too!

⚘

"Zakhor: Memory, Ritual and Gender," by Norma Baumel Joseph reprinted here with permission, was originally published in *Canadian Woman Studies/les cahiers de la femme*, 16/4 (Fall 1996)

NOTES

1. This is the edited version of a lecture first developed in Montreal for Women's Federation, Federation Combined Jewish Appeal in 1994, and then expanded and delivered in Toronto, at the conference "From Memory to Transformation" in January 1996. It was previously published in *Canadian Woman Studies/les cahiers de la femme* 16/4: 28–32.

2. Yosef Hayim Yerushalmi, *Zakhor: Jewish History and Jewish Memory* (Seattle, WA: University of Washington, 1982), xiv.

3. Judith Plaskow, "Jewish Memory from a Feminist Perspective," in J. Plaskow and C. Christ, eds., *Weaving the Visions* (San Francisco: Harper, 1989), 40. For an interesting exploration of the theological role of history see Arthur A. Cohen, "The Religious Center of the Jews: An Essay in Historical Theology," in Mary Douglas and Steven M. Tipton eds., *Religion and America* (Boston: Beacon Press, 1982).

4. Brevard S. Childs, "Memory and Tradition in Israel," *Studies in Biblical Theology* 37 (1962).

5. Jonathan Boyarin, "Voices Around the Text: The Ethnography of Reading at Mesivta Tifereth Jerusalem," *Cultural Anthropology* 4/4 (1989), 398–421.

6. This commandment to remember is based on the incident as described in Exodus 17:14–16, in which we are told that God will blot out the memory of Amalek from under the heaven.

7. Rabbi David Feinstein, *The Anah Dodi Haggadah* (New York: Mesorah Publications, 1993), 69. There are variations of this English translation, but they all maintain a male profile.

8. Babylonian Talmud, Sota. 11b, Berakhot 24a, Kiddushin 70a.

9. For an interesting exploration of the personal meaning of ritual, see Allan Lazaroff, "A Rationale for Ritual," *Midstream* 40/2 (February 1994): 20–22.

10. Chava Weissler, "The Traditional Piety of Ashkenazic Women," in Arthur Green, ed., *Jewish Spirituality: From the Sixteenth Century Revival to the Present* (New York: Crossroad, 1987), 245–275; "Women in Paradise," *Tikkun* 2/2 (April 1987): 43–47, 117–120; "Prayers in Yiddish and the Religious World of Ashkenazic Women," in Judith Baskin, ed., *Jewish Women in Historical Perspective* (Detroit: Wayne State, 1991), 159–181.

11. Translation by Chava Weissler, "On Putting the Sabbath Loaf into the Oven," in Ellen Umansky and Diane Ashton, eds., *Four Centuries of Jewish Women's Spirituality* (Boston: Beacon, 1992), 55. Reprinted with permission of translator.

12. This is a markedly different context than the mishnaic [pertaining to the Mishnah, the first written compilation of the oral law] one in which the text explains that a woman dies in childbirth if she has not been careful with the ritual of challah preparation that is linked to a remembrance of temple worship (Mishnah Sabbath 2:6). For a similar rift between the classical rabbinical emphasis and women's own view of an issue see: Rahel Wasserfall, "Menstruation and Identity," and Chava Weissler, "*Mitsvot* Built into the Body," in Howard Eilberg-Schwartz, ed., *People of the Body* (Albany: SUNY Press, 1992), 309–327, 101–115.

HE, SHE, IT:

THEOLOGY, LANGUAGE
AND LITURGY

Elyse Goldstein

Since the beginning of the contemporary women's movement, language has always been a major issue for feminists. We have argued that until a more inclusive, less male-focused vocabulary becomes part of society's everyday experience, gender equity would be impossible. A member of the Liturgy Committee for the Reform Movement, feminist Rabbi Elyse Goldstein discusses the inclusion of female imagery and the elimination of sexist language in Jewish liturgy as important steps in creating an equitable Jewish theology.

WHEN I WAS a little girl growing up in Queens, New York, my family would go to the Reform temple every Friday night. I would sit proudly in the front row. I loved the still calmness, the solemnity of the cantor's old European-style singing and the sonorous tones of the rabbi's sermon. As I looked up at the *bimah*, the stage upon which the main participants of the service would stand (and from a little girl's vantage point, that *bimah* looked very high up indeed), I thought that surely God must be paying attention to all those deep and serious voices.

When the Rabbi invoked what he called the "final benediction," standing right in the middle of the *bimah* with his arms spread out majestically, my father would put his hand on mine protectively and give it a little squeeze, his own silent blessing. I felt safe and secure, with God the Father, the rabbi and my own father mysteriously intertwined.

THE ISSUES

Then I grew up. I found out that the rabbi was human, my father was flawed, and God did not take care of everything. Although God as father figure does provide the safety and protection which little boys and girls crave, this image lacks spiritual maturity as we grow older.

The question of language is central to a serious discussion of Jewish feminist issues. For many of us, our first experience of the God of the Bible is through childhood stories. Thus we come to know God as a King, a Father, an all-powerful and mighty Being, mostly referred to as "He." As adults, most of us redefine, re-evaluate and reshape our childhood beliefs. It is then that feminist Jews find ourselves uncomfortable with these simplistic childhood images. And although our spiritual experience, and thus our spiritual "vocabulary," has increased and broadened, somehow our language of prayer has not kept up.

It is extremely difficult to speak about God in a concrete way. We accept that human language is, by definition, limited. But the language of prayer is even more limited by its common use of the male gender for God. Although later Jewish philosophers such as Maimonides championed an invisible, incorporeal God, rejecting the anthropomorphism of the Bible as a mere projection of human need, the dominant representation of God in the Torah has been male; if not physically, then in terms of imagery. The image of God's maleness in the text is expressed not only through the male pronoun, but through the many male characteristics: God as a "man of war" (Exodus 15:3), a shepherd (Psalm 23), king (Psalm 10) and father (Jeremiah 3 and 31). In liturgy, the standard formulation for all blessings is "Lord, King of the world."

Theologian Judith Plaskow has pointed out eloquently that

> neutral and even female images do little to counter this dominant picture. Attributes and actions that are themselves gender-neutral are read through the filter of male language, so that the God who

performs these actions is still imagined in male terms ... when the Exodus narrative is read in the context of the Song at the Sea that celebrates the Lord of war triumphing over his enemies, and when, in a male-dominated society, it is assumed that power is the prerogative of maleness, God comes to be seen as a male throughout. The hand that leads Israel out of Egypt is a male hand, whether or not it is called so explicitly.[1]

Intertwined with male metaphor for God are other fundamental issues of male dominance and male authority, including the hierarchical nature of God and Israel, and the paradox of the dual images of a *partnership* with God with a *servitude* to God.

Language both *reflects* and *creates* reality. As Plaskow suggests, "Religious symbols do not simply tell us about God; they are not simply models of a community's sense of ultimate reality. They also shape the world in which we live, functioning as models for human behaviour and the social order."[2] Shabbat is an example: it is a model of God's action in creating the world, and it is also a model for the Jewish community.

Thus, male images of God serve as "models of" and "models for." They serve as "models of" the male hierarchy of the past, and "models for" the continued male hierarchy of the present. Male imagery of God continues to shape the way we think about God, Judaism and the role of men and women in the religious sphere. On a communal level, a religious society uses its theology to justify what women can/cannot and should/should not do within its social system.

Jewish feminism questions root assumptions and root beliefs about God, and the resulting hierarchical nature of our religion. To do so, it must also challenge the language of those beliefs. Jewish feminism confronts the root conceptions, and the root comfort, of God-as-Father. While on a personal level this challenges the little girl in the front row of the temple who loves the secure familiarity of the Father God, it also enlarges the adult woman's ability to see God in new and inspirational ways, and helps her to grow.

THE SOLUTIONS

The move away from a religious vocabulary that is mostly male involves a number of different strategies. Since English is a non-gendered language, it seems the easiest starting point. We can simply use neutral terms for God; substitute "Ruler" for "King," "Parent" for "Father." We can speak of God as "God" instead of either "He" or "She." Such neutralization works only when the listeners divest themselves of all male stereotypes and archetypes, so that the word "parent" does not automatically conjure up a father, either heavenly or human. Neutral language only works when it doesn't let us hide. And neutral language has limitations. I believe we are created in God's image, as it says in Genesis, and we are not "gender neutral" beings. If we are created in God's image then God, too, has masculine and feminine sides or attributes or characteristics. By de-gendering God we minimize our own human maleness and femaleness.

Another approach is to change the language to include "She." The use of She helps point out the anthropomorphism and ultimate blasphemy of centuries of using He. If we never *really* meant that God was a "He," we should have no problem whatsoever using the term "She." Use of the term "She" often provokes cries of "paganism," while "He" never does. I have yet to hear that "He" is reminiscent of the old gods. But by using "She," we must be careful not to re-stereotype female attributes. "She" becomes the "good God," protecting, mothering, loving, compassionate; "He" is strong, aggressive, victorious, military.

The real challenge in a discussion of changing our theological language is Hebrew. We have to be very creative about Hebrew, which is highly gendered grammatically. For example, in Hebrew, verbs are conjugated differently according to the gender of the grammatical subject. In Hebrew, as well as in English, we *can* change "He" to "She." We can change the masculine form of the phrase *barukh atah* [blessed art Thou] to the feminine form *brukha at*. We can switch back and forth during one service, or use feminine in one service, masculine in the next. Or we can wait and pray that linguists will soon develop a non-gendered form in the Hebrew language!

In the meantime, Marcia Falk has done ground-breaking work in her *Book of Blessings*, offering a new Hebrew which speaks not only in a non-gendered way, but also in a non-hierarchical way. No longer does she use the "Blessed Art Thou, Lord Our God, King of the Universe" formula. Instead she suggests "We bless the Source of Life" (in Hebrew: *n'varekh et m'kor ha-khayim*). In Hebrew the pronoun "we" takes neither the male nor female form. Rather than God remaining the distant King, or becoming a Queen, God becomes the Core of Life, the Fountain of Life and other more imminent (inner) rather than transcendent (outer) idioms. Falk moves the language of prayer not only away from gender but also away from traditional formulations of God as "over us," reigning supreme and demanding our praise.[3]

Falk's formulations, however, have been criticized not only for their bold feminism but because they move people into the "object centre." In other words, when I go to pray, I want to be humble, to lose the individual self and merge into a larger Self. Falk's *n'varekh* [we bless] rather than *barukh* [You are blessed] makes me very aware of my Self, of my own-ness. It is hard to close one's eyes and be transported into a larger reality when one constantly speaks in the "I" or "we" form. And in Falk's text there is no mention whatsoever of the traditional names for God like *Adonai* [Lord] or *Elohanu* [Our God]. For many people, this opens up entirely new vistas of inclusion. The new formulations are ideal for those with less traditional spirituality, or for whom spirituality which finds expression more in an imminent rather than transcendent divinity. But for those with some notion of an outer divine presence — more removed, more supernatural — a balance is needed between Falk's innovations and the traditional texts.

Use of the term "Shekhinah" has also been proposed as a strategy for gender equality in religious texts. Shekhinah literally means "dwelling." The term appears as a name for God's presence in rabbinical literature of the second century C.E. The Midrash [rabbinical parables] speak of God placing "His Shekhinah" in the midst of Israel and of the Shekhinah resting upon individuals when they study Torah. Depicted often as luminous light, the Shekhinah shines with God's radiance; it is a manifestation of Divinity to indicate God's presence. The later medieval Jewish philosophers described the Shekhinah as a separate entity created by God. With the development of the Kabbalah [Jewish mysticism], the Shekhinah takes on definite feminine characteristics. In the late twelfth and thirteenth centuries C.E., the Shekhinah begins to be described as princess, daughter and the feminine principle in the world.

Jewish feminists such as Rabbi Lynn Gottlieb have "rediscovered" the Shekhinah. By "re-mythologizing" the Shekhinah, Gottlieb says we can find a powerful feminine model already existent within Judaism. Our ancient goddess symbols of moon, mother, water, earth are all authentically embodied in the Shekhinah. "The many images associated with the Shekhinah can become a source for women's encounter with the divine today as well as a bridge to our past. Women yearn for this possibility. When women speak of God She, we can finally picture ourselves as created in God's image."[4]

However, the Shekhinah is not a panacea. In kabbalistic tradition, She is a projection of what male mystics believed femininity and the feminine principle in the world to be: passive and receptive. She occupies the lowest rung, the tenth and last of the *Sefirot* or divine emanations which created the world. As such, she is the closest to earth and closest to the "dark" powers. She has no light of her own, but receives the Divine light from the other *Sefirot*. Because the Shekhinah contains so many facets of stereotypical female passivity, we will have to separate the traditional kabbalistic Shekhinah from the Shekhinah we need.

On a metaphoric level, however, the Shekhinah does hold tremendous power for us. She is the divine principle of the people Israel. Together with Israel symbolizing the "wife" and God the "husband," she replaces the goddess. Yet the Shekhinah remains part of the monotheistic vision of the One God. The Shekhinah is the closest first contact in the mystical struggle for communion with God. The kabbalists suggest that the mitzvot [commandments] act as vehicles to reunite the masculine principle with the feminine and as attempts to reharmonize God and the Shekhinah who originally were One. In this light, if Torah study and prayer bring a person into direct contact with Her and thus with God, then the ultimate goal of Judaism is one of harmony. This includes a harmony between God and the Shekhinah, between masculine and feminine, and thus between male and female persons. As the Shekhinah and God ultimately are One, so too ultimately are the masculine and feminine. They need only to be brought back together. We return to the Garden of Eden, to the one being both male and female, created in harmony and equality. We do so through daily acts which reunite the broken fragments of masculinity and femininity. By bringing the Shekhinah "back" into mainstream Judaism, we take one step towards that goal, towards restoring that time of peace and wholeness.

THE CHALLENGES

Can we integrate femaleness into the traditional male imagery of Hebrew descriptions of God? A starting point is the very oldest layers of Judaism and pre-biblical religion. What were the issues when the Torah shunned the goddess? It is important to understand the ancient fear of paganism. However, in uncovering the layers of symbolism familiar to our ancestors, it may be possible to "re-mythologize" and thus to create a new Jewish mythos which includes the feminine along with the masculine aspects of the One God.

The growing interest in the goddess has a special concern with the societal ramifications of a celebration of her positive sexuality and her fertility. In exploring the sources of these images in antiquity, we must ask if there is some light, some possibility, some idea in the "old ways" which can be remoulded, indeed "re-visioned" for us today. Reawakening the actual goddess aspects of YHVH — that is, incorporating goddess symbols for YHVH, who truly Encompasses All Things — can bring back women who in the past have felt that Judaism has not offered them a spirituality or a voice.

Of course, the mere suggestion of even exploring the ancient goddesses threatens the Jewish establishment, evoking the old cries of "paganism." We really have no idea of what biblical paganism was like, for we have inherited its description filtered through biased scholarship predisposed against it. Marcia Falk once asked, in a public lecture given in Toronto, why we continue to be so afraid of paganism. Our task is to research and determine if there are positive aspects of the repressed past that can enrich the staunch monotheism many of us still accept today.[5]

Does changing He to She, or substituting neutral terminologies for God serve to uproot or shift our very beliefs about God? If it does not, then in truth I must agree with its critics: it is only a shallow attempt at "political correctness." What is needed now, if we are to take the feminist challenge seriously, is a whole new imagining of God.

Nelle Morton, an early feminist thinker and writer, advised women:

"Failing to have memory, invent." The very model of Jewish prayer in general — a group of people all saying the same thing at the same time, things someone else has written for them — may be a patriarchal model. Perhaps Jewish feminists have to reinvent altogether Jewish prayer, language, worship experiences, even synagogues. Some of what we do in the meantime may seem surprising. Some of it may seem strange or alien. Some of it may seem wrong for the moment. But we are the generation in the desert, wandering, trying to find the way home.

And how will we know if this new model is "Jewish?" "Jewish" has been defined by men and patriarchal values. We have received a framework of Judaism through centuries of male experience and male interpretation. We have to be prepared to question the boundaries of this primary definition.

THE QUESTIONS

I will conclude in the traditional Jewish way: with questions. The first is: how much are we willing to change the Hebrew when it comes from the Torah? At different Sabbath services that I have led as a rabbi, I have offered participants the chance to chant or say a feminized version of the traditional *Ve'ahavta* prayer. That paragraph in the *siddur* [prayer book] which begins "You shall love the Lord your God ..." comes from the Torah, in the book of Deuteronomy, chapter six. In the Hebrew, it is rendered in the male singular throughout, relating directly to the individual male worshipper. I have placed alongside of the traditional form a form which uses the feminine singular throughout, relating directly to the individual female worshipper. Changing it in a prayer service changes a direct quote from Torah. This change leads to a series of questions for each of us: what is our relationship with Torah? What is its source of sacredness for us? Are its words just words or messages from the Divine? What does changing those words mean for us?

The second question is: how do we write prayers that express a woman's experience of spirituality? Would they be distinctly "female"? Could men say them? Would the structure of a woman's prayer book, written only by women, be different? We know how much women's physicality affects their spirituality. Our bodies are linked with our spiritual selves. In some women's lives, giving birth may be the most spiritual event they experience. Menstruation and its symbolism as partnership with God are completely ignored in our traditional prayer language. How can a prayer book take into account women's spirituality while still being useful and relevant for both men and women?

Third: will changing the words of the prayer book change our perspective about God, or are we just rewrapping the same old problem — how to express a relationship with God through human language — in a new paper? Will changing the language open up new roles for women, new leadership, new paradigms of religious thinking, or end up as an exercise in semantics?

My hope is that discussions and subsequent changes in our God language will indeed "change the world." That is what the rabbis did when they sat at the great academies in the third century, writing a *siddur* for us in the twentieth. I envision Jews, male and female, sitting around in the twenty-first or twenty-fifth century studying *our* words and *our* deliberations in admiration of how the Jews of the twentieth century wrote prayers that made everyone feel included.

NOTES

1. Judith Plaskow, *Standing Again at Sinai* (San Francisco: Harper San Francisco, 1990), 123.
2. Ibid., 126.
3. See Marcia Falk, *The Book of Blessings* (San Francisco: HarperCollins, 1996).
4. Lynn Gottlieb, *She Who Dwells Within* (San Francisco: HarperCollins, 1995), 22.
5. For a more complete discussion of the goddess and Judaism, see "Part III: God, Goddess, Gender and the Torah" in my book *Re-Visions: Seeing Torah through a Feminist Lens* (Toronto: Key Porter Books, 1998).

PANEL:

WOMEN RABBIS TRANSFORMING THE RELIGIOUS ESTABLISHMENT

⊙೫⊙

Elizabeth Bolton, Elyse Goldstein, & Nancy Wechsler-Azen

One of the most profound egalitarian transformations in institutional Judaism has been the induction of female rabbis in all but the Orthodox community. Born of feminism and the fight for social justice and equality, the struggle to create a female clergy has been a major achievement for our generation. Whether they work as congregational leaders, teachers or chaplains, women rabbis are making Judaism more relevant to women as they apply a feminist perspective to communal leadership, personal counselling, religious observance, life cycle celebrations and Jewish text study. As the first generation, women rabbis also have some issues of their own. The following is an adaptation of a dialogue amongst three female rabbis held at the conference "From Memory to Transformation: Jewish Women's Voices."

RABBI NANCY WECHSLER-AZEN:

I AM A RABBI and I am a woman, but in my day-to-day routine I do not always consciously focus on my gender. In fact when public speaking invitations on the subject of women and Judaism come up, it is no longer my pet topic. At the same time, the fact that I am a woman colours everything that I do.

Now and then, I am reminded bluntly and starkly that who I am and what I've chosen to pursue professionally is very unusual. At this time in Canada [January 1996] there are only three female rabbis working full time in our profession. What is our impact now that we have the opportunity to stand on the "inside" of the circle? One of the areas of greatest impact has to do with the next generation: the children of our community.

About a month ago a little girl named Sterling came to show me some drawings she had done in kindergarten. She had drawn pictures for each day of creation. Her drawings were very sweet. But what was more than sweet was how she depicted Shabbat. She had drawn a picture of God resting on the couch — God with a big smile and a pink bow in her hair. The message that has been received by this little girl is that God can be in female form. I keep Sterling's picture right next to my desk in my temple study.

Another vignette: A few years ago, I invited a male colleague to lead the family service. At a family service, the children often come up front and sit right next to me, almost jumping in my lap like little frogs, while I tell them a story. But at this service it was a man who presided as rabbi. The parent who was chairing the service invited the children to sit in front of the rabbi for a story. Although I was in back of the room, they came and sat in front of me. When I explained that they should go to the front to the other rabbi, a confused little boy asked, "Rabbi Nancy, can men be rabbis too?"

I love to tell these stories, because they're so innocent, yet they reveal how perceptions are changing in religious establishments. Why is this happening? It's happening because women rabbis now exist as spiritual leaders. We women rabbis are now standing on the inside of the circle and by our very presence we're helping shift the way Judaism has been seen for over 5,000 years.

There are many areas where the presence of women in spiritual leadership positions is bringing about a transformation in certain areas of Judaism. An obvious example has been the heightened awareness to gender in prayer language and the resulting changes. Another important area is in the creation of experimental rituals to mark important milestones in women's lives. Issues of healing from the private realm to the public are also coming to the forefront. The Reform movement today envisions synagogues as centres of well-being and health. I believe that is due to the women's presence in the rabbinate and our interest in health issues.

The very fact that we're here out front as leaders, centre stage, gives other women the possibility to find their own voices. In my congregation for example, the women have been much more active than the men in education, ritual, fundraising, communication. The men quickly developed a brotherhood and they often play golf. Meanwhile, we've had difficulties in creating a sisterhood in our congregation because the "sisterhood image" of women pouring tea at the Oneg Shabbat [Friday evening refreshment] is in such conflict with our feminist identity.

During the past few years on the High Holidays, the cantorial soloist at our synagogue has been a woman. There we are on the *bimah* [platform from which services are led]: two women guiding the congregation into the new year. Our sign language interpreters, also often on the *bimah*, all happen to be women too. Some people have loved it, some people have quit and some don't mind. But everyone notices. God is not "King" in our synagogue. Humanity is never "mankind." The matriarchs are right there next to the patriarchs in our prayers of ancestry and many of our meditations carry images of the Shekhinah, the female aspect of God. Women leading services at our synagogue are the norm and one cannot help but notice the effect this has on the energy during the *davening* [praying].

What is less obvious is our impact on an organizational level behind the doors of the Jewish establishment. Women rabbis are demonstrating a powerful leadership model that is less hierarchical and more empowering than the male model. This consensual leadership is based on gender consciousness, which demands that we not repeat the kind of experience that once made us feel marginalized. Rather than dominate from our new position of power, we strive to work in partnership.

In a Jewish context, you might call it the *tzim-tzum* model of leadership. According to the Lurianic [mystical, from the Kabbalah] model of creation, in the beginning God filled all space entirely. In order for creation to begin, God consciously withdrew, making space for new growth. This action of pulling back and deliberately making room for others' wisdom and ideas is called *tzim-tzum*.

I have consciously integrated this kind of leadership at committee meetings, in the classroom, in pastoral counselling and even in conducting prayer services. To me, this feels like a transformed model of Judaism, away from the authoritarian patriarchal style. It can be called a feminist model, a *tzim-tzum* model, a horizontal model or a relational model. Whatever it is called, I believe that it empowers if used consciously, that it raises up and invites others to take more responsibility for their Jewish lives. I believe that this kind of leadership is transforming the religious establishment as we have known it.

I became acutely aware of this when my synagogue and another congregation where a male colleague served together planned a family retreat. In my congregation, empowerment is a priority and we have a strong lay retreat committee. We all meet together and the tasks are delegated. At his congregation, the Rabbi was the retreat committee and all the tasks were his responsibility. When I recognized the contrast of leadership styles, I realized how much better I liked mine. We had more energy and more fun.

Of course, when we delegate, when we empower, we don't have the same amount of control any more and we have to make more room for hearing others. The good news is that empowerment is energizing, but it is important that we also recognize the limits of empowerment.

Let's examine the title of "rabbi," as an example. When I was ordained and right out of school, as a feminist, I believed that the title was unnecessary. I believed it created an unnecessary hierarchy between me and the congregation. What I quickly learned, however, was that all my male colleagues used their title. For me not to use my title placed me in a subordinate position. Too many times I've been approached with the comment: "So, you're the *rebetsn* [rabbi's wife]?" "No, I'm the rabbi." "Oh yes, the *rebetsn*."

In the end, I decided that it was important to acknowledge the years of study that came with my title, especially since I was one of three rabbis in the country starting a new congregation. The title was necessary, but to keep from becoming too distant, I made a compromise with tradition: I became Rabbi Nancy.

It needs to be recognized that not all male rabbis are authoritative, nor are all women rabbis feminists. There is a growing number of male feminists whose support in transforming religious establishments must be celebrated and recognized. Because of the support of our brothers (such as past president of the Reform Movement Rabbi Alexander Schindler), women have been ordained in our movement since 1972.

I am well aware that these past twenty-five plus years of women as rabbis is a small link on the long chain of Jewish tradition. How we consciously choose to lead as women rabbis will have a profound impact on how Judaism will look in the next millennium. Suffice it to say that women rabbis are no longer an experiment and as Rabbi Alexander Schindler said, "Welcoming women as rabbis was one of the best gifts we could have possibly given to our religion." To that let us say, "Amen."

RABBI ELYSE GOLDSTEIN:

Rabbi Schindler and Rabbi Wechsler may agree that women rabbis are no longer an experiment, but I disagree. In my opinion, we certainly are still an experiment. There are three things on which I would like to focus. The first is what it's like to be both inside and outside the establishment at the same time. The second is the issue of the feminist model of leadership. And the third is the dichotomy in being a woman rabbi.

Having been ordained in May 1983, I am the "veteran" on this panel and as the veteran, I may sound more jaded.

As one of the women who's been in the rabbinate in Canada the longest, I'm often called upon to represent women in the rabbinate in Canada on all sorts of committees. On a national level, I've been named to two of the most important committees of the National Reform Movement: the Liturgy Committee, which is writing the new prayer book, and the Reform Jewish Practices Committee, which determines Jewish practices for the entire Reform Movement in North America, the latter of which I was privileged to chair for five years. I always joke at these national meetings that I'm the token Canadian non-congregational female rabbi.

One thing that I have learned about being both inside and outside the establishment is that it gives me incredible freedom to be a challenge to the system. People will listen to what I have to say because they perceive that I'm on the inside. But as soon as they start listening, they realize I'm not saying what they want to hear. Therefore, I have the reputation of being both a "bad girl" and a "good girl" at the same time. It's given me the opportunity to make some major changes, especially in the new Reform Movement prayer book that is being written.

At the same time, I experience an incredible loneliness that comes from being both inside and outside the establishment. When I go to these meetings, I'm usually the only woman. Therefore, a question as simple as who do I sit next to becomes a major issue. Is there anyone here who will treat me as a colleague and not as an oddity? Will I be able to raise my hand and speak? If I position myself at the front of the table or at the back of the table, what am I implying? All these sound like trivial questions, but when you are alone as the only woman in a room of sixty or seventy men, they become important.

There is another loneliness which is solved only when I am with other women rabbis. There is the feeling of release when I don't have to speak in a double language. When I'm at the Women's Rabbinic Conference, I can speak my "mother tongue" because my mother tongue is feminism. When I am acting inside the establishment, I have to translate from my mother tongue, if you will stretch the metaphor with me, into a patriarchal language. Yet I am always aware of my sensibilities as a woman and my responsibilities as the token woman. In other words, I must speak Jewish feminism in a patriarchal language, so that those I'm speaking to can hear the issue and move on the issue.

The last point on being an insider/outsider: For the past five years I've dedicated my rabbinate to the academic pursuit: I teach full time. I teach adults Judaism, which I believe is what a rabbi is supposed to do. Instead, I am often defined by what I am not. I have that wonderful title now of non-congregational rabbi. I am now not a male rabbi, no longer an American rabbi and not a congregational rabbi. I've spent the last five years trying to work on positive definitions and to get people to understand that a rabbi without a congregation is not a day without sunshine.

Part of this experience is a female experience and a feminist issue. Why? Because the majority of part-time rabbis, the majority of Hillel rabbis serving university students, the majority of pastoral counsellors and the majority of hospital chaplains are women. Women rabbis, in large numbers, choose not to be in the congregational rabbinate for some portion of their career. As feminists and as women rabbis, we are redefining the non-congregational rabbinate as "real rabbis." As Rabbi Wechsler-Azen has to spend a lot of time saying she's not the *rebetsn*, I have been spending the past five years answering the question: "Oh, so you're not a rabbi any more?" No, I teach Judaism full time; that's what rabbis do. "Oh, but you don't have a congregation, right?" No, I do have a congregation; they are my students. "But you don't practise as a rabbi any more, right?" No, I practise every single solitary day till I get it right. That's what it's like being inside and outside the establishment at the same time.

Number two: I've been struggling with the issue of the feminist model of leadership since I became a rabbi and it's a really important struggle. But I've learned that there are limitations to the feminist model of consensus. I want all models to be co-operative, but too often with consensus democracy, things don't get done. Trying to run board meetings successfully in this feminist model, I often think of this joke told in feminist circles: It's a good thing that Moses led us out of the desert, because if Miriam had done it, we'd still be there, trying to build consensus.

Sometimes I feel like the term "Jewish organization" is an oxymoron. We are by nature a disorganized people; that is our charm. But in trying to do work which will transform people's lives and change the establishment, I've discovered that sometimes it's more expedient to get up in front of a room and move the meeting on, to take leadership, to be assertive or sometimes even to be, that most disfavoured word, aggressive. I try hard not to be hierarchical, but sometimes I find that we'll still be in the desert if somebody doesn't make a decisive move.

And number three, there is a dichotomy in being a woman rabbi. At the moment, Rabbi Wechsler and I are the only women rabbis in Toronto. Together, I am sure Nancy and I could probably log hundreds of phone calls asking us to speak on what is it like to be a woman rabbi. The most recent experience we had was each being asked individually by a CBC radio show to speak on this topic. We both declined for exactly the same reason. If we spent all our time speaking to women's groups and congregations and radio and TV shows on what it's like to be a woman rabbi, we'd never get to be rabbis!

So that's the dichotomy for me. I want to be a rabbi. I want to be a feminist. I want to get on and do the thing I was ordained to do: to be a practising rabbi. I'd also like to bring some depth to the feminist aspect of being a woman rabbi. I try to do this through my teaching, my workshops and my participation on politically relevant panels. I just want to get on with the business of being a rabbi and being a feminist, until it's no longer such a big surprise to be both.

Rabbi Elizabeth Bolton:

I'm the baby on the panel and as a rabbinical student in my last year, I'm just about to emerge through the womb. I'm grateful to the conference organizers for according me the title. At rabbinical school we say the minute you send in your application, people start to treat you as a rabbi. In fact, I will be ordained in June of this year [1996]. I was set to graduate last year but, having given birth to my daughter in the middle of my studies, I'm on what we affectionately call the "*ima* [mother] track." I stretched the six year programme into seven and did the last two years of the programme part time over three years to accommodate my personal and professional life. Perhaps because I'm still close to the school experience where we have the privilege of spending so much time studying, I would like to begin with a consideration of text.

There is a traditional Jewish text, also a process, called Midrash, or interpretation. It involves reading between the lines, filling in the blanks in biblical and other stories. Creating Midrash has been a critical step in the development of our laws, customs and traditions. Traditional Midrash was created by rabbis in the last few hundred years.

One of the challenges for women — and especially for lesbians — in the rabbinate is the issue of finding female role models. There are only a handful of women, in contrast to the hundreds of men named in the Talmud. And the women that we know from biblical stories seem to share a host of limited or negative personality traits; their stories are usually incomplete, truncated or they remain anonymous. We are left with only half a tradition and with the challenge of writing in the margins, to which many of us have been relegated.

So what does it mean for me to be reading the biblical texts and the written interpretations? And, even more pressing, what does it mean to stand within that tradition as a teacher, lesbian and rabbi? I am obligated to struggle with finding models for my rabbinate within a tradition that is based on sacred texts in which I am invisible.

I know I must come to terms with the fact that the traditional Jewish canon is often painful for me as a lesbian. I also know that I must get beyond my anger at not being acknowledged in order to carry on with my love for Jewish learning, ritual and community. I carry within myself both the love and the anger, but always the determination to go on in my field. I accept that biblical stories are *my* tradition as well, even if not all of them *were* written down or transmitted, even if "between the lines" is the way that I keep myself focused in my work.

The challenge is laid out at the very beginning of the Torah in Genesis: "So God created man in His image, the image of God He created him, man and woman He created them." For me, it immediately becomes problematic to be confronted with a formative relationship model, with a paradigm which is so resolutely heterosexual. Where and how do I find a reflection of myself, the created-in-the-image-of-God person I believe myself to be, but embodied in me as a Jewish woman who loves women? How can I write myself and others like me into Jewish tradition?

To counter this, we can use Midrash, both traditional and contemporary, and bring Lilith into the Garden of Eden, for example. We can dance the same dance but with different steps. The rabbis were able to take a biblical text and elaborate and embellish to suit their own purpose — and their material became another layer in the sacred canon. So I think if they can do it, we can too!

Out of necessity and because this is part of the Recontructionist learning process, I have also looked to other disciplines for inspiration. An outside source for me has been bell hooks, an African–American feminist writer whose model of moving from margin to centre has become very important for me. If I stand where I am, with my own integrity in who I am, I am moving the margin — and myself — to the centre, the place of importance and power. To me it is also a matter of civil rights: It is my right to assume any role I choose for myself with pride — and I believe this choice must be extended to everyone. This is my political work. I am here in the rabbinate partly because of those who went before me, who couldn't attend rabbinical school because of homophobic policies; those who have not been able to come out as lesbians or gays in their pulpits or those who were not permitted to retain their jobs after coming out. I want to proclaim that lesbians can and should move from the margins to the centre and claim their place.

Another model that I employ to see myself standing in the tradition of the rabbinate is the hermeneutics of politics. How you study or interpret the Bible is for me a powerful tool, because it gives me a radical way in which to organize my experiences. Politics are an organizing principle for me. As a long-time feminist activist, I have spent a lot of my life working for social change. Activism is an important piece of the text I want to include in my rabbinate. As part of my work, I want to help transform other people's lives through dialogue, inclusion and accepting differences.

I received a gift last Friday night, when a woman came to me after the Shabbat ritual and said that she and her husband, who is not a Jew, had attended the High Holiday services I had led two years ago. And for the first time ever, they both felt included. They and their children have since joined that congregation and are still members. The possibility of doing that kind of meaningful work, which I call the hermeneutics of the situation, makes it worthwhile for me to continue in the rabbinate and to offer my experience and knowledge — gained through who I am in life.

The last model I use I learned from Judith Plaskow, author of *Standing Again at Sinai*. She uses the term feminist Judaism, instead of Jewish feminism and challenges us to reshape the tradition while continuing to stand within it, to create community and to name the Divine as we experience it. Ultimately, this means learning how to speak more than one language; the language of tradition as well as the language we speak to each other as women. We must learn well and learn enough so that we have the authority to use the language of tradition as well as men do, connecting Jewish women's voices with power and tradition. Then we can create the environment to create feminist Judaism wherever we work and insist that women who love women are also part of the Jewish community.

⟨ॐ⟩

ANOTHER FOUR QUESTIONS:

NURTURING A JEWISH LESBIAN FAMILY

❦

Susan G. Cole

One of the most revolutionary consequences of the feminist and gay/lesbian movements is that women couples are openly having and raising children. Along with this development comes a whole range of different ways of expressing Judaism in the home and in the community. Journalist and writer Susan G. Cole discusses her experiences in bringing up a child in a Jewish lesbian environment and the range of new Jewish rituals and traditions that have evolved in their home and community to address their unique needs.

WHAT HAPPENED when I was born? Molly might ask. And we'll tell our daughter about birthing too long at home, and having trouble getting to the car so we could get to the hospital and crying when she came out and me falling asleep on Leslie's bed afterwards, the nurses trying to get me to move. Who was I anyway? When does a labour coach lie on the bed and fall asleep and not go home? When she's the mother's lesbian partner, that's when.

Tell me how you first met, Molly might say. I tell her that I had one of my first encounters with my partner Leslie at a workshop for Jewish lesbians at a lesbian conference. It's a convenient bit of lore — our daughter knows Jewish identity threw her mothers together so it starts out in her mind as a good thing. Mind you, Leslie admits she hadn't registered for the workshop and, though she could claim some genuine interest in her Jewish identity, she'd probably say her main motivation was the sight of me sitting there.

But who can say? These kinds of issues never used to possess me at all. To be honest, I too attended that workshop on a whim. You know what I mean — it had the right time slot and I didn't qualify for whatever else was slated. I hadn't spent much time at all thinking about Jewish anything. I realize, now that I'm assessing where I stand with these things, an astonishing thing that at the same time is obvious — thinking about how best to make Jewish identity matter to Molly was what made me think about my own for the first time in years.

You never know when these questions will hit. I like to tell another story. It's about a similar shock of recognition, which came to me late in my first year at an American college in the spring of 1970. I was meeting with the women's caucus of the campus anti-war organization, still going strong after the student strike of 1969. As a feminist and lesbian in training, I had distanced myself from any formal Jewish activities, including the campus Hillel group, and dived into the radical student movement — and its anti-imperialist principles — with typical teenage abandon. As I sat with the leaders inside the women's contingent, I was faced with having to explain my absence at an upcoming series of meetings.

"I'm going home for Passover," I explained. "It's the Jewish holiday when ..."

"Me too," said one sister radical.

"Me too," said another.

What with trying to make a mark on campus within a fledgling feminist movement and having to fashion Dick-and-Jane type explanations for our anti-war brothers as to why a women's caucus was necessary, we never had a context for imagining that Judaism would ever be a bonding factor among us women. But then I took inventory: Fleischmann, Freedman, Kaplan, Rosenkrantz — why did it never cross my mind that these women were Jewish? And what about our Jewishness had brought us to oppose the war in southeast Asia? Probably much the same things in Judaism as brought both Leslie and me to feminism — an appreciation that collective action in history matters and that acts of imperialism, whether by modern Americans against the Vietnamese or by the crusaders of the Middle Ages against the Jews, violated the human right to self-determination and personal identity.

Statistics Canada still does not ask specific questions about same-sex couples, so the data on lesbian mothers is sparse. Still, in 1990, *Newsweek* reported that there were nearly 10,000 lesbians in the USA who had their children after they came out and the numbers have blossomed since then. Given the huge diversity in gay culture in North America, my story is very specific. It even has some fairy tale-like qualities. Two politically sophisticated Jewish lesbians living in a major North American metropolis, both with loving family backgrounds and strong roots in the left and lesbian communities, decide to have a baby.

This is, however, the only story I can express with any authenticity. As I write these thoughts, I don't pretend to know what it would be like to be lesbians in a small town wanting to have a baby. I can only guess what frustrations would beset two women with no roots in a lesbian community and no connection to other lesbian mothers. And I'm sure that a lesbian with an Orthodox upbringing would have very different insights into the complexities of nurturing a Jewish lesbian family. Still, even in what appear to be our optimal circumstances, certain themes emerge that bind all Jewish lesbians with children: the understanding that visibility and community — both Jewish and lesbian — are the key to our kids' security and the sense that identity comes out of a conscious day-to-day practice of reaffirming who we are.

I. FAMILY: WHERE DOES OURS FIT IN?

In a way, Leslie and I made it a bit easier for our families of origin. In my case, my brother donated sperm so that Leslie could carry the child, and so, though I am not the birth mother, I do have a blood connection to my daughter, which makes my parents feel like real grandparents in that blood-is-thicker-than-mud way. I can't say that involving a brother guarantees a smoother ride, and there are specific drawbacks to using any donor who is known, but the direct link proved a window our parents were more willing to walk through. Plus, Leslie and I are both Jewish, so at least we weren't throwing a mixed lesbian marriage into the mix. We fit easily into each other's family celebrations and from our earliest days together went to the movies on Christmas day — a tribute to another kind of shared childhood tradition.

But diversity is deep in the Jewish community and so lesbian lovers can be Jewish, yes, and different. My partner Leslie has strong roots in the Jewish left, coming from a family involved in the founding of the United Jewish People's Order (UJPO) in Toronto, a community-based Jewish cultural and political organization with headquarters in the Morris Winchevsky Centre and at the country retreat Camp Naivelt. The centre's Shule [school] has created fertile ground for new ideas in secular Jewish education and for radical Jewish celebrations. I remember being astonished at a Purim Cabaret that took the dress-up theme to its logical conclusions and made some of the city's Jewish drag queens feel right at home.

Not that I had an Orthodox upbringing. My parents too have a progressive bent — being among the first to join the Reform congregation at Holy Blossom Temple. Holy Blossom has become one of the continent's most powerful and influential Jewish establishments and so obviously it has a very different relationship to power — and to the concept of God — than the UJPO. But if Holy Blossom could be called more religious, and even as it is, to be sure, comfortable with its prestige, it can take some credit for expanding some of Judaism's theological boundaries. It has also become a ground-breaker in gay-sensitive and AIDS-related programming.

Equally influential to me, though more on the subconscious day-to-day level, is the fact that my maternal grandmother had a commitment to the Jewish community that was almost legendary. She is known for having originated programmes to provide kosher meals for patients in hospitals, giving shelter to the poor through the Halbushes Arumin societies and being among the founding mothers of the Baycrest Home for the Aged and Mount Sinai Hospital in Toronto.

What if we had been brought up in strict Orthodox households? Hostility to lesbianism is huge among fundamentalists — the lesbian-positive book, *Bread on the Seder Plate* by Rebecca Alpert, takes its title from a *Lubavitsher rebetsn*'s [ultraorthodox rabbi's wife's] dismissive comment that lesbianism was to Judaism as bread was to the seder table. It would be excruciatingly difficult to reconcile my Jewish education with who I was. But for both Leslie and me, even though we were politically radicalized in our teens and sought community among our like-minded hippie and political friends, our Jewish educations did not make us want to turn away from our roots.

Then again both Leslie and I have always been close to our families. Our fathers were gentle men who loved strong, smart women, especially their wives, and they and the rest of our birth families consistently supported our life choices. Our families integrated Jewish values into our upbringing in different ways. In Leslie's experience *tzedakah* [charity, righteous deeds] translated into political action — you fought social injustice as part of your commitment to the world around you. Within my more liberal traditions, *tzedakah* meant that you volunteered your time and your talent to help others and create a better world. In both cases, you give back to your community because your community is what feeds you.

2. COMMUNITY: WHERE DO WE BELONG?

As with many lesbians who grew through feminism and who came out in the days before lesbianism was even a little bit chic, lesbian community was what nurtured us as adults. I mean, look how Leslie and I met, at a lesbian conference. If you asked me before Molly was born how I described my identity, I would have been uneasy — lesbian, sure, with middle-class privilege, I guess, Jewish, definitely. But if you had asked how I identified my community — I would have answered lesbian almost immediately. That has shifted since Molly was born. For one thing, in Molly's early years we enjoyed life in a daycare community and a lot of new heterosexual friends.

More important, when it came time to think about rearing a child in a household that paid proper respect to our Jewishness, we were lesbian, yes, but we had other life experience that we shared with all kinds of progressive-minded Jews of our generation. Many of us have left the mega-synagogues of our middle-class youth, some looking for more women-centred alternatives, some looking for more gay-positive alternatives, some wanting more focus on community, all resenting the tithing techniques of Toronto's institutional behemoths. You don't have to be lesbian to realize that Jewish institutions had to respond to changing values and find a way to expand their political awareness as well as their social class range if they had any chance of keeping their wayward children of the 1960s involved.

In keeping with these circumstances, Toronto has seen a flurry of alternative congregations trying to build new communities, some of them peeking out only during the high holidays. They tap into a new kind of longing among the Jewish baby boomers who lived out radical ideas through the 1960s to the 1980s and then had kids when they reached their mid-thirties. For many of us, that's when the how-to of Jewish life gains new meaning, when children start asking questions. The Morris Winchevsky Centre has itself experienced a mini-renaissance since 1990, attracting new families to its community-minded organization.

At the Winchevsky Centre, kids get grounded in Jewish culture, history, holidays and the value of social justice. The Shule eschews the individualist B'nai Mitzvahs that are still typical at most traditional congregations and replaces them with a collective graduation event for the grade seven class. The class prepares a presentation based on a chosen theme — honouring the women in their lives, say, or celebrating Jewish cultural heroes — and the parents organize a party of varying scale, depending on the desires of the families of the kids.

So, with Molly now approaching junior high, Leslie and I find ourselves crossing two communities — our Jewish community at the Morris Winchevsky Centre and the lesbian community that brought Leslie and me together. Accordingly, we have multiple celebrations on every holiday — at least three. For Hanukkah, we have one major gathering for immediate family, another that's called a Family Sunday at the Morris Winchevsky Centre and yet another for our Jewish and non-Jewish friends.

This gathering brings together what we refer to as our "chosen family." This is the phrase we use to describe the people who are so present in our everyday lives that it feels natural and logical to celebrate simkhas [joyous occasions] and holidays together. A few, like some ex-lovers, have been fixtures for some time; some are work mates who have blossomed into friends, some are current collaborators in artistic projects and therefore only temporary members of the chosen family. So we stay consistent to the value of inclusiveness that we learned at Passover — let those who are hungry, come and eat. At Hanukkah the guest list for our chosen family party must meet two basic criteria — the invitees must have a particular connection with Molly and they must show proper appreciation for my latkes [potato pancakes].

Tell me the story of Hanukkah, or Purim, or Passover? Molly might say. At Purim, we used to read her a charming children's book called *It Happened in Shushan*. It tells a story in pictures and poems that conveys the subtext of Vashti's rebellion and gives you the sense that Esther entered a beauty contest and married a narcissistic king with her eyes wide open.

Now Molly tells the tales herself to our friends who come to celebrate. For the sake of our non-Jewish friends, we tell the traditional story. And for our Jewish guests we branch out a little by showing a few pagan influences now and again. In our household we don't disavow the power of the myths that predate Jewish history. Molly tells a source tale for the holiday of Hanukkah in which an ancient people respond to the decreasing numbers of daylight hours before the winter solstice by camping out on the hills and lighting fires while praying to the powers of the sun. For eight days, their fires blaze, says Molly, and at the end of that time, the amount of daylight increases with every rising sun. It's a story that shows what can happen when people come together in a united cause.

Our family is fortunate in that we haven't experienced the kind of alienation from our birth families that so many gays have to deal with. Passover is agony when you're in the closet, especially when the seders act as instant updates on everybody's personal lives — or when you're out of the closet and face intolerance from your blood relations. Taking care of your chosen family becomes a survival tactic in the face of these anxieties — it provides an important anchor and a sense of connectedness.

But the idea of a chosen family carries with it even more resonances among those of us who have decided to have children within the context of our gay and lesbian relationships. For one thing, we made this choice specifically because we reject the nuclear model, its gender assumptions about roles and who does what work, and the assumption that blood ties are the only ones that should influence our kids or create authentic emotional bonds.

For another, becoming a lesbian parent doesn't just happen. Unlike many heterosexual couples who cope with unplanned pregnancies, or who have children because that's what's expected, or who don't even think too much about why they have kids, our specific choice dictated how we would conceive our children — after seeking sperm donors, maintaining ovulation charts and inseminating on the appointed days on the dot as planned, trust me, there are no such things as accidents.

In turn, many of our lesbian and gay friends will not make this choice for themselves and have had to face a future in which they seek alternative ways to develop close connections to kids. Because they are our friends — and because, I can't forget, Molly is so extraordinary — even if their relationship to their own birth families is strong and solid, they have chosen us for a special kind of closeness. We honour these kinds of choices in specific ways in the context of our Judaism.

3. EMPOWERMENT: WHAT HAPPENED WHEN YOU TOLD PEOPLE ABOUT WANTING A BABY?

When my partner and I first began talking about having a child, we were met with two basic responses. From the less imaginative came the claim that children needed men in their lives — as if not having a father and not having men in their lives were the same thing. Other people just worried. They worried that we were saddling our child with our issues and that our daughter's unusual circumstances would work against her. The theory was that, like the products of miscegenation in the 1950s, the children of lesbians would be plagued all their lives by bias, cruelty and all kinds of conflict.

This view came across strongly when a well-meaning television producer in Los Angeles expressed a fleeting interest in my play, *A Fertile Imagination*, the story of two lesbians trying to conceive a child. The producer in question, charmed by the fact that my brother was the sperm donor in our case — a tidbit missing from the play which features no male characters at all — wanted to know more about our situation.

"Has there been a problem keeping your brother out of the picture?" she asked enthusiastically.

"Well, no, actually," I allowed. "He lives on a farm outside the city and has his own complicated life to get on with."

"What about the school yard?" she tried, earnestly. "Has it been hard on your daughter?"

"Well, no actually, aside from the usual sexist playground pressures — which should bother any parent with a pulse — specific incidents of discrimination were pretty rare."

"Oh well, there's not much story line there."

So much for my brush with Hollywood.

But there was more at work here than the long-held artistic belief that drama can't exist without conflict. The producer believed that, art theory be damned, the subject of lesbians with kids automatically had conflict built into it.

I do see her point. If we operate under the assumption that we live in a homophobic society that cannot tolerate difference — if we understand that fundamental dynamic — then how can we imagine the lives of our children as anything other than trouble-laden? For the most part, it hasn't worked out that way for us.

This is Molly's life. The word lesbian is a word she has breathed with ease since day one. She understands Gay Pride — and has celebrated it with us every year since she was born — although she doesn't much like the guys in chaps with the bums cut out. What this means is that she doesn't embrace or understand all aspects of gay community. But then neither do her mothers. We use the moments when she gives us one of those telltale quizzical looks to let her know that we ask some of the same questions as she does — dissent has its own value — but that fundamentally we respect the diversity and complexity in our communities.

Leslie and I knew from the start that having a child would mean coming out in new ways all the time. We knew that in making the choice we automatically took on the never-ending task of educating the people we encountered — the job came with the territory. A lesbian teacher friend of mine — not yet officially out, as is the case with so many in her profession — recounted a revealing anecdote in which a well-meaning high-school principle wondered aloud whether there were any gay teachers on the staff. Yet when asked if there were any kids with gay parents, the answer was immediate — "Definitely, and we know who they all are." Why? Because the parents in every case had declared themselves in order to ensure that teachers took an inclusive approach — on Father's Day, for example — in their children's classrooms. They had all — as have we with Molly — made the connection between coming out and being advocates for their children at school.

I don't know how we would have handled that part of parenting if we had not known beforehand the political implications of what we were doing, or how we would have managed if becoming lesbian mothers had been the first political action we had ever taken.

In the midst of all this openness, Molly is not naive. She says that she doesn't tell everyone that she has two mums — she knows how to sniff out the ones who will have bad reactions. Sometimes she has to contain the enthusiasm of her friends, who like us and like to talk about us and have occasionally come out for her before she's ready.

In the end, the problem isn't so much living with oppression as it is living with the knowledge that oppression exists. In that way it's a lot like being Jewish in North America. During the first ten years of our children's lives, a minority will experience an overt act of anti-Semitism. But somewhere along the road, they all must discover that the Holocaust took place. In fact, a central issue for Jewish parents I know is how to introduce the historical fact of anti-Semitism to our children. We want to share our history so they learn from it, but we don't want to terrify them at the same time.

Leslie and I got this message when Molly first saw the movie *Fiddler On The Roof* and was introduced to the word "pogrom."

"Where are the anti-Semites now?" she asked.

"They could be anywhere," was our way too candid response.

Wrong answer — we could see it in her eyes. So we covered up quickly and talked about how people came to the Americas for religious freedom, and how our political cultures nourish anti-hate laws and that society has learned from history and atrocities can't be covered up the way the used to and that the collective we will never forget.

You can never predict how the child of lesbians will respond to a product of popular culture. Take that now famous coming out episode of *Ellen*.

"It's the most important thing for lesbians ever to happen on TV," we gushed, making special stay-up-late plans. There were invitations to

Ellen parties, galas at the bars in gaytown and Molly got the distinct impression that this was one big deal.

But that was our perspective. Molly's was quite different. From the point of view of a child of two lesbians, raised in an unremittingly lesbian-positive — maybe "lesbian-regular" says it better — household, the show wasn't an exercise in empowerment at all. It was an unsettling lesson in the heaviness of homophobia. I could see the confusion clouding her face. Molly wondered why Ellen couldn't get the word "gay" out of her mouth. Are things really that bad? Not, as I've said, that she doesn't know that her situation is unusual or that hatred is out there. But gay living is a day-to-day fact of life for her. Now she had to figure out why it is that she's having an easier time living with two mums than a famous stand-up comic with her own TV show has living with her lesbianism.

4. VISIBILITY: WHY DON'T THEY EVER MENTION HANUKKAH ON TV?

By the time Molly was six she was clear enough on who she was to notice what was missing from commercial culture, especially during the month of December. I think it was one of those "Give Like Santa, Save Like Scrooge" ads for Canadian Tire that made her insist, "Calling it 'the holiday season' doesn't count as including Hanukkah."

Already she was expressing her longing to see some reflection of her identity and culture in everyday mass media. We knew she would have the same desire when it came to being a girl with two mothers, so from the start we read her every existing children's book that reinforced our life choices. Our favourite is a story called *Heather Has Two Mummies*, written by Lesléa Newman, someone who — is this coincidence? — otherwise writes fiction for adults from a Jewish and lesbian perspective. *Heather Has Two Mummies* made headlines in the early 1990s, when it appeared on the Rainbow Coalition, a political grouping of gays, Blacks and other progressives inspired by Jesse Jackson's mid-1980s presidential candidacy, as recommended reading for teachers in the New York School Board district. That drove the conservative contingent around the bend.

The book also made a major impression on Molly, as we discovered on one extraordinary reading. The story begins with Heather's mothers moving in together and then deciding to have a child. They seek help from their family physician who inseminates sperm from an anonymous donor. At Heather's first day of daycare, the kids are asked what their fathers do and Heather gets confused and then worried. However the daycare workers make a learning experience out of it by asking all the children to describe their families. Together they discover that almost no two families are the same. It's a nice little liberal tale about tolerance and diversity.

We began reading the book to Molly long before we were ready to give her specific information about how she was created. In fact Molly was around for a long time before we even told my brother's much older kids that they had a half sister via unusual circumstances. We thought we'd try a fairly organic approach to information-giving with Molly and hoped reading her Newman's book might twig some questions. Every time we came to the part about Heather's mums going to the doctor to get the sperm, we'd wait for the penny to drop — "So how did I come to be?" The words would come out of Molly's mouth any day now, we were sure of it.

But it never happened. Not once did Molly ever bring it up. We saw intriguing situations at daycare in which kids would insist that you need a man and a woman to make a baby, and so Molly had to have a dad. However no amount of social pressure or even personal curiosity — which Molly brought to bear on just about everything else — moved her to pop the question.

Finally we could bear it no longer.

"Do you ever wonder where we got the sperm to create you?" we asked one day.

"You went to the doctor and he gave it to you," she said matter-of-factly.

It was the only story she knew and she was sticking to it.

We set her straight with the real story — her uncle had given us the gift — which surprised her only because the thought had never crossed her mind that the source would be somebody she knew. Otherwise, the revelation was something of a non-event. The experience filled us with relief — we had approached this moment of discovery with some trepidation although I'm not sure now why. It also filled us with awe at the power of those rare stories that speak to our mostly invisible lives — Molly claimed this one as her own from the start.

Lesbian life is not that visible in Jewish culture. It's one thing to see it denounced in the Orthodox community, but the Bible is not exactly eloquent on the subject. It speaks of strong women — Miriam, Deborah, Judith and all the inspiring heroes reclaimed by feminists — and even intimacy between them, as in the case of Naomi and Ruth — but these appropriations sometimes feel strained. They will feel less so as more and more lesbians write their own Midrash with their own lives. Others are reinventing our past so as to make lesbianism a part of our cultural and community mosaic. I'm appreciating creative literary approaches like Alana Dykewomon's in *Beyond The Pale*, a novel that imagines lesbians living and loving at a key moment in the Jewish American experience — the turn of the century immigration from the old world.

But our stories will surface when there are more of us coming out, more of us having children and more of us wanting to make a lesbian imprint on the culture. Then we and our children will see ourselves reflected back with all the richness of our experience, insights and creativity.

This is one of my deepest desires for Molly. After all, she has never once wished she had a dad — only that she knew more kids who had two mothers.

SUGGESTED READING

Alpert, Rebecca. *Like Bread on the Seder Plate: Jewish Lesbians and the Transformation of Tradition*. New York: Columbia University Press, 1997.

Arnup, Kathy, ed. *Lesbian Parenting: Living with Pride and Prejudice*. Charlottetown: Gynergy, 1995.

Dykewomon, Alana. *Beyond the Pale*. Vancouver: Press Gang, 1997.

Newman, Lesléa. *A Letter to Harvey Milk*. Firebrand, 1988.

Newman, Lesléa. *Heather Has Two Mummies*. Los Angeles: Alyson, 1989.

MINYAN OF CRONES:

NEW RITUALS FOR
JEWISH WOMEN

❧

Pearl Goldberg

*With the increased interest in spirituality and ritual, Jewish women
are forming support and study groups to help them shape their Jewish
identity in this time of transition and change. Based on their own
knowledge of Jewish history, religion and culture, they are adapting
traditional customs and developing new ones to meet their own group
and individual needs. The Minyan of Crones is one such group. In
this article, group members describe some of their communal and personal endeavours, from the marking of a parent's death to full participation in synagogue ritual.*

THE MINYAN OF CRONES is a Jewish feminist study group consisting of
fifteen women ranging in stage from mothers of teenagers to grandmothers, and including married, divorced and remarried women. We
came together in 1989 with a common need to apply feminist perspectives to our lives as Jews, and we have been meeting on a regular
monthly basis since then. We were, and are, all synagogue members,

with varying levels of background, observance and spiritual orientation. A unifying bond was our dissatisfaction with the traditional roles of women in the synagogue and with the dominant patriarchal interpretations of biblical text. There was a good deal of anger in our early meetings. Anger against the benevolent paternalism of our synagogues, anger against the writing out of history, and out of biblical text, of women's lives and experience, anger against our own passivity in accepting this status quo.

It was not easy to find our way. We were a diverse group of professional women with family responsibilities and limited time for study. Our early efforts included reading and reviewing the texts that have become the mainstays of Jewish feminist perspective, such as Judith Plaskow's *Standing Again at Sinai*, Henry and Taitz's *Written Out of History*, Heschel's *On Being A Jewish Feminist* and Reuther's *Religion and Sexism*. We learned that we were not alone in our concerns. Women scholars were reinterpreting text and history to include our mothers as well as our fathers. The pursuit of the relevance of Judaism to modern educated women, and the search for pertinent role models and meaningful new roles was not ours alone. We spent many hours exploring our own attitudes and feelings, sharing the experiences that created our hostilities, as well as those we felt validated us as Jews. We discovered the wealth of interest and scholarship among women in our own community, and invited speakers, at first for only single sessions, and then as we clarified our own needs, for series of sessions. With the help of these fine women scholars, we are learning to apply feminist perspectives to biblical text, to holiday observance and to life cycle events. Most importantly we are learning to take the initiative and make the changes for ourselves that are immediately possible. Most of us are now members of egalitarian congregations, where full participation by women in synagogue ritual is taken for granted. An increasing number of our members wear *tallitot* [prayer shawls] and kippot [head coverings], read Torah and haftorah, act as *sheliakh tzibbur* [lead services] and prepare and present *divrei Torah* [commentaries on a Torah reading] with a feminist perspective.

Along the way, we have become a cohesive and stable group, concerned for each other's physical and spiritual welfare. Our group has seen many changes over the years. We have celebrated *simkhas* [joyous occasions] together, comforted each other in our losses and provided support in times of distress. Out of the need to give personal significance to events in our lives that go unrecognized in traditional Judaism, we began to develop rituals that were meaningful to our immediate concerns, yet tied to the traditions we cherish.

SEEKING WOMEN'S RITUALS

Anthropologists tell us that ritual and ceremony are an integral part of human groups worldwide. Rituals vary widely from community to community, yet their general features are surprisingly constant. Ritual occurs at a moment significant to the community, and is marked by special symbolic acts, acts which become uniquely powerful simply by being evoked for the occasion. The members of the group anticipate and participate in a set sequence of events with a freedom that comes from knowing what to expect, and in an emotional state appropriate to the event.

Rituals reflect the group that generates them. For the individual, participation in ritual serves as a means of identification with the group, and provides an enriching experience. For the group, ritual provides an important role in preserving the cohesiveness of its members. Some rites endure, often with new meanings ascribed to old traditions. Some rituals simply fade away through lack of use. And in every community, new customs, rites, traditions constantly evolve to address the new needs of the community.

WHAT MAKES RITUAL SO IMPORTANT?

Ritual provides the architecture of life in general, and in our case, of Jewish life in particular. It creates difference. It creates space for us to mark the events of the calendar year, to single out the significant happenings in our lives. It creates space for us to pause, to reflect, to wonder, to appreciate, to rejoice, sometimes to mourn. And it gives us patterns to do all this. Patterns that we can and should adapt to meet our needs.

An event that is marked by the performance of a ritual is defined, acknowledged, given status and merit — whether that event was a long life, a week of work, a completed course of study, even a meal. In such observance, the event itself is shared with community — be that community nuclear or extended family, academic or synagogue community — thus giving public recognition and validation to a personal experience.

Ritual provides closure to what went before and permission to proceed further. It gives us tools to live our lives and to celebrate the events that define us as individuals and as Jews. As Jews, we have a vast repertoire of ritual to draw on — our Jewish traditions, our unique family traditions, the poetry and prose we are drawn to, our own creative urges.

WHY NEW RITUALS FOR WOMEN?

Judaism, with its long history, its wealth of teachings and tradition, generally subsumes women as part of mankind. As a result, women who see themselves as persons in their own right, with full responsibility and obligation as Jews, find gaps in ritual that cry out to be filled. Further, the use of the masculine form throughout the language of prayer and ritual creates the overwhelming image of a male God. The apologist view that this is mere metaphor does little to lessen the impact of the constant portrayal of divinity as "He" on the female self-image. Hence the effort in many circles to create rituals that are specific to women and that incorporate "God language" that is gender-free.

PERSONAL RITUAL

Jewish tradition marks the birth of a boy with *brit* [circumcision ceremony] and his coming of age with bar mitzvah. No parallel ceremonies mark the birth and coming of age of a girl. "*Simkhat bat*," the celebration of the naming of a daughter, and bat mitzvah for a girl coming to adult responsibility in the community, are relatively new but already very significant rituals intended to make a young woman feel a full member of her Jewish community. The life events unique to women — menstruation, childbearing, weaning, menopause — are only recently being marked in ceremony as women take the initiative to create their own rituals beyond the generic *she-he-kheyanu*, the blessing with which we recognize first time, happy occasions.

Events common to all humanity take on special significance as ceremony is invoked. For example, while the Kaddish [mourner's prayer] marks a death, a piece written specifically to comfort the mourner, or words by the bereaved to express her grief, deepens the meaning of the mourning process. As one searches within for the deeper significance of an event, the process of creating the ceremony becomes as valuable to the creator as the product will become to the recipient. Making ritual specific to the individual takes it out of the realm of the impersonal and allows the individual to experience more fully the impact of the event being marked.

When the mother of one of the members of the Minyan of Crones died in 1994, "Blessings on the Death of a Mother" was created to comfort and support her. A special gathering of the group was held, and the blessings were read by members of the group in turn.

BLESSINGS ON THE DEATH OF A MOTHER

Let us enfold and comfort our sister, our friend, who mourns
the death of her mother as she joins us tonight.
Everyone has a mother.
More than husband and wife, we are one flesh with the mother
who bears us.
In her body we are conceived, sustained and nurtured, until we
explode newborn in to the world.
And our mothers continue to nurture us until we separate
ourselves, become our own persons, declare our independence
of maternal ties.
We grow up, we grow away, we deny and neglect and sometimes
forget the bonds that link us.
Yet there are ties that bind:
    the memories of experiences shared,
    the good times, the bad times,
    the loving times, the hostile times,
    the celebrations, the grieving,
    the frenzy of preparation for Passover, the seder meals,
    the new shoes for Rosh Hashanah, the fought-over dress,
    the calm of the freshly cleaned house, the gleam of polished
    candlesticks,

the daily routine, the weekly tasks,
the values, explicit, implicit.
We break the ties. We forge our own lives.
Our mother's presence grows stronger as her life grows dimmer.
She dies, as all mortals must, and the broken ties emerge whole,
knit into our very being,
embroidered onto the fabric of our daily lives,
so that she is always with us, more present in death somehow,
than in life.
She stands at our elbow, encouraging, reminding, sometimes
even nagging, so that to deny her presence is to deny ourselves.
Her immortality is in us and in our memories of her very being.

Let us bless our sister, our friend, as she moves forward in her life, bearing the memory of her mother.

Dear _____,
May your friends and family comfort you in your loss.
May good health and good friends renew your zest for life.
May the sun warm you, the breezes caress you and the rains refresh you.
May your mother's pride in you and your accomplishments comfort you.
May the memory of your mother's sturdy self-reliance and her loving kindness to all around her be a model for you to emulate.
May the good years you shared with your mother and the devotion and care you gave so unstintingly to her sustain and keep you.
May the memory of your mother be for you a blessing and a comfort always.
And let us say "Amen."

PEARL GOLDBERG:

Our relationships with our mothers had often been discussed in the group. Two things always surprised me in these discussions. First, the wide variety of feelings, ranging from hostility and anger to love and admiration. Secondly, the similarities in our experiences over the years. Even though my own mother had died several years earlier, writing this blessing on the death of the mother of one of the members was tremendously evocative and cathartic for me, as the reading of it proved to be for the whole group. As well, knowing the bereaved and her mother made the whole process, and the final result, very specific, very personal and very emotional.

Other rituals the group developed include blessings on becoming a grandmother for the first time, and a renewal of spirit healing service for a member facing serious illness. The former included reciting the *she-he-kheyanu,* incorporating Marsha Falk's formulation of *n'varekh'kha* [Let us bless the Source of Life] rather than *barukh atah* [Blessed are You (Lord)] as a gender-neutral way to express the gratitude this traditional blessing invokes.

Such ceremonies, are, of course, very personal rituals, developed for specific women in specific situations, sometimes written by a single member of the group, sometimes as a collaborative effort. These efforts personalize relevant Jewish ritual and attempt to fill the gap where such observances are lacking, for men as well as for women. Men also lose parents, become grandparents, face illness. The traditional generic responses — the Kaddish, the *she-he-kheyanu,* the *mi shebeirakh* (the prayer asking for God's blessing for an individual or a group in a particular situation, sometimes joyous, sometimes stressful) — all strike a meaningful chord. Personalizing the event becomes a source of support and enrichment for all those involved.

FAMILY AND COMMUNITY RITUAL:
WE MOURN AND WE CELEBRATE

Judaism is a religion of "loving kindness." There is much focus in the traditional 613 commandments on the importance of one's relationships with others, and the word "mitzvah," although technically meaning "commandment," has come to refer to any good deed or kindness, as well as to acts of piety. Such customs as comforting the sick and consoling the mourner have long been the domain of women. The pots of soup, the main dish casseroles, the baked goods, the shopping for provisions, the gift of a relevant book, the gift of time — all are ways of reaching out and helping the ill, the bereaved. And here, also, there can be space to create and add new and special observances.

Shivah is the traditional seven day mourning period for the death of a family member. It is customary during *shivah* to visit the mourner, and this visit often becomes a time to reminisce and share memories of the deceased.

TEMMA GENTLES:

I recall my grandfather's *shivah*, when so many wonderful stories were told, mostly about events which happened outside my awareness. I told myself I would remember these and write them down as soon as I got home ... but I didn't. Now, years later, as I search for ways to celebrate the lives of those I have lost, the "*Shivah* Box" has materialized as a way to assist mourners to make a transition by way of memory from the immediately painful experiences surrounding a person's death to the reflections which help us to affirm life.

The box is a place to record and keep these healing memories as they surface during the week of *shivah*. I envisioned that each day a volunteer "scribe" would write down or tape these anecdotes. This would, of course, take some planning and probably require a coordinator, but people do sincerely offer to help out, and the family can eat only so much food. In the long term, the memories might prove more nourishing! Sometimes people also bring memorabilia or send letters, and so there is also a section for photos and small objects. My *Shivah* Box evolved in collaboration with other artists. Any sturdy and attractive receptacle, even an album, would also serve the purpose.

To provide a sense of closure to the *shivah* and tangible evidence of communal respect and honour, the family would receive the box at the end of the week of mourning in the hope that they would come to celebrate their loved one's life and rejoice in it through their tears.

Life cycle events give us cause to rejoice with family and friends, and none is more significant on a personal, family and community level than the celebration of a wedding. When a child is named, parents pray to be able to help this new life find his or her way to Torah [Jewish learning], huppah [the marriage canopy] and *ma'asim tovim* [good deeds].The prayers for huppah include the wish that the parents will live to bring their child to the wedding canopy. The requirements for a Jewish wedding are few. The bride accepts any object of value (usually a simple gold ring of minimal value); the groom recites a ritual formula of consecration ("Be thou consecrated unto me by this ring according to the law of Moses and Israel"). These two actions must be witnessed. Everything else about the wedding is *minhag* or custom.

The wedding is more than a personal commitment of two people to spend their lives together. As a public announcement of their intent to create a Jewish home, the wedding ceremony is part of the ongoing process of ensuring Jewish survival. Customs change over time, and in the Minyan of Crones we have been privileged to see our children create ceremonies that incorporated their personal commitments along with the traditions they cherish into their weddings.

MIRIAM WYMAN:

My children marked the announcement of their intention to marry with *aliyot l'Torah* [being called up to the Torah]. Since our *shul* [synagogue] is egalitarian, they were both called up, as were their parents and siblings, to formally and publicly mark this new step in all of our lives.

In the week before the wedding, on a day when Torah is read, the groom is usually called to read from the Torah in a custom known as the *ayfruf*. For our children, their *ayfruf* was a major community event, with both bride and groom reading Torah and with friends and family singing, dancing and enjoying lunch together. For many of our guests, including the mothers of the children-in-law, we celebrated their first ever *aliyah l'Torah*, which gave an additional dimension to our *simkha*.

Every Jewish wedding takes place under a huppah, a canopy supported by four poles, usually one that the synagogue provides. Its symbolism is manifold. Its open sides evoke the memory of Abraham's hospitality, its roof symbolizes the home the couple is about to establish. Although the huppah is a required part of the marriage ceremony, there are no *halakhic* [legally binding] requirements about its shape, dimensions or decorations, thus making it the perfect venue for personal expression. The use of the groom's *tallit* [prayer shawl] as a canopy is favoured by many couples, and wrapping the children of their union in the same *tallit* for their naming ceremonies provides a lovely sense of family growth and continuity.

MIRIAM WYMAN:

Our son and his fiancée made a unique choice for their huppah. I quote from a letter they sent to relatives and friends:

"We would like you, who have helped create us as the woman and man that we are, to help us create the huppah under which we will wed. We have included with this letter a square of fabric, and we have sent similar squares to other relatives and friends with whom we feel a special connection. We ask you to prepare this square to be joined with the others into our huppah. Your square will help create the holy space in which we will wed, and through it you will stand with us under the huppah."

As the squares arrived, we were overwhelmed at the outpouring of affection and creativity that was embedded in every piece of fabric. The huppah sheltered them during their wedding, and they now mark their anniversary each year by hanging it as a canopy in their living room.

There are many other traditions to consider in planning a wedding. One is the *ketubbah*, or marriage contract. The standard synagogue issue is a small, printed, unadorned certificate, which, duly signed and witnessed, is a legal document. The creation of illuminated *ketubbot* — custom designed works of art incorporating personal preferences of style, along with the words of the contract — is experiencing a resurgence as couples search for ways to make their wedding reflect their individuality. It is increasingly common to add to the traditional wording of the *ketubbah* statements of the personal commitment of the partners, and to ensure that in case of divorce neither partner can withhold the *get* [religious divorce] necessary to dissolve the religious marriage. Both bride and groom and two witnesses sign the *ketubbah*. In the Orthodox tradition, women cannot act as witnesses. To ensure that the marriage is considered valid by the Orthodox community, and still include women friends as witnesses, the bride and groom often choose to increase the number of witnesses, and to include among them the two required men.

Once the *ketubbah* is signed and witnessed, the *badekn* [veiling of the bride] takes place. Some couples choose to dispense with the veil entirely; others feel the veil creates a special space for the bride and cherish the practice. Still others seek out new ways to make this tradition their own. In a different but equal *badekn*, one bride removed the kippah [head covering] her groom had been wearing and replaced it with a new one before he covered her face with her veil, thus marking the transition in their relationship from not-yet-married to married.

Finally, both parents take their children to the huppah, where they meet and circle one another. The circling tradition has many interpretations, some magical and mystical. Traditionally it is the bride who circles the groom. Out of vogue for some time, perhaps because of its magical connotations, perhaps because this seemed to indicate the bride's submission to the groom, this custom too is finding new favour. Some see the circling by the woman as defining the space the couple will share, some make the circling mutual to demonstrate both their independent and complementary roles in the relationship.

It was the custom in the shtetl [small Jewish towns in Eastern Europe] to set a table at every *simkha* for people who were poor or hungry. The donation of a proportion of the food costs of the wedding, as well as arrangements to pick up any left-over food for distribution to food banks is a modern adaptation of this custom which emphasizes the ongoing connection of individual, family and community. Many families also choose to extend their *simkha* by sending the flowers to hospitals and institutions. *Tzedakah* [deeds of righteousness] thus becomes an integral part of wedding process.

SYNAGOGUE AND PRAYER RITUAL

Synagogue ritual is the most public realm of Judaism. Involvement in synagogue ritual is a community event, and, unlike personal ritual, the impact of the community view of ritual practice cannot be underestimated or ignored. Egalitarian synagogue ritual means sharing these activities with men and women, not reserving them for segregated situations of women alone. Full religious equality for women in synagogue ritual is a necessary validation of women's status as Jews.

TEMMA GENTLES:

Before the seder this year, a neighbour knocked on our door and said he needed two Jews for a minyan [quorum of ten adult males traditionally required for liturgical purposes]. "Fine," I said. "My husband and I will be right over." "No, no," was his response. "I didn't mean you." He didn't ask for two men. He asked for two Jews. Am I not a Jew?

PEARL GOLDBERG:

I said Kaddish for my mother in 1987–88 in the synagogue of which I had been a member for many years. On one particular Saturday evening, there were eight men and some fifteen women — at least five of whom had been saying Kaddish on a daily basis — waiting to *davn* [pray]. The *parnas* [lay leader of prayers] insisted we could not begin, because there was no minyan. After twenty minutes or so, he found a youngster who had just become bar mitzvah to join us as the "ninth man." According to *halakhah* [Jewish law], the Torah itself can be called the "tenth man." The *parnas* did so, and we were able to proceed. Click! Did I count as a Jew everywhere except in my own synagogue? I think now that this *parnas* did me a great favour. It was at that moment that I decided I needed to find a place where I counted.

It is precisely because of the very public nature of synagogue worship that it is the ideal forum to effect change. Beyond the significance of egalitarian practice for women, the synagogue environment where children and adults come together can play an important role in modelling practices for the community. In a non-egalitarian environment, boys and girls can experience a synagogue where both are included and encouraged to participate and lead in ritual activity until the age of bar/ bat mitzvah, when suddenly, all doors in synagogue participation open wide for the boys, and shut tight for the girls, regardless of their experience up to that point.

In an egalitarian minyan, children have the opportunity to see both men and women participate equally, thus providing role models for their own continuing participation as adult members of the community. This kind of role modelling also affects adults. After an initial period of discomfort with both the concept and the actuality of women's inclusion, most men come to take it for granted. For women who were never given the opportunity to become bat mitzvah, this can provide the impetus to study and learn in order to participate. Women who were bat mitzvah at twelve or thirteen years of age often experience a resurgence of interest in renewing and practising their buried skills.

Every branch of Judaism is currently struggling with the greater inclusion of women, in liturgy, in prayer groups, in ritual. The wearing of the *tallit*, customarily donned by adult males for morning services as well as for Yom Kippur [Day of Atonement] services, is one of the more visible areas of this concern.

RICKI GRUSHCOW:

The greatest advantage of wearing a *tallit* is to enrich and enhance my prayer and to allow me a more intimate and spiritual fulfillment. The *tallit* embraces and surrounds me; it provides a sense of envelopment and enclosure, a setting apart from the world. When I first wore my *tallit*, I endured a fair amount of teasing and pressure designed to embarrass me out of wearing it. It was very threatening and hard for me to persevere. I'm very glad that I did persevere; to be able to commit oneself to a mitzvah out of religious conviction and to participate in a centuries-old way of prayer has increased my sense of spirituality and attachment to Judaism.

Closely associated with the wearing of the *tallit* for the weekday Morning Service is the wearing of *tefillin*, or phylacteries, traditionally worn by Jewish males over the age of thirteen. *Tefillin*, like *tallit*, are another physical reminder of the covenant between God and the Jewish people, a direct connection to spirituality, and another important ritual to model for our young people.

RICKI GRUSHCOW:

Shortly after I began to wear my *tallit*, I found myself at a Rosh Khodesh [New Month] service, and there I was, *tallit* in hand, and no *tefillin*, which on a weekday, would, of course, be part of the prayer service. This made me feel very strange, and I had to deal with the concept of *tefillin*, which was much more difficult and uncomfortable for me. Putting on *tefillin* is very awkward at first. It takes a lot of practice to learn, requires considerable coordination, longer arms than I have, or shorter straps! Watching men don *tefillin* had always seemed somewhat pagan to me. Once I took the initiative to become a participant and to be actively involved in this mitzvah, I discovered the beautiful prayers involved in the wearing of *tefillin*, and a whole new meaning and relevance became clear to me.

The reading of the Torah (literally, the Law) is the core of the Shabbat morning service. The Torah itself is the physical embodiment of holiness in the synagogue. Our prayers are directed towards the ark which houses the Torah, and to the east towards Jerusalem, and we rise in honour of the Torah when it is revealed in the sanctuary. Thus, to be close to the Torah is the most sacred place in the house of prayer. Accordingly, to perform an *aliyah*, literally "going up to the Torah" is the greatest honour in the service. An *aliyah* also functions to mark such major life events as a baby naming, a wedding, special anniversaries.

Although no *halakhic* argument prevents a woman from being called to the Torah, it was not customary to call her up because of the "dignity of the congregation." (Megillah 23a) This apparently means that for a woman to participate in the Torah service, thus showing her knowledge and ability, was inappropriate, lest she shame the less able men of the congregation! Accordingly, until the thirteenth century, the person called up to the Torah was always a man, who recited the blessing and read the portion himself. By the fourteenth century, it became the custom for a *ba'al koreh* [Torah reader] to be appointed to read the portion for all so as not to shame those unable to read, and the person called to the Torah recited the blessing only. Customs harden into "law," and the perception that women are forbidden to be called to the Torah, to read from the Torah, even to touch the Torah, is still widespread in some circles.

With the exception of the *mi shebeirakh*, the person being called up to the Torah was named by his first name and his father's name. Our tradition very specifically tells us to "honour thy mother and thy father." There is no *halakhah* which dictates against the naming of both parents in ritual situations. The standard omission of the mother's name has been, for many women, a confirmation of their conviction that women are indeed invisible in traditional synagogue practice. Honouring women with *aliyot*, and with the opportunity to read from the Torah, as well as naming both men and women by their matronym in addition to their patronym is now an accepted part of ritual in Reform, Reconstructionist and many Conservative synagogues. *Aliyah* remains the purview of men in most Orthodox congregations.

LIEBA LESK:

I belong to an egalitarian traditional congregation that has existed for ten years, and I have been privileged to offer and facilitate their first *aliyah* for many young, middle-aged and older women. Their joy at having this honour is often celebrated in tears and dancing. Standing at the Torah and looking at the writing on the parchment during an *aliyah* is a moving experience for me. I feel a connection with the individual Hebrew letters, with the words, the text, and then with the people and the situations described. I feel as if I am a continuing thread in a long line that goes back thousands of years ...

Reading Torah is an even more emotional experience for me. When I get the text, I feel very anxious about whether I'm going to be able to learn it in time. I practise the reading over and over,

I become more and more involved in trying to understand the text, in order to give meaning to the Torah reading when I chant it. Every year I find more insights in almost every Torah reading, so the responsibility to read from the Torah allows me the opportunity to increase my understanding not just of the particular *parsha* [the reading of the week], but of the very sentences and words I study.

Formal prayer in Judaism is led by the *sheliakh tzibbur*, the delegate of the congregation, traditionally an adult male. The original role of the *sheliakh* was to ensure that those who were unable to pray had the prayers said on their behalf. In contemporary practice, the *sheliakh tzibbur* leads the congregation in prayer. Since there is no requirement for formal training for this role, the daily prayers and minyans at *shivahs* are often led by capable lay congregants, a task often undertaken by women in egalitarian congregations.

LIEBA LESK:

My experience leading services began as it does for many children in the Junior Congregation of the Conservative Movement, and ended when I became bat mitzvah. Ten years ago, when my own congregation in Toronto started, I began to learn the form for the different services, and have been leading services ever since. The challenge for me is to give the prayers relevant meaning and context, and I strive to create an atmosphere of spirituality and participation, so that the *davening* [praying] is as alive as possible. It is a particular joy for me to teach the children of our congregation, the girls as well as the boys, how to lead the *davening*.

I enjoy singing very much. It is a warm and emotional tie to *davening* that I have always had, perhaps because my mother's beautiful voice is an integral part of my childhood synagogue memories. I doubt that the idea of being a *sheliakh tzibbur* ever entered her mind. It would have been beyond the realm of possibility.

The involvement and inclusion of women in public ritual activity is a necessary, but not a sufficient condition for a totally egalitarian experience of Judaism. The benefit that any individual, man or woman, adult or child, can gain from ritual participation is dependent on the power of that ritual to create identification with the group, and the group benefits accordingly. Jewish women are finding their places in ritual participation. We are still searching for our voices in Jewish history, theology, liturgy. There have always been women in Jewish life. Hearing their voices by study and reinterpretation of text is a motivating force for the Minyan of Crones. The voices are there if we can only listen.

CONCLUSION

Talmud Torah [the study of Torah] is considered a positive religious duty of the highest order and there are various blessings for fulfilling this precept. As we study and seek to bring women's experience and perspectives to bear on our lives as Jews, the Minyan of Crones have chosen to bless ourselves and one another with seven blessings for our learning. The final blessing refers to the custom of providing candy, cake or a taste of honey when a young child begins to study traditional texts.

BLESSINGS FOR OUR LEARNING

May we create for ourselves a community of seekers and learners.
May our creative ideas and thoughts be grounded in study and flow generously.
May we find ways to give meaning to our life experiences.
May we support and accept each other as we create and try new ways.
May others accept our ways as we have accepted theirs.
May our work be honoured by future generations.
May our learning always be fulfilling and sweet.
And to all of this, let us say "Amen."

☙

NOTE

This article is adapted from a workshop presentation at the conference "From Memory to Transformation" given by Pearl Goldberg, Temma Gentles, Ricki Grushcow, Lieba Lesk and Miriam Wyman, all members of Minyan of Crones.

PART FOUR

ACTIVISM

AND

SOCIAL

CHANGE

DIASPORISM, FEMINISM AND COALITION

౨ఌఄ

Melanie Kaye/Kantrowitz

Although the State of Israel does exist as a homeland for Jews, current politics make aliyah *[immigration to Israel] anything but a simple choice for many progressive Jews. They remain instead in the diaspora, committed to their respective communities. Progressive diaspora Jews must find ways to continue the struggle for universal civil rights and social justice in these communities. Melanie Kaye/Kantrowitz argues that, on the eve of the twenty-first century, Jewish women in the diaspora have a very important and rich role to play in creating a better future, and a better world.*

DIASPORISM

WHAT IS this word? What does it mean and why invent it?[1]

I am a secular Jewish feminist committed to the complexities of life in the diaspora, and to the struggle here to end all systems of oppression, including anti-Semitism. I call this commitment Diasporism, and I do so partly because of another word, also invented but older by one hundred years or so: Zionism. The concept of Jewish nationalism, Jews in the historic land of our origins and aspirations, has become an integral part of contemporary discourse. But, though the majority of Jews continue to live outside the Jewish state, there is no name for the ideology that backs up the political choice to do so. It's as if the millions of Jews who continue to wrestle with minority status in Buenos Aires or Lodz or Minneapolis or Toronto, or even, though this hardly counts as minority, New York City, are pitifully stuck in *golus, galut,* exile. Through a Zionist lens, authentic Jewishness resides in Israel: out here in *golus* lurks only oppression, assimilation and an attenuated identity. Jews belong in Israel. We should leave the *golus* and make *aliyah* [immigrate to Israel], or at least do penance for *not* making *aliyah*: by sending money, and by granting the Zionist's exclusive claim to authenticity.

Yet most Jews remain in diaspora.

HISTORY

In Europe, the modern period — roughly late eighteenth century up until our own time — offered various strategies to combat anti-Semitism. Assimilation, kind of a non-strategy, an attempt to evade the problem. Endurance, of course. Immigration, escape of another sort. Territorialism, which, like Zionism, aspired towards a Jewish state, but was indifferent as to location (Uganda was a serious contender). Zionism, committed to biblical Zion and nationalist normalcy. And socialism: class struggle would create a new free world and anti-Semitism would disappear.

Yet the eruption of pogroms in Eastern Europe led some Jewish socialists and communists to organize *as Jews*, and in 1897, the same year as the first Zionist Congress, a small group founded the Jewish Labor Bund. Their attention to explicitly Jewish organizing did not go uncontested. In one famous conflict, the Bundist leader Vladimir Medem, arguing the right of Jews to defend themselves, was challenged fiercely by none other than Leon Trotsky (born Lev Bronstein).

Bundists — like, for the most part, their ideological foes, the Zionists — were anti-religious. They believed in the Jewish people. For those early Bundists, the experience of organizing among Jews, of speaking with them in Yiddish, the language of the Jewish common people (a language which some of the early Bundist intellectuals had to learn), created a pride and a commitment to Jewish language and culture. Bundists remained committed to class struggle, evolving a complex implicit notion of identity, community and coalition predicated on working-class unity but also on cultural and linguistic autonomy. Bundists were thus distinct, on one hand, from other leftist Jews who, from a Jewish perspective, employed the classic bourgeois tactic of trying to assimilate (into the left), and, on the other, from Zionists, who assumed that anti-Semitism could not be eradicated, but could only be avoided by emigrating from non-Jewish sites to biblical Zion.

BUNDISM AND DIASPORISM

Why do we need a new word? Why can't we just invoke an honourable history and revive the term Bundism?

One reason is that the Bund still exists, with its own platform and parameters. But I find other significant arguments for a new term, a new concept. While the Jewish Labor Bund is the clear intellectual, political and moral ancestor of the Diasporism I am trying to articulate, North America approaching the twenty-first century is not Europe at the beginning of the twentieth. It's probably an oversimplification to say that European countries where Jews lived were bicultural and we were the *bi*. But North America is wildly multicultural. Jews are not the only — or even the primary — minority.

The Bund grew in a context that was largely working-class. The class base of the Jewish community, its centre of economic gravity, has shifted. Though not all Jews have become rich or even middle-class (and the economic insecurity of even middle-class Jews can lead to progressive class positions, as well as such fruitful anomalies as professional unions), Jewish self-interest, narrowly defined, no longer largely or automatically lines up with the interests of the working class and poor. While contemporary Diasporists draw on Bundist analysis of Jews serving as a convenient scapegoat for the ills of capitalism (anti-Semitism as "the socialism of fools," in German Socialist August Bebel's phrase), we also face a task unknown to Bundists: to articulate the meaning of self-interest in the largest sense, as in, what kind of world do we want to live in?

Finally, Bundism is strongly identified with *mame-loshn* [mother tongue; Yiddish]; the Jews of Eastern Europe who responded to Bundism were steeped in *yidishkeyt* [Yiddish culture]. We can't assume this about Jews in North America. Linking Diasporism too closely to Yiddish ties our hands. The revival of Yiddish language and culture is a splendid phenomenon, but assimilation has left many Ashkenazic Jews alienated from their Yiddish heritage. Most important: the Jewish communities of North America are multicultural communities. Ashkenazi is only part, not the whole. An ideology, a movement that includes all of us, can't assume — as Bundism could — *yidishkeyt* as our common culture.

DIASPORA AS CENTRE

Diaspora means dispersion; its premise, we were once a gathered people in our own land, the land of Israel, and now we are scattered, an inherently negative condition.[2]

What would it mean to conceive of diaspora *as* the centre of a circle that includes but does not privilege Israel? A paradox, an oxymoron, putting the margin at the centre. The image evokes the work of African–American feminist bell hooks (one of whose books is entitled *From Margin to Center)*. But unlike people of colour, whose collective global status as majority might suggest a "natural" centrality, we diaspora Jews are truly a minority, no matter where we stand. Diasporism means embracing this minority status, which leaves us with some serious questions: Can we embrace the diaspora without accepting oppression? Does minority inevitably mean oppressed? Do we choose to be marginal? Do we choose to transform the meaning of centre and margins? Is this possible?

One thing Diasporism definitely means: We're not looking to go home. We're not really looking *to be* at home. Given the multicultural nature of the Jewish community forged in diaspora, even in the Jewish community we experience the simultaneity of home and strangeness. If we are at an event that claims to be for the whole Jewish community, at any given moment *something* must feel unfamiliar to *someone*; it just shouldn't always be the same people. I recently bought a tape of Iraqi Jewish music, oud and violin. It doesn't feel like my music; it's new to me. But it is just as Jewish as klezmer, which to an Iraqi Jew probably doesn't feel like hers. Too often anthologies, performances, book lists, conferences entitled "Jewish culture, history, experience," etc., include only Ashkenazic culture, history and experience. At best, there is a small postscript for diversity, into which the one or two Sephardic or Mizrachi items are tokenistically slotted: as though Sephardic and Mizrachi Jews are diverse, while Ashkenazic Jews are what? Normal?

Two years ago Jews for Racial and Economic Justice were organizing in New York City a teach-in on progressive Jewish history, which we named *In gerangl*, Yiddish for "In Struggle."[3] I invited a friend to join one of the panels, and she —a Jew of mixed Sephardic–Ashkenazic heritage — remarked that the Yiddish title signified to her that the event was not about or for Sephardic Jews. When I shared this observation with our organizing committee, some simply dismissed its relevance on the grounds that the vast number of Jews in the USA are Ashkenazim (somewhere between 85 and 97 per cent). Yet even the high end, 97 per cent, leaves 3 per cent Jews who are *not* Ashkenazim, which is greater than the percentage of American residents who are Jews of any sort (about 2.5 per cent). Don't we press for, and would like to expect, inclusion in all our 2.5 per cent glory? If we count as a minority, then our minorities must also count.

Let me stress a basic point. If in our planning we excluded a whole community of Jews, we failed. Failed, let me be clear, not as bad people, or politically incorrect, or any of the guilt-and-shame apparatus which obscures the real problem with certain political choices. Failed because *we need* the unity of progressive Jews. Failed too because those Jews who are cultural minorities within a hegemonic Ashkenazic community are often best equipped to help the Jewish world reckon with our multiculturality. And this multiculturality is an enormous asset when it comes to combatting racism and anti-Semitism, and to building social justice coalitions.

This doesn't mean we shouldn't have events focused on Yiddish culture or history. I am as impatient as the next Yiddish-lover with dismissals of Yiddish on the grounds that it is just one more European culture. Yet when we turn to the relationship of Yiddish culture to contemporary progressive Jewish politics, we cannot, as I suggested above, assume *yidishkeyt* as *the* Jewish cultural norm that accompanies Jewish progressive politics.

I don't claim it's simple. The shape of most Jewish thinking on progressive Jewish history and culture has been defined by Ashkenazic experience. For example, for our next teach-in, we tried to find the
equivalent to "In Struggle" in Ladino.[4] *En lucha,* someone said, the obvious Spanish equivalent, but when we finally tracked down someone
whose Ladino was idiomatic rather than bookish, she howled. *En lucha,*
she said, conveyed wrestling. *Con peña* is what she told us, and that's
what we used, but I notice as most people talk about these annual
teach-ins, *in gerangl* has stuck and *con peña* has dropped out of the
shorthand.

Nevertheless, in the process of searching, we discovered an old
phrase book for Yiddish-speaking trade unionists trying to organize
Ladino-speaking workers, in which Yiddish is translated into Ladino
and English, all, including the English, in Hebrew characters (though
unfortunately for us these predecessors did not feel the need to say "In
Struggle"). We made contact with a number of Sephardic women,[5] and
with the department of Sephardic Studies at Yeshiva University, got on
some mailing lists. We are now able to include many Sephardic cultural
and community events in our newsletter, and even co-sponsor some.
We can also draw on a larger pool of Sephardic contacts in planning
our events, thus taking us another step towards authentic multiculturalism.

Beyond the Ashkenazi/Sephardi nexus, our multicultural community can help us past simplistic dichotomies: Jew/Arab? Over a million
Israelis, and a significant number of Canadians, are both. Ammiel Al-
calay's brilliant scholarly exploration *After Jews and Arabs: Remaking
Levantine Culture* demonstrates the entwined culture and history, and
the impact on Europe of the two "natural opposites." What about
Black/Jewish? Between one and two hundred thousand American residents are both African–American and Jewish. Full inclusion of our bicultural members strengthens our ability to form coalitions where we
need them most.

TENETS OF DIASPORISM

Diasporism means work. Work to retain the fullness of our identity, be-cause we cherish our culture and history; because we understand how shame and covertness diminish human strength, and feed racism and bigotry. Work to protect cultural variety, because we understand the dangers of mono-cultural pressure; because difference attracts and in-terests us. Diasporists are not against intermarriage or mixed race, mixed culture babies. We are anti-assimilation. We want to raise *truly* bi- and multicultural children, knowledgeable, proud and connected. Our vehicle is not the bloodline but culture, history, memory.

Diasporists support refuge for all who need it, a solution not of homeland (though we can never forget the critical significance of the passport), but of safe harbour for everyone. We strongly support the vital struggles of immigrants, documented and undocumented. While recognizing the role of nationalism and national integrity in the process of liberation, we challenge the concept of borders. We disrespect the boundaries of the imperial nations, and say people should be free to cross where they will. We resonate with post-colonial voices in Eng-land, who defend themselves by invoking history: *We are here*, they say, *because you were there.* (In the mega-global-capitalist states one might update it, *We are here because you are everywhere.*)

Diasporism means envisioning a community and culture that is al-liance seeking and *totally relational.* We seek allies and we seek to *be* al-lies. Yet we recognize that Jews, still traumatized by the Holocaust and our sense of collective isolation, are terrified of being ally-less. Indeed, Jean-Paul Sartre reported that when he simply included Jews on a list of victims of Nazism, he actually received letters from Jews thanking him.

But since Jews rarely expect inclusion, we often fail to situate our experience in a larger context that includes other groups. Diasporists seek to strengthen our practice at contextualizing, at cross-cultural rela-tions. Recently I spoke on a panel in New York City where a Jewish man asserted a clumsy sameness between the experience of Jews and African Americans: "We were slaves in Egypt," he insisted. "We have to listen to Christmas carols in Macy's." (It was that time of year, and Christmas can be grueling for non-Christians, but this was New York City, where the public schools close for even minor Jewish holidays.) A young African–American student stood to respond, angry, I think at his glibness. "You know your culture," she said. "Can you imagine that I might have a culture I don't even know about?"

I was struck by two thoughts. At least I know something of my cultural loss, and am able, through the labour of scholars, linguists and musicians, to reconnect with some of this loss. The young woman could not even name her ancestors' language. But she had not a clue that Jews have also suffered traumatic cultural losses. And how, I went on to wonder, *should* she know, when Jewish education has targeted only Jewish children, and left the multicultural arena to others.

Diasporists, however, committed to working across our differences, conceive of Jewish education not only for Jews, but also to educate non-Jews about us. Similarly, we are committed to learning about the cultures of others.

Finally, Diasporists seek visibility. We want to be seen and known as Jews; to speak as Jews; to organize as Jews.

Why?

CONTEXT: THE END OF THE TWENTIETH CENTURY

I am writing this essay in Spring 1998. California has just voted to end bilingual education, the third in a series of racist and punitive ballot measures which stigmatized immigrants and smashed affirmative action. In my home town of New York City, the mayor usurps power daily. He has forbidden groups of more than thirty people to gather on the steps of City Hall. He slashes public funds, while pressing to privatize the public hospitals, schools and housing, and insisting that the city's billion dollar surplus go to build two new baseball stadiums, moving the Yankees from the (impoverished) South Bronx to Manhattan's (wealthy) upper west side.

These are the pace-setting coasts of the most powerful nation in the world, where we spend more money building prisons than schools. The word *revolution* is paired most frequently with, on one hand, advertising — soap, soup, fabric — and, on the other, a sweeping backlash, as in the *Right Wing Revolution*, with its relentless Christianity, legislation of fundamentalist morality, pro-life rhetoric and lust for capital punishment, pro-family hype assaulting families not under white male protection. On the rise: Holocaust revisionism, neo-Nazi racism, queer bashing and immigrant bashing, militia and other terrorist activity. The concept of entitlement to the means of basic survival disappears into a Manichean struggle pitting productive and deserving (white) folks against the dead weight of (criminal) poor men and (lazy and breeding) poor women. *Poor white* is considered an oxymoron, because in the popular consciousness and discourse race and class have so merged that *poor* simply equals *African American* or *Latino*. The illusion of a tightening economy — the loss of jobs through down-sizing, exporting production, shifting to a part-time unorganized labour force without health insurance or other benefits for blue, pink and white collar workers, while those with wealth increase it astronomically, so they do better and better while most of us struggle harder and harder just to stay afloat.

This is our terrain, and frankly the word fascism is not that far-fetched. Surely I'm not the only person trying to understand this historical moment, lying awake at night wondering, *Is this like Berlin 1933? 1931? What will I wish later I had understood?* Most haunting, *what will I wish I had done?*

A JEWISH/FEMINIST/DIASPORIST RESPONSE

In the gathering storm, Jews *qua* Jews are not primary targets, though women are, and the continued encroachment of (Christian) religion into formerly secular spaces should be flashing a huge danger signal. We have no unanimity of Jewish opinion, even about issues which seem (to me) so clear, like church–state separation, on which Orthodox Jews weigh in blithely on the side of Christian fundamentalism against the godless secularist agenda: against sex education, gay rights, condom distribution; and for school vouchers and school prayer. When people of colour are targeted, too many Jews ignore it, or even bask in the implied comparison. I have not heard anywhere near the appropriate level of Jewish outrage about the pseudo-scientific racism of *The Bell Curve*, which claims IQ superiority for Ashkenazic Jews and inferiority for African Americans.

Yet eugenics — including philo-Semitic eugenics — serves white supremacy directly, and male supremacy indirectly. From eugenics to control of our bodies, the places where genes get reproduced into new little organisms, is a slippery slope indeed. Furthermore, white supremacy targets Jews. In *The Turner Diaries*, the wacko — and popular — futuristic novel about race war to impose apartheid, Jews are race mongrels, and, along with other race mongrels, need to be exterminated first — *because we confuse things.*[6] So the question I ask is not idle; it is guided by fear and need: How can we meet these threats?

The Jewish Right (everything from neo-conservatives to fundamentalists) *is* organized, and they claim to speak for all of us. It's up to us to disrupt their claim.

I've been reading a book called *The Imaginary Jew* by Alain Finkielkraut, a French intellectual. For Finkielkraut, an imaginary Jew claims the name "Jew," even proudly, but ignores the content of Jewishness. So he locates, at last, a Jewishness he considers real, not imaginary: "The past, from which I refuse to avert my gaze, reflects more than an embellishment of my looks. For if Judaism has a central injunction, it should be thought of not as a matter of identity, but of memory ..." Memory. History. And, implied, but let me make it explicit, *larger than oneself.* No surprise, the idea that Jewishness is about connection to other Jews.

What *is* surprising is how Finkielkraut draws from this observation an injunction to repudiate his past commitment to socialism and liberation struggles, as if these commitments were inauthentic, were refusals to be fully Jewish. I interpret these same commitments on the part of my younger self — civil rights, anti-imperialism, women's liberation — as foreshadowings. I would say, I *was* being a Jew without claiming it, without knowing it.

And I think this is more than a personal difference between myself and Finkielkraut. The so-called great shift rightward on the part of Jewish radicals and liberals in the USA — to the extent that it exists — is sharply gendered. I do not hear the same sarcasm, pessimism, rejection and dejection in the voices of leftist Jewish women of my generation — or in those of the generation of women now in their twenties and thirties, who have, after all, their own history of activism. Many Jewish men are trying to cut a deal with the larger Christian society. They identify with a sort of victim-privilege of Jewishness — a *we've suffered so we have no responsibility* Jewishness — blurring the time lapse between mid-century and the present, standing apart from contemporary struggles for social justice.

As women we cannot stand apart from these struggles because *as women* we are in struggle, connected to the struggles of other women. We recognize our common oppression by gender. In addition, many of us understand — some from our own experience and location, some through the experience of those we love, and some through education in why and how to be allies — where oppression by gender, race, class, sexual orientation intersect and reinforce each other.[7]

Thus, while many Jewish men aspire — with some success — to occupy centre stage, many Jewish women are still marginalized — I am tempted to say, *are still Jewish*, as the margins have offered such a determining and valuable vantage point in Jewish diasporic life. When I ask, then, why Jewish women are proving so important to Jewish renewal, to feminism and to progressive political movements, I try not to answer essentially: *because we're so cool* — but analytically: *because we're so positioned*.

In my work I talk to countless women working very hard in their communities and in communication with each other. Popular media in the USA stress conflict, especially between Jews and Blacks; rarely do they interview women. In practice, I don't find Jewish women and African Americans particularly at odds. For example, affirmative action is often invoked as evidence of implacable difference between our communities, yet Jewish *women* have always supported affirmative action.

The Jewish community is most often represented by powerful, wealthy men, who speak for the interests of the wealthy and powerful. If, instead, the Jewish community were represented by the full range of voices inside that community — women, and working and poor people, people of colour, seniors, lesbians and gays — there would be a different set of interests and priorities. A lot more concern about employment, health insurance, daycare, schools, housing, rape, AIDS, hate crimes. An agenda very close to the agenda of the African–American community. Democratization of the Jewish community would go a long way towards healing the Black–Jewish split in the USA, and towards challenging the hierarchy and sexism of the Jewish community. What if *we* spoke for the community?

Why don't we?

And, in fact, where there is consciousness and aspiration I consider Diasporist, in groups, organizing efforts, cultural events, etc., you find women actively participating and even leading mixed gender groups. As feminists, we must be aware of the dangers of working in mixed gender formats. Always the risk of men claiming the credit, of women's issues being ignored, tokenized or marginalized, our voices ghettoized, relegated to the "women's" issues, panels, corners, while the "big picture" is presented by men. Yet though I am sometimes sorely tempted to work in women's venues, in the end I am not willing to leave the Jewish world to the men. I am inspired by state-by-state struggles in the USA against anti-gay ballot measures, by the strong alliance from the Jewish community, and among lesbians, gay men and feminists. Diasporism asks us to interrogate separatism. We need unity. We need strength. We need to believe we can hold our own even when men are there. I believe that Jewish women must continue to assert our participation and leadership in the larger Jewish community for the following reasons:

1. Material resources: men have more.

2. Philosophical: It is not as though they are the real Jews and we are not. We must not cede the Jewish future to them.

3. Tactical. Men can be allies, comrades and teachers. I am thinking especially of the gay men and women whose skill and militancy has been honed in AIDS activism, an experience Esther Kaplan, writer and activist, credits with teaching her how (middle-class white) men's sense of entitlement connects to the belief that winning is possible, and thus contributes to demands for effectiveness.[8]

Finally, having praised my brothers as comrades, let me say one more reason why women's leadership is critical:

4. Practical: Not to essentialize women as inherently progressive, but a lot of what's happening in the male-dominated political arena is *wrong*. Often through our education as feminists, in political work, in women's studies classes, in multicultural communities, often in cross-cultural lesbian relationships, women are politically way ahead of the men. The community sorely needs our leadership.

A DIASPORIST DREAM

Mine is not, like Dr. King's, a long-range dream of a free society, but a short-term vision of how to move towards that dream.[9] In my dream, to meet the palpable nightmare of a growing Christian fundamentalist right wing, a new human rights movement emerges from the separate movements into which the 1960s and 1970s dwindled. The smaller movements still function as community or issue-bases, as channels between each community and the larger movement. But the larger movement can *MOVE* like a mighty wave. There's a feminist wing, and an African–American wing of the movement, a Latino wing, a First Nation wing, all the other people of colour. Crisscrossing there's a labour wing, and a wing of the movement for not-yet-unionized workers, queers, youth, a health care wing, AIDS activists and women's health activists, teachers, environmental groups, homeless people, immigrant rights: all the ways that people organize for freedom and justice come together. In this movement, rape, environmental racism and poverty are deemed crimes against humanity. Housing and food, health care and education are considered basic human rights. Artistic expression and participation are considered basic human needs.

As this movement pushes and bumbles towards the world we want, Diasporist Jews form one wing. We are not segregated. Like others, we participate also in all the appropriate places where our multiple identities and concerns lead us. But Jews in this new movement know and are proud of our history. We know our foremothers. Our leaders are not all Ashkenazic men in suits who belong to a synagogue. Our women lead. We recognize and embrace our diversity of race, culture, sexual orientation, observance and secularism. Ladino and Judeo–Arabic are valued along with Yiddish and Hebrew, for themselves and for the bridges they make with other Spanish and Arab cultures. Indeed, we have a wildly expanded notion of what it means to "look like a Jew."

I said, women are key leaders; also lesbians and gay men, bisexuals and transsexuals, mothers, young Jews, old Jews, workers and poor Jews, artists and writers. Jews of colour lead towards alliances with the communities they span. The coalition work between Israeli and Palestinian women, and the pressure it continues (in my dream) to exert towards completion of the project of Palestinian liberation, is an honoured model of feminist leadership and of radical boundary crossing.

We bond with Japanese and other Asians against the use of the term JAP, and against any *model-minority-we-made-it-why-can't-they* co-optation. We bond with Muslims, Hindus, Buddhists, Sikhs and other non-Christians against Christian hegemony. We bond with immigrants to preserve cultures and languages. In the USA, with our history of enslavement of Africans, we recognize the frequent leadership of African Americans in progressive struggle; but we do not imagine that the issues of other communities of colour, and of all working or impoverished people, are magically included under the category of African American. We are not obsessed with being liked by African Americans, but rather with contributing our part to create the world where untainted human relations will be possible. We form a human chain of commitment between those able or willing to give money or time, those who risk their careers or freedom, and those who risk their lives. We comprehend the process whereby activists edge and are edged towards greater commitment, greater and greater risk.

In this movement, Jews are visible. Non-Jews know that we are not whites/Europeans who go to Jewish church, but a people whose history, culture/religion and sometimes complexion situate us shiftingly between the categories of white and colour. Non-Jews know and respect the history of Jewish oppression and resistance, of Jewish allies. Through our crisscrossing identities, friend- and loverships, families and concerns, and most of all through the political change which we accomplish together, we come to trust the power and joy of solidarity. We are who we are, where we are. We don't need to go home.

❦

NOTES

1. I recognize that Diasporism isn't exactly catchy. I'm using it until something catchier comes along. Since writing this essay, I've discovered the Diasporism of Philip Roth's brilliant satire *Operation Shylock*; Roth's Diasporism solves the problem of anti-Semitism by forcing the Jews to leave Israel and return to Europe. As should be apparent, this is not my meaning.

2. I am indebted to recent discussions of the Chinese, Indian and African diasporas, which, if not welcoming permanent status as minority (on the contrary, often asserting majority status, as people of colour), do embrace the new identity and context that has been created through cross-cultural encounter.

3. I learned the term from Irena Klepfisz, and she and I used it as the title of a handbook on resisting anti-Semitism in the anthology we co-edited, *The Tribe of Dina: A Jewish Women's Anthology* (Boston: Beacon Press, 1989).

4. Joanne Lehrer, our blessed intern at that time, and I conducted the amazing and frustrating linguistic search.

5. Thanks to Emily Levy, who supplied us with "*con peña*"; we reached Mrs. Levy through her daughter, writer Gloria Kirchheimer, whose story, "Food of Love," appears in *The Tribe of Dina*.

6. Timothy McVeigh, convicted in the Oklahoma City bombing, carried around copies of this book to hawk. More than 200,000 copies of this book have been sold, a scary miracle of small press distribution.

7. I think that lesbians and bisexuals who truly identify with and stake their claim with queers often see these interconnections most clearly because our movement and communities, while far from fully integrated, still are more inclusive and multi-racial than most other places.

8. Esther Kaplan, "The Feminist Diaspora," unpublished talk, Hamilton College, Clinton, NY (Fall 1995).

9. An earlier version of this section appears in "Stayed on Freedom: Jew in the Civil Rights Movement — And After," in Marla Brettschneider, ed., *The Narrow Bridge: Jewish Views on Multiculturalism* (New Brunswick, NJ: Rutgers University Press, 1996).

ACTIVISM FOR CHANGE
IN ISRAELI SOCIETY

Rachel Leviatan

While the standard of living in Israel has risen significantly over the last decade, poverty and its incumbent inequities remain an integral part of the hidden life of Israel which few tourists see. Israeli kibbutznik and activist Rachel Leviatan began her life in the slums of Tel Aviv and escaped from her family's poverty by joining a kibbutz youth programme and moving to a kibbutz which cared for and educated underprivileged children. She never forgot her childhood experiences; as an adult Leviatan went on to work in education and grass-roots politics.

BOTH MY PARENTS came from families rooted for many generations in Israel. Both had had very ugly encounters with their Arab neighbours during their childhood. My father was born to a family originating from Iraq and Bulgaria who had lived in Hebron since the middle of the nineteenth century. During the pogroms of 1929, he and his parents were forced to flee Hebron to Gaza. The pogrom began when a gang of Arabs attacked a group of young Jews on their way to pray at the Wailing Wall in Jerusalem. Riots against Jews continued in three cities simultaneously, Hebron among them. One hundred and thirty-two Jews were killed and three hundred and forty were injured. Following the pogroms, all Hebron Jews were forced to leave their homes. My father's family sought refuge in Gaza where they had to start all over again. Unfortunately, I have no knowledge of my father's experiences in Gaza since he never spoke of this period in his life.

Though it may seem ironic, I was a strong supporter of the return of Hebron to Palestinian rule in 1997, even though I have a personal claim to this place. In order to truly achieve peace with our Arab neighbours we must be willing to give up land which is located in predominantly Arab areas.

My mother was born in the town of Tiberias on Lake Kinneret (the Sea of Galilee), the oldest daughter of a strongly traditional and prominent family in the town. My grandfather was a wealthy wheat merchant who did business between Jordan and the town of Tiberias. He owned a mill on the southern shore of the lake with windows overlooking the water. Though the family had very good relations with their Arab neighbours, there was always the danger of conflict. One day, in 1926, an old Arab woman whom my grandfather had previously helped confided to him that she had overheard a plan by an Arab gang to kill him and burn the mill that very night.

It was already evening and my grandfather did not hesitate. He gave the woman one of his gold coins and put the rest of them — all the money he had — into a belt around his waist. Then he jumped through the window of the mill into the cold dark waters of Lake Kinneret, swimming towards the town of Tiberias — a distance of about ten or fifteen kilometres. Swimming steadily towards the shore, he looked backward and saw his mill going up in flames. He exclaimed to his God: "Thou hast given, Thou hast taken away." He was a good swimmer but the belt of coins was very heavy. Mid-way to Tiberias, he understood that he had to choose between his life and his money. He opened his belt, looked up and again exclaimed: "Thou hast given, Thou hast taken away," and let the gold fall to the bottom of the lake. He was thus able to make it to his home in Tiberias. Almost crawling, wet and exhausted, he was greeted by his six daughters and smiling wife, who announced that his first son had been born. He looked again up to his God and exclaimed for the third time but with a twist: "Thou hast taken away, Thou hast given."

This story is true. There may even be a moral to it. But its simple outcome was that my family overnight became poor and had to start all over again. My mother was only twelve at the time. As the oldest daughter of a large family (eventually numbering nine children), she had to help with the family upkeep. She quit school and started work; she continued working till she retired at the age of sixty-five.

My father eventually settled in the southern part of Tel Aviv. My mother's family moved to Hadera, north of Tel Aviv. When my father and mother married they lived in an apartment in a neighbourhood in the south of Tel Aviv. My father worked as a cook in a British army camp. Great Britain at that time had a UN mandate in Palestine. I was born in 1947 in that apartment, the year before Israel became an independent state. Shortly thereafter my family moved to Hadera to be close to my mother's family.

My recollections from my early childhood are of a crowded room with toilets in the yard outside. We were four children very close in age. My father could not keep any job for long, and was unemployed most of my childhood years. Working as a house cleaner for well-to-do families, my mother was the main breadwinner. This had an adverse effect on my father's self-image. Sephardic culture emphasized that men were the heads of the household, the major (if not the only) breadwinners, proud, stable figures. My father's low self-image adversely affected his ability to function effectively as a father to his children and as a role model for them.

As the oldest daughter, I was in charge of helping my mother with her housework and taking care of my younger brothers and sister. In fact, it was largely my responsibility. I had difficulty combining these responsibilities at home with my school obligations. I dreamt of finding a way to build a different future for myself. The opportunity came when, at the age of twelve, I joined the youth movement Ha-Shomer Ha-Tza'ir. Ha-Shomer Ha-Tza'ir was associated with the left-wing kibbutz federation, Ha-Kibbutz Ha-Artzi. The group discussions and visits to our counsellors' own kibbutz introduced me to the concept of the kibbutz. A kibbutz is a community usually consisting of fifty to three hundred families. Kibbutz life is guided internally by principles of communality and solidarity among members. The kibbutz is run according to the dictum "from each according to their abilities, to each according to their needs." External dealings are derived from values of social justice and the ideal of Zionism as well as a commitment to leading the general society in accomplishing these goals.

These meetings brought me to make my first major independent decision — to move to a kibbutz and continue my high-school education within it. With the help of my youth counsellor in the movement, I was accepted into a youth group within the framework of Aliyat Ha-Naar [Youth Aliyah], a branch of the Jewish Agency, whose original goal had been to find homes for Holocaust orphans. Youth Aliyah continued its work by helping needy Israeli families educate their children within kibbutz environments. I was sent to Kibbutz Ein Ha-Mifratz, which is my home to this day.

This group was composed of children from dysfunctional homes or children whose parents could not afford a high-school education, which at that time was still a privilege in Israel. Many kibbutzim were, and still are, committed to providing homes and education to less fortunate children. We were adopted into families, our needs were taken care of, and within a short time we felt transformed in an environment rich with opportunities, an environment very different from the ones from which we came.

Despite this idyllic life situation, most of us were in constant conflict within ourselves. There we were, experiencing heaven on earth, while our families continued to struggle for their meagre existence. Why did we deserve more? How could we enjoy what we had while the rest of our family lacked the basics? Filled with guilt, I often thought of giving up my life on the kibbutz and of returning to my real home, to help my mother and take care of my little brothers and sister. My mother, however, encouraged me to stay on the kibbutz, believing that this was a wonderful opportunity that should not be missed.

When I graduated from high school, I served in the military for two years, then returned to Kibbutz Ein Ha-Mifratz for a new phase in my life as a full member of the kibbutz with all rights and obligations, rather than as a student.

Teaching in a Kibbutz

As a high-school student and during my first years as a kibbutz member, I worked in the kibbutz's educational system. This experience made me decide to become a teacher. I studied at Oranim, the kibbutz college for teachers, and became a kindergarten and elementary school teacher.

One of my major goals in education was to expose the children to life outside the secure environment of the kibbutz. I believed that even very young children should learn about people and surroundings different from their own. We established contact with a large Bedouin family that had its tin huts set up nearby our kibbutz. I took each of my classes to visit the family and they became friends with the children who were their own age.

When workers barricaded themselves inside a very large textile factory near our kibbutz that was slated to be closed, I talked about the situation with my class. The children joined me in bringing cooked lunches and sometimes evening dinners to the workers. On one of these occasions, I gave my first political speech expressing support for the workers. After all, I myself had a father who had been laid off from work and was unemployed for a long time. I myself had experienced first hand the traumatic outcome for my family.

After working for about ten years in education of the very young, I volunteered to work with a group of disadvantaged high-school students from outside my kibbutz. This was within the framework of the same Youth Aliyah organization which had brought me as a child to Ein Ha-Mifratz. Having myself been in this position, I understood and appreciated this programme. This particular group consisted of youth who came mostly from dysfunctional families, or from very problematic social circumstances. The education of a Youth Aliyah group on a kibbutz is not just a job; it is a twenty-four hour mission. The educator is the one to whom the children refer with problems in their studies, or with their social and emotional problems. The educator often serves also as a bridge between the young boys or girls and their parents and as another bridge between students and their parents and the kibbutz institutions and its community.

I remember one girl who was very quiet and introverted, whose only wish was to study. At the beginning of the first year, I went to visit the home of each student. The door to this girl's house was locked and no one could be contacted. One of the neighbours explained with a chuckle: "You surely must know what the mother's profession is. It is the oldest in the world." The girl's mother was a prostitute who was "working" on the highway not far from our kibbutz. We put extra effort into this girl's education, and she successfully graduated with her university degree.

There was another child I remember especially, a boy whose mother was living in a slum area of one of the big cities with an Arab partner. The boy had been living in a foster home. He hated Arabs and was extremely violent. We were under constant pressure to kick him out of school. His adoptive family on the kibbutz, myself and the entire faculty invested a great deal of energy and love in rebuilding his trust in adults. Gradually his violent behaviour ceased. He finished school, served in the army, and became a productive individual. I will never forget the emotional way in which his mother thanked me the day he graduated.

Most often these children came to us with a feeling of inferiority which I recognized from my own experience. I chose to put emphasis upon their uniqueness, to develop their pride in what they were and what they had achieved. In this work, I felt I was bringing my life to a certain closure: I was now able to give to others what I myself had been given.

POLITICAL ACTIVITY IN SHKHUNAT HA-TIKVAH AND SHKHUNAT EZRA

When the Likud party (a conservative anti-labour party) came into power after the general elections of 1977, I felt that I needed to be involved in political activity outside the kibbutz boundaries. During that year, still working as an educator, I organized our kibbutz political activities during the elections for the Histadrut. The Histadrut is the General Federation of Labor in Israel. At that time, close to 80 per cent of the Israeli population participated in Histadrut elections, which took place every four years. I started by mobilizing members of our kibbutz (mostly female members) for house-to-house visits in a nearby town, mostly in run-down neighbourhoods, to persuade prospective voters to vote for the MAPAM party (a left oriented Zionist–Socialist party). This was at the time the only Jewish party which gave equal standing to its Arab members.

My political activity focused for many years around voluntary work during the election campaigns for the Knesset [Parliament] and the Histadrut. I was elected to represent my kibbutz as a member in the Central Council of the MAPAM party and also became an active member of several of its acting committees.

My political activity took a much more active turn after a year's stay in the USA, just before the election campaign of 1989. This time I volunteered for full-time political community work within the framework of the MAPAM party. I was asked to work in two neighbouring communities in the south of Tel Aviv — Shkhunat Ha-Tikvah and Shkhunat Ezra — that were considered among the poorest slums in the city. When I told my mother, she exclaimed that Shkhunat Ezra was the very neighbourhood where I had been born and which my parents had left when I was still a baby. Not much had changed in the neighbourhood in the forty years since my parents lived there. When I arrived in the neighbourhood, I immediately felt at home. The fact that I had been born in Shkhunat Ezra opened many hearts and doors for me in the neighbourhood.

Fate was bringing me a full circle and giving me closure on yet another plane. I went willingly back to some of my childhood experiences, to the pain but also to the tastes and odours that I had almost forgotten during my years on the kibbutz: the warm hospitality of these earthy people, their ever ready, home-made tasty food.

The people living in that area were of Sephardic origin and on the whole strong supporters of the Likud party. They saw MAPAM as "Arab lovers and Jew haters." Many Sephardic Jews in Israel have strong negative feelings against Arabs as a result of their adverse experiences with the Arabs among whom they had lived.

My first effort was to gain entry into the community through personal connection and to be accepted as an individual before dealing with ideological and political matters. After I became known as an individual, the people in the community would organize informal meetings in private homes. I would invite various political figures from the MAPAM party to these meetings to discuss more general issues of the country but also to discuss concrete issues of the community.

These efforts paid off: voters for MAPAM in the area rose from less than 1 per cent to 30 per cent. But even more important for me and for the local community was their awakening awareness of their power to control their own lives. They organized themselves from being just individuals in a neighbourhood to being an active community.

In Shkhunat Ezra, which was the less organized community, we were able to establish a local — elected — leadership team which worked together to improve the quality of life in the community. We started by organizing a demonstration to call public attention to the deterioration of neighbourhood services such as roads, school buildings, garbage disposal and street illumination, and to urge for removal — or at least cleaning — of the garbage trucks' cleaning garage that was located in the middle of the neighbourhood. National TV covered the story of the neighbourhood and the demonstration, and so did some newspapers. As a result, the mayor of Tel Aviv had to take action. People in Shkhunat Ezra suddenly saw that it was in their power to effect change. One Saturday I invited the community leaders to visit my kibbutz. It was the first time they had ever seen a kibbutz and the first time they were exposed to the possibility that a small community of people could build their lives with their own work. The kibbutz members received them warmly and they responded by referring to me as "one of us, who was even born amongst us."

During the summer of that year, economic mismanagement by the Likud backfired. They had decided to make strengthening and extending settlements on the West Bank their first priority, and had put social justice and employment opportunity, as well as the economic well-being of the poor, as their last priority. As a result, unemployment almost doubled to about 12 per cent, and many young couples had no place to live, for government money was not directed towards building low-rental housing. "Tent-towns" of those without housing began to appear. One of the first such "tent-towns" was established near Shkhunat Ha-Tikvah since it was among the poorest neighbourhoods in Tel Aviv.

MAPAM had established a special task force to deal with the "tent people." I was surprised to discover that I, who was the member most identified with this cause, was not invited to participate. The task force was composed exclusively of men. When I asked the chairman of that committee why, his answer was clear and matter-of-fact: "But surely you have no time for meetings as you are constantly out in the field." I soon became a member of that task force, but I had learnt a lesson: It is not enough to be active; you must also assert yourself. And as a woman, you must do so among other women activists.

It was summer, and a particularly hot and humid one. The conditions were deplorable. It was very difficult for the children as it was summer vacation and they had no organized activities. My own kibbutz and other kibbutzim had responded to my request for books and toys, but still the children needed supervision. I came up with the idea of inviting kibbutz high-school students to come to the tent-town and take charge of creating a summer camp within the camp itself. Some of my friends were sceptical about the willingness of our youth to "waste" their precious summer vacation time in a Tel Aviv "tent community." But our youth proved them wrong. It immediately became the "in" thing to do, and teenagers competed to be the ones to go to Tel Aviv for the programme.

BACK TO EDUCATION

The experience I had with our high-school youth at the tent-town was a major factor in my decision to switch to high-school education when I returned home from Tel Aviv. Our high school (grades seven to twelve) is run as a children's community governed in many of its aspects by the children themselves through a web of committees and youth counsellors. Older pupils guide the younger ones. The upper high-school classes also board in our high school. Part of my work was organizing extracurricular enrichment classes, but I saw as an additional goal helping the students get involved in the important social agenda of Israeli society.

During the aliyah [immigration into Israel] of Ethiopian Jews in the early 1990s, I thought of involving the children in helping the national effort of absorbing the Ethiopian immigrant children. We chose the ninth graders as the focal group in our school to deal with this challenge. These particular classes were considered especially problematic in school and many among the school faculty did not believe they would be willing to contribute their free time. These classes had a particularly high percentage of problematic children with disciplinary and learning problems. However, with the help of their teacher, a small number of students went several days a week to the trailers where a group of Ethiopian immigrants lived. Our students helped the immigrant children with their homework and played with them. With time, more and more of our students joined in the work and the number of children involved increased. We also helped the Ethiopian children in their preparations for holidays. During summer vacation, they had a summer camp on our kibbutz grounds. This activity continued over the next year with equal success. Eventually our school received a special commendation from the Israeli Knesset. Our activities with the Ethiopian children gave them the opportunity to meet Israeli-born children in an experience in which they felt both equal and unique.

I also developed student activities around the sensitive political issue of peace with our Arab neighbours. We organized several panels of presenters of differing political views about the fate of the Golan Heights, and about the Oslo peace agreements with the PLO. We organized a petition, both in school and in the neighbouring kibbutzim, supporting the Rabin government in its effort towards peace.

I thought it of utmost importance that our youth understand the antagonism between religious and secular Israelis — especially as expressed by religious West-Bank settlers. I remember an interesting meeting with a couple of rabbis (husband and wife) from one of these settlements. They talked about what it meant to live in close proximity to Arabs, about their attitudes towards peace, about the meaning of being religious. Our youth were very impressed by the candid talk. These meetings also sharpened their own critical views. They became open to other views, but also developed critical thinking on the topics discussed.

Believing that a major component of high-school education is exposure to the outside world and to the real issues that make it function, I encouraged students to change their local monthly paper from a strictly internal organ to one which brought in the outside world. I also helped students secure interviews with political, cultural and social leaders.

This work has made me a strong believer in young people's ability to get involved in socially meaningful action, if they are exposed to it in a sincere way. When approached in the right way, teenagers do have compassion for others and do want to be part of events and actions that are real and of importance to their society.

I have no doubt now that political activity can take place within the framework of educational work, but also that educational work can be accomplished within the framework of proper political activity.

Looking back, I am sure that my interest in community activism is a direct result of my childhood experiences and my family's unique history. A common denominator is my wish to combine educational work with social and political involvement. But I was also able, in my activism, to bring to closure two stories that opened up in my childhood. I returned to the neighbourhood where I was born, to reconnect with the unique traditions of the people who live there, and yet to effect changes for improving their lives. And I became an educator of students from the Aliyat Ha-Naar who underwent the same experiences I had had as a child. My past experiences helped me to understand where I came from and gave me guidance about where to go.

There is also one more final lesson for me: I have discovered that people like me who are not part of the political establishment can make a major difference in the real world of politics and effect change in society. It means that many others also can contribute to changing their society. For me, it is an expression of hope for the future.

⚬⚭⚬

WOMEN IN THE
MOROCCAN–JEWISH
COMMUNITY OF
MONTREAL

෴

Yolande Cohen with Joseph Yossi Lévy

*Moroccan Jews who live in Quebec are part of the diverse spectrum of
the Jewish diaspora. Yolande Cohen and Joseph Yossi Lévy provide us
with an overview of the history and issues of Moroccan–Jewish immigrants in Quebec and the challenges to their community that current
rapid social changes present. A major factor in these changes is the
emergence of a new breed of women: better educated, more professionally employable, and caught between modernity and tradition.*

SUCCESSIVE WAVES of emigration have put an end to two thousand
years of common history for Moroccan Jews. Fifteen thousand Moroccan Jews are now living in Quebec — only one of many destinations
where members of our community came to settle since 1948, when
there were still 300,000 of us in Morocco. Like so many young people
whose identity was formed under the French protectorate, we looked
with contempt on anything too reminiscent of our Moroccan origins,
opting instead for a universalism that would allow us to hang our hopes

on a utopia whose borders extended well beyond the nation-states of which we were renegades. Being neither entirely French nor entirely Moroccan, we found that a Canadian nationality provided us with an identity that was malleable enough to fit our own fluctuating identities.

We did not feel as if we had lost our roots, though, in spite of two successive emigrations. To extend a metaphor used by Bernard Shapiro, President of McGill University, during a recent conference on the future of the Jewish community in Montreal, we are like the farmer who does not have a problem finding his roots, since they are always under his feet. So, too, our feet are rooted in our communities. Our Moroccan–Jewish identity is rooted in culture and tradition. It can be taken along and transplanted to the soil of the host country, and thrive here as it did in Morocco under the Muslim dhimma and the French protectorate.

COMMUNITY AS CENTRAL REFERENCE POINT

What else could explain the speed and determination with which the first Moroccan–Jewish immigrants set to the task of reproducing inside existing community institutions those that characterized their life in Morocco? Is there not a striking continuity between the community institutions that in Morocco for centuries and with complete autonomy governed our everyday life, life cycles and social security and also ruled in all religious, judicial and educational matters, and those that today regulate marriages, henna rituals, burials, schools and so on, in strict observance of the traditions particular to specific Moroccan cities? There is no doubt that the community institutions which were founded by those first immigrants in Montreal gave them a support structure if not the support they expected. No doubt there were differences in sensibilities between the Ashkenazic and Sephardic communities, the latter being older and better established than the former, but that is not enough to explain why Jews from Morocco felt the need to found the CSQ (*Communauté sépharade du Québec* [Quebec Sephardic Community]) and its various branches, the Maimonides School with its two campuses, and separate synagogues in the suburbs of Montreal. The main explanation lies in the fact that Moroccan Jews saw their attachment to their own brand of Judaism — brought to maturity in

Morocco, then transformed by the French regime with its discriminatory legislation, and later by the process of de-colonization and the founding of the State of Israel — as the only possible way of integrating themselves into Quebec society.

The community's projects were carried out under the Canadian policy of multiculturalism and pushed along by the momentum gained from affirming our separate Sephardic identity within the Jewish diaspora. An integral institutional foundation was built on the affirmation of a separate Sephardic–Jewish identity, rooted essentially in traditional religious practices and an unshakable attachment to the State of Israel. Today it is easier to understand the reasons for this, one of which was the attachment to the French language of the entire Sephardic community.

This affirmation of the Sephardic identity would have created a ghetto, however, if at the same time Moroccan Jews had not pursued integration into the larger community, albeit in less explicit and more individual ways. Education was one key element of this strategy. Statistics show that the Jewish community as a whole is, like the Asian, among the most highly educated groups in Quebec. Most young Moroccan Jews, who generally had between two and seven years of secondary education when they arrived here, quickly realized the need for further studies. More than 40 per cent of the members of the community now have a BA, with 6 per cent holding a MA and 2 per cent a doctorate — a very well educated group. Investing in education, including that of girls, is seen as an important key to upward mobility within Quebec society, and the quickest way to gain access to the different economic sectors, whether these be the service or manufacturing sectors or the liberal professions.

Our generation gave expression to the community's identity by building institutions, giving it at once cohesion and strength. We succeeded in surfing between tradition and modernity, but not without many sleepless nights ... aware that we were developing our own identities while constructing our communal space. Maybe not as post-modern as surfing the net, but akin to it ...

These days our crucial preoccupation has shifted to finding ways to ensure that a Jewish identity is transmitted to our children and to determining what we should transmit. We wonder whether our children will succeed in combining their attachment to family and community with their professional and personal ambitions. We are facing critical choices. In the new economy, jobs, rather than links to community and culture, are paramount, and English is the main language of work and communication, with spoken French — which our children still consider a prestigious language — being relegated to the private sphere. What should we say to them, what should we do to ensure the survival of this identity of ours — our wealth and legacy, after all?

IDENTITY, GENERATIONAL DIFFERENCES AND GENDER

Several studies have been done on the development and transformation of Moroccan–Jewish identity. The work of Elbaz[1] and a collection of life stories from three generations of Moroccan Jews[2] have thrown some light on the conjunctions and disjunctions in the definition of our identities. What is clear is that our relationship to Israel provides a common base. Identification with Canada and Quebec remains weak, however, while the adoption of a Sephardic identity — a label used to distance oneself from the North African referent — is affirmed in opposition to the identity of the Ashkenazic Jew.

A distinction should be made among the generations, however. For the first generation that came to Quebec, the Sephardic identity is rooted in a relationship with the country of origin as both a point of reference and of comparison, as well as the locus of the socio-cultural heritage, a relationship to Quebec that is at the same time close and distant, an ambivalence towards Israel and towards anglophone Jews, and an affirmation of their Jewishness, even though it sometimes deviates from orthodoxy. The analysis provided by Berdugo et al.[3] partially reiterates the above description but shows that the referents vary even among the first generation of immigrants. Depending on the age when they arrived in Quebec, those whose identity is based on nostalgia and on the maintenance of cultural and religious referents, in spite of certain concessions to the culture of the host country, can be distinguished from those whose identity is based on mimesis and, while not in opposition to the primary identity, incorporates all the elements of modern life while appropriating the challenges of North American society. There is also a third approach, taken by the younger generation, which consists of cobbling together a new identity located somewhere between those two poles. According to Elbaz, the young feel attached to Quebec but are also concerned about the Jewish condition. They try to meet its challenges, most often by returning to tradition. These studies, however, did not attempt to differentiate between men and women in the community.

Very few studies in fact deal directly with the role and place of women in the transmission of Jewishness, which, in terms of its religious form, is women's responsibility. Dinelle and Barrette-Dalphond's thesis,[4] which deals explicitly with Sephardic women immigrants in Montreal, is the exception. The authors use a feminist analysis and qualitative method which provide a glimpse of the major changes going on in the life of women immigrants from Morocco. Women bear the burden of responsibility for transmitting religious heritage, whether or not they work outside the home, are practising Jews, or live alone or with a partner. This produces complex relationships in terms of their own identity and that of their family, which is nearly always the extended family.

The division of labour along gender lines and the roles that go with it are an example of the burdensomeness of the traditional models and of the difficulty women have in divesting themselves of these. The division of labour between men and women tends to reproduce Jewish ideological models. However, in practice, the greater participation of women in the labour force has increased their autonomy and affected the observance of religious traditions by forcing them into the confines created by the work environment rather than by the family. This change is noticed throughout the community but affects different classes differently. It accelerated during the 1980s and has led to the present identity crisis.

How do women — who as mothers are not only the pillars of the family but also of the community — see their role now? A comparative study using leaders of ethnic groups in Montreal[5] reveals several marked tendencies. The role of the mother remains essential in the transmission of ethno-religious identity. Entry of women into the labour market and the influence of feminist ideas have modified the division of labour between the sexes, resulting in some cases in a new balance, and in others, in greater exploitation. This conjunction of factors has increased women's demands for recognition of their status.

Relations within the couple tend to be more egalitarian, especially among younger people, and conflicts can be resolved by divorce as it no longer carries a stigma. As one of the respondents in the study explained in her conclusion

> Sephardic women play a central role in the family. The problem lies in the lack of recognition of their status, which is that of a companion, in the best of cases, or that of an inferior. Nevertheless, there continues to be a real division of the roles. This must always be seen, however, in the context of a power game that is much more subtle than just plain submission of one to the other.[6]

The birth rate is decreasing. The importance of the extended family network is also decreasing, except in times of crisis. Several people also note increasing similarity between the characteristics of immigrant family systems with those of the host country, depending on when they settled in Quebec.

The results of a comparison between francophone Jewish women and women whose ancestors are from Quebec show that the former still attribute more importance to family values, while the latter favour their own freedom.[7] A comparison between men and women from the francophone Jewish group confirms that the women continue to put the well-being of their families first, giving priority to values such as responsibility and emotional bonding, while men prefer freedom.

As far as changes in this area are concerned, longitudinal and comparative studies might throw light on what is particular to the situation of Sephardic women in Quebec. It would be interesting in this respect to compare our results with those of Arlette Berdugo's study of Jewish women in Morocco.[8] Her study, which surveyed three groups of women, measured their influence on their immediate and extended family networks, as well as their role in the structuring and survival of the community in Morocco. The author notes that, in spite of the massive exodus that has marked that community during the past thirty years, women's increased participation in community affairs corresponds to a period of enormous change in their lives (assuming tasks, paid labour, etc.) and in the community. A comparison between the two groups (in Quebec and Morocco) would allow us to determine the conjunctions and disjunctions along their journeys. It would also allow for more nuanced interpretations of what is due to adaptation to a new environment and to the specific cultural background of the men and women who emigrated.

In all the stories there is one common denominator, however. They convey great anxiety about the children's future, which in turn reflects an underlying apprehension about transmission of values. In both regions, people expressed similar anxiety about what values to transmit and how to transmit them. However, juxtaposed to this feeling of disempowerment and helplessness in the face of a completely uncertain future is the will to maintain close family ties. This shows in the importance that is still assigned to life's celebrations and rituals.

COMMUNITY AS EXTENDED FAMILY

Women continue to occupy a central symbolic role in the domestic and religious spheres, often providing the link between generations and between family and community. Their community activities are today to a certain extent displacing activities that in the past were performed exclusively for the benefit of their families. Community provides them with an extended family context and fills a space that used to belong entirely to the private sphere. In Montreal, too, this activism is common currency, whether we are talking about fundraising by professional women — who put much energy into this type of activity — or about the seniors' clubs, summer camps, etc., at the Jewish Community Centre, which are organized by professionals and volunteers of mostly Moroccan–Jewish origin. The involvement of Moroccan–Jewish women in the community has even resulted in one of them, Maryse Ohayon, being elected president of the CSQ.

Nevertheless, there is a keen sense of malaise within the institutions. There is not enough of a renewal among the community elites that run them, which means that they are no longer all that representative. As a result, the clans remain strong, making it difficult for community leaders to mediate to reduce tensions within the community and help its members deal with the contradictions they face.

These few elements make us realize how important tradition and the culture of origin are in determining the behaviour of communities (there is, for instance, obvious similarity between the methods used to recruit members of the elites in Morocco, France and Canada) and the transmission of identity. These questions must then be linked to the history and culture of these communities if we want to understand the transfer of influences and change in identity. The present cross-fertilization in the diaspora is making short shrift of the long-established schemes that were born of a desire for integration and which until now mostly succeeded.

By way of conclusion we would like to look ahead. In our opinion the fundamental tendencies that characterized the last two decades are bound to grow stronger. Education will continue to play a leading role in the career choices of young people. Employment and career opportunities will continue to be the main causes of the dispersal of families and their move to certain areas, with concurrent changes in identity. It is more difficult to predict the future of the communities and whether they will be able to assume the difficult task of mediating between people's private identities and social and political realities. In any case, more than ever they will be called on to play the role of guardian of tradition and bridge between generations and communities.

TRANSLATED FROM THE FRENCH BY MYRIAM JARSKY

NOTES

1. M. Elbaz, "D'immigrants à ethniques: analyse comparée des pratiques sociales et identitaires des sépharades et achkénazes à Montréal" [From immigrants to ethnic groups: A comparative analysis of the social and identity practices of Sephardic and Ashkenazic Jews in Montreal], in J. C. Lasry and C. Tapia, eds., *Les Juifs du Maghreb, diasporas contemporaines* [The Jews of Maghreb: Contemporary diasporas] (Paris: L'Harmattan and Montreal: Les presses de l'Université de Montréal, 1989), 89–101; M. Elbaz, "La seconde génération des juifs–marocains à Montréal" [Second-Generation Moroccan Jews in Montreal], in Kacem Basfao and Hinde Taarji, eds., *L'Annuaire de l'émigration* [Emigration annual] (Morocco, 1994), 176–178.

2. M. Berdugo, Yolande Cohen and Joseph Yossi Lévy, *Juifs–marocains à Montréal. Témoignages d'une immigration moderne* [Moroccan Jews in Montreal: Testimony of a modern-day immigration] (Montreal: Éditions VLB, 1987); Yolande Cohen and Joseph Yossi Lévy, "Élites juives–marocaines à Montréal" [Jewish–Moroccan elites in Montreal], in Kacem Basfao and Hinde Taarji, eds., *L'Annuaire de l'émigration* [Emigration annual] (Morocco: 1994), 158–160.

3. Berdugo et al., *Témoignages*.

4. J. Dinelle and A. Barrette-Dalphond, "Femmes et judaisme: les femmes immigrantes sépharades à Montréal" [Women and Judaism: Sephardic immigrant women in Montreal] (Master's thesis, Department of Sociology, UQAM, 1994).

5. M. Labelle and Joseph Yossi Lévy, *Ethnicité et enjeux sociaux. Le Québec vu par les leaders de groupes ethnoculturels* [Ethnicity and social stakes: Quebec viewed by the leaders of ethno-cultural groups] (Montreal: Éditions Liber, 1995).

6. Ibid., 219.

7. Joseph Yossi Lévy and J. M. Samson, "Acculturation, Religiosity and Tradition among French-Speaking Jews in Montreal," in Simcha Fishbane, Stuart Schoenfeld and Alain Goldschlaeger, eds., *Essays in the Social Scientific Study of Judaism and Jewish Society*, Vol. II. (New York: Ktav Publishing Co., 1992), 78–95.

8. Arlette Berdugo, "Images et représentations de la communauté juif marocaine" [Image and representation of the Jewish–Moroccan community] (PhD diss., Paris X, 1995).

THE STREETS ARE PAVED WITH CUTBACKS:

JEWISH WOMEN AND ECONOMIC JUSTICE

༒

Shlomit Segal

Despite the stereotype of Jewish affluence, many Jewish women are dependent on social welfare programmes and the generosity of Jewish social services. One of the basic tenets of Judaism is the concept of tzedakah, a term which refers not simply to acts of charity, but to a whole notion of community based on social justice. What is our role and responsibility as Jewish feminists in dealing with the issues of poverty, both within and outside our community? Shlomit Segal demonstrates the impact that economic restructuring has had on the lives of Jewish women, as well as its implications for social activists.

IN A RECENT workshop with Jewish women I asked participants how many of the women in the room felt that their jobs were threatened by current economic policies. Instantly, almost every hand in the room went up. Among those whose hands were not raised, I recognized students and retired women who had no job to lose. And of course, some women in the room may already have become unemployed.

Recent years have seen the advent of economic restructuring. Through economic globalization, the economies of different countries are becoming more and more inseparable, so that the idea of a "national economy" becomes meaningless. An increasing number of the products we buy come from far away; businesses and factories are becoming increasingly mobile. As well, in the last fifteen years, there have been a series of international trade agreements, first GATT (General Agreement on Tariffs and Trade) and the WTO (World Trade Organization) and NAFTA (North American Free Trade Agreement). These agreements have weakened the abilities of national governments to make laws concerning trade and given more power to large corporations.

Accompanying economic globalization are the policies of "structural adjustment." Structural adjustments were first demanded by the International Monetary Fund (IMF) and the World Bank as a condition on which they would lend money to national governments. The IMF and World Bank are international bodies dominated by the USA and Western Europe that lend money to national governments, mostly southern hemisphere countries. In the 1970s and 1980s, the two bodies began to demand that borrowing governments reduce spending. They also pressured borrowers to bring in foreign investment and large-scale industry, usually subsidiaries of multinational corporations. Now these policies are also being followed by many other governments, not only ones that borrow from the IMF and World Bank. To a large extent, this is because these are the policies that are supported by large banks and corporations, who are influencing policy-making in the industrialized Northern countries.

Political scientist Isabella Bakker describes the principles behind these policies, also known as neo-liberal economics. Neo-liberal economics assumes that institutions such as the state and the market should reflect the motivation of individual self-interest. States should provide only a minimum of public goods. This view of economics also proposes that the most efficient allocation of resources and maximization of utility occurs through markets.[1]

The application of restructuring or structural adjustment usually involves privatization of services that are owned by the government such as electrical companies, public transportation and resource industries. Cutbacks in government spending on health, education and other social welfare services and increasing privatization for these services also occurs. This often means that services that were once free now charge fees. Subsidies on basic foods and to farmers, where they exist, are ended. Regulations concerning labour standards, environmental protection and foreign ownership of local companies to encourage foreign investment are loosened. And free trade policies, as mentioned above, are instituted.

Controls on the value of national currencies and controls on stock market and bank activities are also loosened. Loosening of controls on currency means that, instead of the government setting a dollar value to their money, it is left for the international market in currencies to decide. Thus traders who buy stocks and bonds and currencies decide what a national currency is worth. The economy becomes oriented towards exports, such as cash crops and primary resources like minerals and wood. Taxes, especially for businesses and higher income individuals, are lowered.

The most severe impacts of these policies have been on the poor people in the most destitute countries where severe poverty and environmental devastation has increased in recent years. This is a critical issue for Jews and feminists. Although Jewish women in North America generally live privileged lives compared to people living in absolute poverty in Asia or Africa, I think it is worth looking at the impact of economic globalization on our lives and making the links.

WOMEN AND RESTRUCTURING

Traditionally, economics and economic policies has been seen as something "gender neutral," not having anything to do with issues of gender (or of race). Political scientist Marjorie Griffin Cohen writes that "its representation as a universal force makes 'restructuring' appear apolitical and, in conjunction with this, gender, race and class neutral."[2] However, in recent years numerous feminist social scientists have critiqued the gendered nature of economic theory and practice.[3] Many of the most basic concepts in economics, such as *homo economicus* [economic man] and seeing the household as one unit, are based on male-centred and sexist ideas. They assume that every household is made up of an altruistic husband who provides for his wife and children. They also assume that everything that goes on in the household is consumption, as opposed to production. Today, the household with an employed husband, homemaker wife and children is by far the minority in North America. Yet politicians have yet to put into place a comprehensive child care programme. Why are certain types of work rewarded with a salary, while other types of work (those mostly performed by women) not rewarded monetarily? As more and more women, including those with young children, have entered the paid work force, child care and housework simply make up an uncounted "second shift."[4]

Other aspects of restructuring also have an impact on women. When cuts are made to health care, education, child care and elder care, it is usually women who "take up the slack." When there's someone waiting to be placed in long-term care, or someone is shipped home early from the hospital, women relatives are generally expected to take care of them. Women are also being asked to spend more volunteer hours in their children's schools and to participate in other community volunteer work. Tax cuts are another policy that generally benefits men at the expense of women because men on average have higher incomes, and so pay more taxes.

IMPACT ON THE JEWISH COMMUNITY: LOW-INCOME WOMEN

The most severe impact of structural adjustment policies worldwide has been on low-income women and children and seniors. These people are the ones who are most dependent on social services such as health care, education and pensions. In the Jewish community, as well as in North American society as a whole, low-income women include immigrants, elderly women, women with disabilities, single mothers and women from low-income backgrounds. Women worldwide earn lower incomes than men and are expected to take on the main responsibilities for child care, housework and care for older or ill family members. In Toronto's Jewish community, women are twice as likely as men to have low incomes (under $25,00 a year).[5]

ELDERLY WOMEN

Elderly women make up a significant group of Canada's poor and this is reflected in the Jewish community. In 1991, 34 per cent of Jewish women over sixty-five were living at or below the poverty line; 72 per cent of elderly Jewish women who lived alone were poor.[6] This reflects the fact that most elderly women were homemakers and thus don't have employee pensions. Those who are widowed, divorced or single are particularly vulnerable because they don't have their income supplemented by a higher male income.

IMMIGRANTS

For the last twenty years, Toronto has been the favoured destination of Jews immigrating to Canada. The main sources of Jewish immigration are the former USSR, Eastern Europe, Israel, the USA and South Africa. Other areas of origin include Northern Africa, South America and Asia. The Jews immigrating from English speaking countries tend to be well educated and middle-class and therefore don't fit into the category of low-income immigrant. However, poverty rates are high among other groups of Jewish immigrants. On average, over 20 per cent of Jewish immigrants to Toronto live at or below the poverty line. The largest group of immigrants is from the former Soviet Union. Among this group the poverty rate jumps to 35 per cent.[7] This can be partially explained by the fact that this group includes many elderly people. Among immigrants from Israel, the poverty rate is 17 per cent. This relatively high rate of poverty is probably due to the job market disadvantage of those not fluent in English as well as xenophobia and racism in the workplace. At the same time, many of the traditional workplaces of Jewish immigrants, particularly the "*shmate* business" of clothing and textiles, is in decline. And the new immigrant head tax is likely to increase immigrant poverty in every community.

SINGLE MOTHERS

In Canada, 58 per cent of single mothers are poor.[8] In the Jewish community in Toronto, single parent families (the vast majority of which are single mother families) are twice as likely to be poor than two parent families. In 1991 they formed 6.6 per cent of the families, but 11 per cent of the Jewish poor.[9] For single mothers, access to affordable child care, as well as enforcement of fair child support payments, are critical factors for their economic well-being.

Women with Disabilities

Though I have been unable to find a study that describes the average incomes of disabled Jewish women, there have been studies that look at Canadian women with disabilities. It is likely that the high levels of poverty among disabled women[10] affect those who are Jewish. Disabled women have high rates of unemployment and the levels of disability support almost guarantee poverty for those who are unable to work.

Middle-Class Jewish Women

It is well known that Jewish women in North America are disproportionately found in the "helping professions." Many Jewish women are teachers, social workers, legal aid lawyers, health care workers and counsellors. About one-third of Jewish women work in education, human services and government.[11] The percentages of involvement in these fields are almost identical in the Toronto and Canada surveys, and represent about double the employment rate of the general female population in these areas of work. Traditionally, this has meant that Jewish women have higher incomes on average than non-Jewish women, who are more likely to work in lower paying sectors. This also reflects the fact that Jewish women have more formal education but have tended to stick to traditionally female professions like teaching and social work.

However, the location of Jewish women in the work force is now a vulnerable one. Education, health care and other social services have been a significant target for cutbacks by federal and provincial levels of government. Some workplaces have also been targets of privatization, which generally leads to lower salaries and the end to unionization. To a large extent the cuts have been passed from the federal level to the provincial by cuts to transfer payments that cover education and health care costs. Throughout Canada, government workers are being laid off, school boards are being cut back and in some areas whole hospitals are being closed. The only new jobs in the area of health care and social services that are being created are ones at the lowest pay scale, such as home care worker.[12]

ECONOMICS AND JEWISH FEMINIST ETHICS

The underlying principles of economic restructuring policies and neo-liberal economics are a belief in the supremacy of the market, the primacy of self-interest and minimum involvement of the state in providing services to its citizens. These principles are very much at odds with traditional Jewish ethics concerning wealth and human welfare. The prophets and subsequent Jewish scholars have portrayed human wealth as a temporary divine loan which carries with it community responsibility. "Since Judaism is a community-oriented rather than individual-oriented religion, that means that the group at all levels, communally, nationally and internationally, is thereby made a partner in each individual's wealth."[13]

Within traditional Judaism, one is expected to share one's wealth with the needy in the community; to refuse this responsibility is a sin. Indeed, though the epithet "Sodomite" has been used against gays and lesbians, the rabbis of the Talmud believed that the sin of the Sodomites was their refusal to share their wealth with others.[14] Jewish law obligates the community not just to give *tzedakah* [charity/acts of justice] but to provide community services in order to meet basic physical needs and spiritual needs of community members. The Talmud states that a Torah scholar can only live in towns that have a communal fund for *tzedakah*. Traditionally, Jewish farmers were required to leave the corners of their fields for the needy so no one would go hungry. This practice is recalled in the Book of Ruth. Maimonides stated that the most important form of *tzedakah* was to provide a person with a job, or a loan to start a business, so that the recipient would be released from the cycle of poverty. It is noteworthy that Jews are obliged to give *tzedakah* to gentiles as well as other Jews, though the commandments surrounding charity to Jews are more strict.

For Jewish feminists, who may not embrace every word of *halakhah* [traditional Jewish law], these teachings of our ancestors are ones that ring true today and correspond with the beliefs of most feminist writers, Jewish and gentile. Judith Plaskow reminds us that while the creation of woman-affirming Jewish communities is an important element in the quest for social justice, it is just one piece of a larger struggle for justice that is being carried on in every corner of the earth.[15]

Indeed, many Jewish feminists such as Michele Landsberg, Melanie Kaye/Kantrowitz, Irena Klepfisz and Felice Yeskel have been active in the struggle for economic justice and have written about this issue. As well as drawing on Jewish prophetic tradition, the work of these feminists draws on the writing and activism of feminists of colour and socialist feminists, some of whom are and were Jewish. Women's rights and the end to racism and anti-Semitism are tied to the struggle for economic justice and equality.

In recent years, there has been an abandonment of liberal and progressive politics by many Jews. Yet it is clear that right wing economic policies are not serving the interests of Jewish women, or of society in general. It now appears essential that Jewish feminists join in coalition with other feminist and progressive groups that are challenging the ideology behind restructuring and articulating the alternatives. Drawing on the traditional Jewish imperative to share individual wealth with the community, it is also important for Jewish groups to use their assets to support economic justice projects. These can include activities such as loans to community development funds for low-income neighbourhoods or sponsorship of housing co-operatives.

The changes that have been brought about with economic restructuring are not inevitable, nor are they just. In the spirit of *tikkun olam* [repair of the world], it is imperative for us to work towards realizing an alternative social and economic order which reflects a vision of *tzedek* [justice].

NOTES

1. Isabella Bakker, "The Gendered Foundations of Restructuring in Canada," in I. Bakker, ed., *Rethinking Restructuring: Gender and Change in Canada* (Toronto: University of Toronto Press, 1996), 4.

2. Marjorie Griffin Cohen, "Democracy and Trade Agreements: Challenges for Disadvantaged Women, Minorities and States," in R. Boyer and D. Drache, eds., *Markets Against States: The Limits of Globalization* (London: Routledge, 1996), 274.

3. Suzanne Bergeron, "The Nation as a Gendered Subject of Macroeconomics," in Bakker, *Rethinking Restructuring*; Nancy Folbre, *Who Pays for the Kids?: Gender and the Structures of Constraint* (London and New York: Routledge, 1994); Marjorie Cohen, "The Problem of Studying 'Economic Man,'" in Angela Miles and Geraldine Finn, eds., *Feminism in Canada: From Pressure to Politics* (Montreal: Black Rose Books, 1982).

4. Arlie Hochschild, with Anne Machung, *The Second Shift* (New York: Avon Books, 1989); Marilyn Waring, *If Women Counted* (San Francisco: HarperCollins, 1988).

5. James L. Torcyner, Shari L. Brotman and Jay Brodbar, *Rapid Growth and Transformation: Demographic Challenges Facing the Jewish Community of Greater Toronto* (Toronto: McGill Consortium for Ethnicity and Strategic Social Planning, 1995).

6. Ibid., 148 and 149.

7. Ibid., 21.

8. Michelle Landsberg, "Is Canada Really the Best Nation for Women?" *The Toronto Star*, 28 June 1997, J1.

9. Torcyner et al., 149.

10. Morley Gunderson and Leon Muszynski, *Women and Labour Market Poverty* (Ottawa: Canadian Advisory Council on the Status of Women, 1990), 101.

11. Torcyner et al.

12. Pat Armstrong, "Unravelling the Safety Net: Transformations in Health Care and their Impact on Women," in Janine Brodie, ed., *Women and Canadian Public Policy* (Toronto: Harcourt Brace, 1996), 45.

13. Meir Tamari, *With All Your Possessions: Jewish Ethics and Economic Life* (New York: The Free Press, 1987), 37.

14. Ibid., 51.

15. Judith Plaskow, *Standing Again at Sinai: Judaism from a Feminist Perspective* (San Francisco: Harper, 1990), 224.

DEVELOPING JEWISH THEMES IN CHILDREN'S LITERATURE

༄

Phoebe Gilman, Rhea Tregebov & Sharon Kirsh

Social activism can take many forms, but perhaps the most transformative acts are those which reach the very young. The writing of children's literature can be seen as one of the most fundamental vehicles for transforming the future. When children see themselves reflected in stories rich with Jewish subjects, experience and history, with Jewish images and language, their sense of personal and cultural identity is strengthened. In this compilation, three critically acclaimed children's book authors discuss their backgrounds, the evolution of their stories and their personal motivation in writing children's literature.

INTRODUCTION

Rhea Tregebov

FOR MILLENNIA we were a people without a land, and our cultural survival depended upon memory, upon remembering and interpreting the lessons of the past. Our pockets were empty but our heads were full.

Each of the following essays by authors of children's books examines the creative power of this tradition of remembering and evaluating the past.

Although Sharon Kirsh wisely points out the impossibility of writing for children without being in contact with one's own child within, how far into the past we reach for the richness of memory varies with each author. The sources of Phoebe Gilman's acclaimed picture book, *Something From Nothing*, go deeply into the peasant, preliterate origins of the folk tale. But while the folk tale resides, inevitably, in the achronicity of the eternal, immutable past, there is an added layer of memory, of specific time and place, in *Something from Nothing*. Gilman's essay outlines the origins of her images in documentary photographs of pre-Holocaust shtetls [villages].

Sharon Kirsh's young adult novel, *Fitting In*, also draws its strength from the specificity of time and place, in her case, the anti-Semitism of her own childhood in Halifax, Nova Scotia, in the early 1960s. In the current rhetoric of achieved equality, it is easy to forget how recently Canada itself had institutionalized anti-Semitism. My own picture book, *The Big Storm*, grew out of a desire to memorialize not my own childhood, but that of my mother, whose childhood was spent living above the family delicatessen in Winnipeg during the "Dirty Thirties."

Remembrance is a gift as well as a burden. When we present Jewish children or children belonging to any minority with authentic images of their own culture, we not only arm them against prejudice, we nourish their sense of identity and worth, and protect them against the amnesia that a denial of cultural difference engenders.

THE CREATION OF *Something From Nothing*

Phoebe Gilman

I've come to accept that stories develop a life and a will of their own. Even a story like *Something From Nothing*, which is adapted from an old Yiddish story, changed as the characters created themselves in my hands.

I first heard "The Tailor" at a conference in Montreal. Janet Lunn (author of *The Root Cellar* and *The Story of Canada*) and I were talking about the mystery of the creative process. "You know," she said, "it's like that old Jewish story, 'The Tailor.' Anything can be the catalyst for a story, even a lost button." I was intrigued. No. I didn't know the story, which was kind of ironic because I am Jewish and Janet is not.

The story was a perfect parable for the creative process. At the time this happened, I was struggling to write something completely different, a fairy tale about the aurora borealis ... trying, but not succeeding. As I struggled, the tailor kept whispering in my ear, "Write my story. Write my story." All right already. I'll make you happy. I'll write your story. It shouldn't take long. After all, the plot's ready-made. Ha! Was I mistaken!

I began to gather as many versions of "The Tailor" as I was able to find. Eventually a song surfaced. Since I believe it to be the oldest of them all, I pass it on to you:

> I have a coat
> From yesteryear's cloth
> Tra la la la la la
> In it there is not
> One single stitch
> Tra la la la la la
> Therefore I reflected on what to do
> And made from the coat a little jacket
>
> ... from the little jacket a little vest
> ... from the little vest a pocket
> ... from the pocket a little button
> ... from the little button a little nothing
> ... from the little nothing a song

As I was retrieving the many old versions of "The Tailor," I began writing my own. Can I put a child in here someplace? After all, it is a children's story that I'm making. Why not turn the tailor into a grandfather? As soon as I did that, the grandfather wanted to make all these things for his grandson instead of himself. He wanted to give his grandson the moon and the stars. (This was drawn directly from my own experience of my grandparents.) Okay. Grandpa will make the jacket for his grandson. Hmm, I thought. Why not add another layer to the tale? If it's for a grandson, why not start with a very young child and have Grandpa make him a blanket? And so the first lines were born:

> When Joseph was a baby, his Grandfather made him a wonderful blanket to keep him warm and cosy and to chase away bad dreams.

The internal logic of these changes dictated further changes. It takes time for things to get old and worn. That time would make visible changes in an infant. Joseph would be growing and changing as much as his blanket would. And what about the rest of the family? The whole *mishpukha* [family] wanted to get in on the act. Enter a father, a grandmother and even a little sister several years later. When I was growing up, my younger brother Mark had a blanket. He loved that blanket. It was his tent, his cave, his Superman cape and his magic carpet all rolled into one. No matter how much our Mother begged and pleaded, he refused to part with it. It was known as his *shmate* [rag]. That bit of family history found its way into my story. Joseph's mother became the one to insist that he throw it out. What would Joseph do? Run to Grandpa and ask him to fix it.

Since Joseph was growing older as my story progressed, it occurred to me that he, not Grandpa, could be the one to turn the lost button, the nothing, into a something, a story. Through love and the power of example, Grandpa had taught him to use his own "noodle." Or, as my father used to say to us, "The eggs are getting smarter than the chickens."

Up until this point, I had no idea that I was writing a Jewish story. The text, read on its own, could take place anywhere, any time. Illustrating a story is a bit like solving a mystery. Where does this happen? When? What do the characters look like? What can the pictures do to *illuminate* the text? What is happening between the lines?

Since the story originated in the shtetl [village], why not set it there? One does not enter the world of my grandparents lightly. As I worked on the research for the pictures, I became filled with sadness for this world that was destroyed in the Holocaust. The people in the photographs called out to me to act as their witness. The book took on another dimension. It became a way of remembering and recording the lives of my people. Although the shtetl is a composite, put together from many different sources, it is not generic. The house, the furniture, the street, the bagel vendor, the organ grinder, the knife sharpener, the woman bringing water from the well, the people in the marketplace, the river where the clothes are washed, once did exist. I painted their portraits to the best of my ability.

To solve the illustrator's problem of how to portray the repetitive action in the text (Grandpa cutting and stitching), in a visually dynamic manner, I decided to mirror the repetition in the text by repeating the image of the house interior and the exterior of the street, laying it out like a stage set. This allowed me to move the people around, creating mini-picture stories while remaining consistent with the form of the text. By doing this, I was also able to create a panorama of shtetl life.

At this point, two questions began to concern me. One: was my story becoming too sombre and adult for its intended audience, for children? And two: where was the button? The child *in me* was not completely satisfied with the book's solution of turning it all into a wonderful story. I wanted to know where the button went!

The solution to that mystery was the creation of a family of mice under the floorboards of the house. They became the ones to find the button. This created another subtext to this many-layered tale. The mouse family story. As Grandpa cuts and snips, the mice collect the bits and pieces that fall between the floorboards. As the story progresses, and the wonderful blanket shrinks, the mouse house material expands. In the end it is the mice who find the button and bring it home to their Papa, who uses it as the cushion of a little chair.

The final page shows Joseph reading his story to his family. Down at the bottom, a little mouse sits on the button chair reading his story to his family. If you want to hear and see the stories they wrote, simply turn back to the front of the book and begin again.

A good story can be reused and recycled by generations of readers as long as there are generations of good listeners. Not too long ago, a stranger said to me, I wish someone would look at me with the same look of love that is on Joseph's Grandpa's face. That look is not an invention. It was there for me on the faces of my family when I was growing up. *Kvelling!* [Doting.] Our families are our first audience. All artists need an audience. We do not speak to the wind. We wait, holding our breath, for response. I have been overwhelmed by the response to this book which has far exceeded my greatest expectations. I am grateful for this opportunity to thank you, my audience, in print. Thank you for listening. Thank you for hearing, seeing, understanding and appreciating what I did.

Origins: Writing *The Big Storm*

Rhea Tregebov

Children's books with Jewish content as they exist now can be loosely divided into three categories: holiday books, which generally tend to be picture books for younger children; traditional folk tales, which also tend to be picture books; and books about the Holocaust, which are almost exclusively young adult fiction for older children.* As a parent, I value all three categories. I have been grateful to find well-written and informative books that fill in the details about the traditional holidays and that help us as a family celebrate what is ignored or distorted by mainstream culture. I am also grateful for the traditional tales that pass on what is to me a remarkable and valuable world view. My son is now approaching in more depth issues relating to the Holocaust, and I value the excellent literature available to assist us in moving through this rite of passage.

However, what still tends to be missing, and perhaps most particularly from *Canadian* children's books, are those books in which there is a greater integration between Jewish content and artistic intent. We need more books that address the varieties of ways of being Jewish that contemporary life in Canada offers. We need books about intermarriage as well as orthodoxy, about rejecting as well as affirming parts of Jewish culture, about the ongoing anti-Semitism that challenges the continuation of our culture. Stories that convey the particularities of Jewish culture, the ethos and mythology, the kinds of family interaction, the history of Jewish immigration to Canada — all of these are, unfortunately, in short supply.

I look at the dearth of available literature and wonder about what factors continue to prohibit us from bringing into our writing our inner sense of Jewishness. I don't wish to dictate to any writer what they write or don't write. But I do find it very curious that writers who are titans of contemporary children's writing (Vera B. Williams, Maurice Sendak and Arnold Lobel) do not demonstrate more explicit evidence of their Jewishness in their books. And this makes me wonder whether

---

* Special thanks to Toronto Public Library librarians Joanne Schott and Joanne Schwartz for their assistance with my research.

a false dichotomy of literary quality *versus* ethnic content is being set up. That, lingering somewhere in our consciousness as writers, there is a sense that "ethnic" content precludes literary quality.

With these background questions in mind, I'd like to go on to describe a my own experience of writing my children's book, *The Big Storm*, which is about a little girl growing up above the family's delicatessen in Winnipeg in 1935. The plot originated in a family story; the emotional resonance I was able to bring to the plot came from my deep attachment to the mythic stories of her childhood that my mother told me when I was a child. Growing up in Winnipeg in the 1950s and 1960s, I had experienced a sense of dislocation, of the absence of roots: the ties with Europe were abruptly cut with my grandparents immigration near the beginning of the century and their lack of interest in telling stories about the "bad old days." Of course any remaining connection was then further eradicated by the Holocaust, into which much of my remaining family vanished. My sense of being shut off from any family history was somewhat alleviated by the stories of my mother's past, by the fact that the North End of Winnipeg was identifiable even beyond its cultural centre (this part of town is the equivalent of the Lower East Side in New York City), and, even more particularly, that my grandfather's delicatessen was known, recognized, *seen* by the North End, Jewish community in which I continued to live.

In mainstream society, however, as a Jew, I felt invisible. We are now accustomed to the reluctance of the larger society to recognize our minority status by virtue of our so-called invisibility as a minority, but what I'm talking about goes even further into the psyche. The invisibility of being Jewish was a product of looking out into the available cultural paradigms and seeing next to nothing that reflected my own experience. I remember the shock of delight when I came across the All-of-a-Kind Family series of books, in which the family was recognizably Jewish. Even in these books, the barrier of location (the books were situated in New York City) remained an impediment to full identification with the protagonists.

My sense of continuity with the past, the absence or difficulty of any answer to the question, "Where do I come from, Mom?" (a question my own son, three generations Canadian-born, asks in turn) came from a sense of not belonging *here*. This not-belonging was assuaged somewhat by the family mythology about life in the delicatessen and the fact that this mythology was reinforced and asserted outside the family structure by recognition within a larger community (albeit a small and isolated one).

Furthermore, these tales of my mother's childhood in the delicatessen asserted many values that seemed somewhat at odds with the values I was offered as a child and which, at the close of the millennium, are even more at odds with the values our children are surrounded by. The children were independent. They were valued in the family because they contributed economically; their labour was worth something. As a child I always felt superfluous (loved, but superfluous). Then there was the closeness of community facilitated by the urban environment of the time that the suburban environment of the 1950s and 1960s in which I grew up did not allow. In writing *The Big Storm*, I hoped to get all these values across.

So these were the inner drives that led me to come up with the book. While initially there was some concern that *The Big Storm* had a limited market because of its articulated ethnic content, the book found a wide audience of both Jewish and non-Jewish readers. I feel more and more strongly that the particular has a universal appeal; that by refusing to be homogenized and by asserting our difference in fact we call up a response to the authentic in every individual.

One final footnote regarding the importance of children's literature with ethnic content. Anti-Semitism and bigotry are still out there, as we all know, particularly in these times. There are battles that still need to be fought. Jewish content appears not only in books written by Jewish authors. In particular in some of the older books still on the library shelves, we may find ourselves very uncomfortable with the portrayal of Jewish characters and culture. We need not only to preserve and express our culture, but to defend against the negative stereotypes that continue to survive.

A HANDFUL OF MEMORIES

Sharon Kirsh

Halifax is where I grew up, what I refer to as "home." In my mother's apartment, in the living room, sits a large mahogany hutch which dates back to the time of my parents' marriage over fifty years ago. The top half of the hutch has three long glass doors, each of which opens with a tiny gold key and makes a soft clicking sound when it closes. Behind the doors is an array of pretty china cups and saucers, a set of crystal wine glasses, extra pairs of *shabes* [Sabbath] candlesticks and an assortment of cake plates, mugs and dishes, many of which were wedding gifts from people now deceased. I never tire of peering through the glass at these artefacts which have been sitting in their designated locations ever since I was a little girl. Through all the seasons of my family's history, the hutch and its contents have remained steadfast, teapot on the top shelf, miniature cream and sugar bowls on the second, and so on.

I do not own my parents' hutch. I do not own any of the shiny perfect objects that are housed in it. I own only one thing: that is, the memory of the hutch and its contents. The image of it from childhood, while murky, serves as the backdrop to other more stirring recollections of family life. It was one prop in the scenery of my childhood, a significant prop because it sat large, looming and majestic in the livingroom which served as our playroom and as our dining room all rolled into one. It was through those glass doors that my mother took out the wine goblets for *kiddush* [the blessing of the wine] every Friday night, where she removed the fancy glasses for special company for Rosh Hashanah [the Jewish New Year], where she took out the candy bowl and filled it with chocolates when she wanted to treat us.

Almost everything in that hutch is old, part of my parents' past. And now the memories associated with it are growing older. Now often I ask my mother questions which I would never have thought to ask when I was fifteen, or twenty-five, or even thirty-five. Now I want to understand who gave each item to her and what her relationship was to them at that time, and how it has changed over time. Now I recall specific family events associated with specific dishes or cups or candlesticks. I think of the guests who sat around our table at *yontev* [the holidays] of my mother working in the kitchen, cleaning up long after our guests went home and the rest of us went to sleep. And then the next morning she would march from the kitchen to the hutch carrying with her the cleaned and polished items that would now be placed gently in their rightful locations.

Sometimes the contents evoke memories of foods — I think of the *teyglekh* [honeyed dessert] on this plate and the *mandlbroyt* [almond biscuits] on that one and the *compote* [stewed fruit] (which for years I thought tasted more like compost) in the other one.

I feel as though I own the hutch without actually owning it. I feel entitled to it. I feel entitled to it because it is part of my treasure chest of very personal reminiscences. It is through the same mechanism that I have come, in recent years, to feel entitled to my memories of growing up Jewish in a small city in Canada in the 1950s and 1960s. At the time the experience seemed in no way extraordinary, just as the hutch seemed in no way extraordinary back then, and of course in most ways neither one was.

For many years after moving to Toronto in the early 1970s my growing up experiences in Halifax remained lodged, abandoned, in the vaults of my memory bank. Then twenty years passed. I had a child and I began to observe her in her world, defined in part by her school experience in a secular Hebrew day school, in part by the books she reads and, of course, by many other factors. When she was very little, she asked whether everyone in Toronto was Jewish. When I was little I thought the whole world, with a few notable exceptions, was Presbyterian, Anglican and Catholic. I was convinced my name had been MacKirsh, and that my grandfather had dropped the "mac" when he came over from the old country. My daughter reads books that acknowledge the existence of Jewish children, that are rich with Jewish words and expressions and images. She knows about the Holocaust, about Jewish heroines, about shtetls [villages], about characters from contemporary Jewish literature.

Growing up in Halifax we had no exposure, as far as I can recall, to children's literature with a Jewish theme. While the series of books All-of-a-Kind Family by Sydney Taylor, a Jewish version of *Little Women*, was published in 1951, it was not until five years ago that I read the series. Similarly, I. B. Singer's writings for children might have been available, but we were not introduced to them. During our childhood and adolescent years, the books we read in school and for leisure were of subject matter, imagery and language which in no way reflected any aspect of our private or communal lives. It was our great fortune to have been on close terms with the likes of the Brontës, Dickens, Shakespeare, Twain, Dumas, Montgomery and Alcott. The subject matter was as varied and colourful as the palette of human concerns, but who among us can recall even a word about the tragedies and triumphs of religious or ethnic diversity? The imagery of the classics carried us away to worlds where women lay dying of consumption on chaise longues, where orphans struggled for physical and emotional survival, where rapscallions outsmarted their elders. But who among us can remember an image of a Jewish child living, struggling, laughing? And the language, too, was from a world far away from the one in which we lived. Some of it was the most perfect language I've ever read or heard, but never were there words, special words or expressions or cadences of dialogue that reflected our culture. We were absent.

During the past three decades a rich crop of books has sprung up geared towards the young reader written by Jewish women and men about the experiences of Jews, both young and old. One category has been autobiographical recollections of the Holocaust and post-war period, often in fictionalized form. There are literally hundreds of books of that genre, informing young readers about life in Eastern Europe prior to the Holocaust, during it and then after the smoke had settled. Some of these thinly veiled fictions have been written by Canadians (e.g. Lillian Boracks-Nemetz and Jack Kuper). While today's children might not know anyone who survived the Holocaust, they are given an entree in that world, into their own history, through literature. Similarly, through a second category of books, the retelling of Jewish folk tales, especially those which vividly depict shtetl life, today's children can travel back to a time that predates their parents and perhaps their grandparents. Contemporary interpreters of folk tales (such as Chapman, Hirsch and Adler) paint a dynamic picture of a nineteenth century world which provides an historical passageway for children's imaginations, and which allows them to situate themselves in a context.

My novel *Fitting In* describes a skinny slice of Jewish life — small city, Canadian, post-Holocaust 1950s and 1960s. It isn't about Toronto,

Montreal or Winnipeg — the self-appointed sculptors of Canadian Jewish culture. It isn't about the USA, where the majority of children's books are written and published. It is about a very narrow wedge of time when the Jewish people, worldwide, were attempting in such isolated Jewish communities as Halifax, Nova Scotia, to reconstruct their shattered bodies and souls and confidence.

My personal history is not unusual. But what I have come to understand about it is my entitlement — both to take the time to recall what life was like for a Jewish girl growing up in that era in that particular place, and to value it as one tiny piece in the tapestry of our modern culture. In the Halifax of the post-war years there were no skeletal remains, no soil soaked with blood. But there was a community that served as a stepping stone for many survivors whose boat first docked in the port of Halifax where they slept for a couple of days or weeks before boarding trains and planes for the greener pastures of big city living.

The main characters in my book are two Jewish girls in their early adolescence — Mollie and Naomi. In most ways they are assimilated with their Christian schoolmates and neighbours. Their cares and pleasures are the cares and pleasures of any twelve- or thirteen-year-old girl. Over time, what comes to set them apart is their burgeoning awareness that not everyone considers their differentness — their Jewishness — to be acceptable. At the same time they learn in *kheder* [Hebrew school] about the Holocaust, and soon they make terrifying comparisons between pre-Hitler Germany and the anti-Semitic slings and arrows hurled at them by certain public school teachers and by certain neighbours right under their noses in Halifax, Nova Scotia, Canada.

Fitting In is about just that — the never-ending need humans have for acceptance by peers and community. As a Jew, fitting into the mainstream in Halifax was not without its struggles. The cruel epithets shouted at us by neighbours whom we thought were our friends, the ugly stereotyping by the teachers whom we were supposed to respect as our elders and superiors, the swastikas smeared in mud on the window of our house by neighbourhood kids, the unrelenting mantra of "Jew as Christ-Killer" by our Catholic friends who learned such lessons in church and at Catholic school, the guilt engendered in us by teachers every time we missed school for Jewish holidays, the exclusion from membership in the most popular summer club in the city, exclusion from all curling rinks, exclusion from riding stables and golf courses because we were Jews — all of these etched themselves upon the minds of Jewish girls and boys growing up in those times in that place.

It was the sense in which we came to view ourselves in the face of such bigotry that I hoped to capture in my book. I wanted the young reader to know that there once existed as part of their history a small city in Atlantic Canada where not very long ago (and perhaps to this very day) being Jewish meant something quite "unique" and not always in the nicest possible sense of that term.

It is my hope that more and more people will look into their own family's hutch and pull out remembrances, and pass on those treasures to the next generation so that children many years from now will be endowed with a lush literature filled with ideas and images and words that reflect their cultural reality. Through the feminist movement we learned the importance of speaking about who we are as women. We must also now recognize the importance of speaking about who we are as Jews.

⊂⊛⊃

CONTRIBUTORS

ELIZABETH BOLTON is a rabbi, cantor, singer, voice teacher and choral conductor. After pursuing a career in classical music, she served as cantor at Temple Emanu-El in Toronto, and then relocated to Philadelphia to attend the Reconstructionist Rabbinical College (RRC). Since her ordination in 1996, she has served a congregation in Princeton, New Jersey and taught as guest lecturer at congregations, elderhostels and college campuses. She is currently on the faculty at RRC and serves as staff chaplain of the Philadelphia Geriatric Center.

ELAINE BRODIE is a photographic artist whose work has been exhibited and published both in Canada and abroad. Her work is in the collections of several Canadian corporations and the Canada Council Art Bank. She is currently on the Exhibition Selection Committee of Gallery 44 Centre for Contemporary Photography and is a part-time faculty member of Seneca College.

YAEL BROTMAN was born in Israel and spent her teen years in Winnipeg. She has been working as a professional artist for fifteen years, specializing in print-making. She prints at Open Studio, a co-operative print-making studio in Toronto. Brotman teaches at the University of Toronto and at the Royal Ontario Museum.

FAIGEL (FLORENCE) BROWN was born in 1927 in Montreal to a Jewish working-class family. Despite the family's economic hardship and with the support of her mother, Brown was sent to the best music and voice teachers in the city. She taught music to support herself for many years. When she retired at the age of sixty, she bought a computer and is now pursuing her ambitions as a writer.

JUDITH R. COHEN is an ethnomusicologist and performer who has been working with Judeo-Spanish ("Ladino") songs for many years. Adjunct Graduate Faculty at York University, she also researches and performs medieval, Balkan, Yiddish and French–Canadian traditions, and is working on a SSHRC Research Grant investigating musical traditions of the Crypto-Jews of Portugal and Spain, and the new traditions of "Jewish Festivals" in Spanish towns.

YOLANDE COHEN is a professor of Contemporary History at the University of Quebec in Montreal. In addition to her academic duties, she is currently working on the production of a CD-ROM on Moroccan Judaism sponsored by the Moroccan–Jewish community. She also remains active in the local municipal scene to ensure that Montreal remains a city tolerant of the traditions of all its inhabitants.

SUSAN G. COLE is a journalist, author and playwright. She is the author of *Pornography and The Sex Crisis* and *Power Surge*, which deal with issues of violence, pornography and sexuality. Her play, *A Fertile Imagination*, about a lesbian couple trying to have a baby, won two Dora Awards and has had six productions across Canada. She is currently the senior entertainment editor at *NOW* magazine in Toronto.

HELENA FEINSTADT is a psychotherapist in private practice who lives in Toronto. She works with individuals and has been facilitating groups of daughters of Holocaust survivors since 1993. She is a clinical member of the Ontario Society of Psychotherapists.

SANDRA FINKELMAN is a psychotherapist and consultant in private practice in Toronto and a daughter of Holocaust survivors. She works with individuals, couples and groups, consults to organizations and offers workshops and training programmes. She has run experientially oriented groups for women since 1980 and for daughters of Holocaust survivors since 1993.

IRENE FROLIC is a Holocaust survivor who came to Canada with her parents in 1948. She lives in Toronto where she operates a glass studio. She is represented by galleries in the USA, Canada, France and Germany and her work is in the Museum of Decorative Art, Lausanne, Switzerland, as well as in private collections.

MIMI GELLMAN is a Toronto-based visual artist, arts educator and curator. She specializes in architectural glass and conceptual art installations. In 1995, she curated the visual art exhibition "From Memory to Transformation: Jewish Women's Voices." Most recently, in 1998, she wrote the catalogue essay for the artists' collective project, "Collective Unconscious." She exhibits internationally and is in many corporate and private collections. She is currently preparing for her solo exhibition at the Canadian Embassy Gallery in Tokyo, Japan, scheduled for May 1999.

PHOEBE GILMAN was born and grew up in the Bronx and lived in Europe and Israel before coming to Canada in 1972. She is the author and illustrator of ten internationally acclaimed children's books, including the award-winning *Something from Nothing*.

PEARL GOLDBERG is a retired educator who has been a member of the Minyan of Crones since its inception. She has had a long-standing interest in women's roles in Judaism and has been actively involved in writing and creating new rituals. Goldberg is an active member of Darchei Noam Reconstructionist Congregation.

ELYSE GOLDSTEIN is the Director of Kolel: A Centre for Liberal Jewish Learning in Toronto, the only liberal adult yeshiva in Canada. Her writings on women and Judaism have appeared in journals throughout North America. She lectures extensively on the subject of feminist theology. Parts of this essay were delivered at the Jewish Feminist Conference in Toronto, 1994, and parts are adapted from her first book *Re-Visions: Seeing Torah through a Feminist Lens*, published in 1998 by Key Porter Books.

NORMA BAUMEL JOSEPH is Associate Professor in the Department of Religion at Concordia University. She is also the convener of the Chair in Quebec and Canadian Jewish Studies and Graduate Programme Director of the MA in Judaic Studies. Founding member of the Canadian Coalition of Jewish Women for the *Get*, Joseph successfully worked with the community and the federal government to pass a law in 1990 that would protect Jewish women in difficult divorce situations and aid them in their pursuit of a Jewish divorce. Author of many publications,

Joseph won the Leo Wasserman Prize from the American Jewish Historical Society for 1995.

MELANIE KAYE/KANTROWITZ is the author of *The Issue Is Power: Essays on Women, Jews, Violence and Resistance* and *My Jewish Face & Other Stories*. She has just completed a novel, *The Exile of Ruby Kaminsky*. Her work is widely published in the feminist, gay and lesbian, and progressive Jewish press. She has taught women's studies, Jewish studies and race theory all over the USA. An activist since the early 1960s, she is the former director of Jews for Racial and Economic Justice in New York City and continues to serve on the board of JFREJ, as well as on the steering committee of the New York City Organizing Support Center.

SHARON KIRSH is the author of *Fitting In*, her first work of young adult fiction. As a former research psychologist, she has written many articles and papers based on her professional work, and only recently took the plunge into fiction.

IRENA KLEPFISZ, a writer, poet and activist in the lesbian/feminist communities, is the author of *A Few Words in the Mother Tongue* (poetry) and *Dreams of an Insomniac* (essays). She is also co-editor of *The Tribe of Dina: A Jewish Women's Anthology* and *Di froyen: Women and Yiddish*. She has published articles on Eastern European Jewish women activists, Yiddish women writers, and translated women's poetry and fiction. She teaches Jewish women's studies at Barnard College and serves as the editorial consultant for Yiddish and Yiddish literature for the Jewish feminist magazine *Bridges*.

SHIRLEY KUMOVE is columnist for *The Book Peddler*, a quarterly journal of the National Yiddish Book Centre in Amherst, Massachusetts. Kumove is also the author and translator of *Words Like Arrows: A Collection of Yiddish Folk Sayings* and its sequel, *More Words, More Arrows*. She is a contributing translator to *Found Treasures: Stories by Yiddish Women Writers*. Kumove is currently completing her translation from the Yiddish of the collected poetry of Anna Margolin; individual poems from the collection have been published in *Writ, Prism International* and *Two Lines*.

WARREN LEHRER is a writer and artists whose books and theatrical works celebrate the music of speech, the complexity of personality and the wobbly line between brilliance and madness. His books include *The Portrait Series, French Fries, i mean you know* and *versations*. Lehrer has received grants from the National Endowment for the Arts, the Ford Foundation and the New York State Council on the Arts. He is an Associate Professor of Interdisciplinary Studies at SUNY, Purchase and a graduate faculty member at the School for Visual Arts.

RACHEL LEVIATAN has been a member of Kibbutz Ein Ha-Mifratz since 1966. She has held different offices in the areas of education and political and community outreach to developing towns in Israel. Under the auspices of the MAPAM party, she also has worked as an activist in the slums of south Tel Aviv.

RUTH LIBERMANN, born in Germany, is an artist living and working in New York. She is currently pursuing a PhD at New York University.

HELENA LIPSTADT was born in Berlin, Germany in 1947 to parents who survived the Holocaust in Poland. She came of age in feminist and anti-Vietnam War politics and continues passionately committed to issues of peace and justice. Author of the poetry chapbook, *Leave Me Signs*, Lipstadt has published her poems, short stories and essays in numerous journals and anthologies.

MINDY YAN MILLER, a Montreal artist, operated a successful textile design business for several years before returning to the Nova Scotia College of Art and Design. She has participated in numerous group and solo exhibitions in Canada and overseas.

THE MINYAN OF CRONES started as a women's Torah study group in 1991 and has become a source for the exchange of wisdom, support and friendship. Current members include Temma Gentles, Anne Glickman, Ricki Grushcow, Lieba Lesk, Jackie Rand, Cyrel Troster, Miriam Wyman and Rena Zayit.

GRETA HOFMANN NEMIROFF coordinates Women's Studies at Dawson College in Montreal, where she teaches in the English and Humanities Departments. She has been teaching women's studies at the post-secondary level for thirty years. She has published widely and edited books in the fields of education, women's studies, women's issues and fiction. Currently she is the vice-president of the Sisterhood is Global Institute, an international non-governmental organization.

NADINE NORMAN is an installation artist who has been residing in Paris, Toronto and Montreal for the past few years. She is a founding member of the Resurgence Collective in Montreal and has exhibited internationally, most recently in Prague and Paris.

ETHEL RAICUS is a painter, industrial designer and teacher who has lived in Toronto for all but two years, which were spent in Israel working on a kibbutz and in a children's village. Simultaneously, and for over thirty-six years, she enjoyed a career in Jewish education. She is the co-editor and one of the translators of *Found Treasures: Stories by Yiddish Women Writers*.

ROCHELLE RUBENSTEIN is a Toronto painter, print-maker, and fabric and book artist. Her work has been widely exhibited in Canada, the USA and Europe, and is in the collections of the Museum of Modern Art, New York, and the Irish Museum of Modern Art, among others.

SYLVIA SAFDIE was born in Aley, Lebanon in 1942 and spent her early years in Israel. In 1953, she came to Canada. She completed her Bachelor in Fine Arts degree at Concordia University in 1975. She lives and works in Montreal and her work is internationally exhibited.

SHLOMIT SEGAL has long been an activist in the progressive Jewish and feminist communities. She was editor of the Jewish feminist magazine, *Bridges*, for five years. Her writing has appeared in *Fireweed*, and the anthologies *Plural Desires* and *Outrage*. By day, she works in graphic design and desktop publishing. Her art work recently appeared on the cover of *Canadian Woman Studies/les cahiers de la femme*.

YVONNE SINGER is a Toronto installation artist who has exhibited both nationally and internationally. Her work is concerned with how language, memory and history construct our identities and with the boundaries between public and private. She teaches visual arts at York University.

JUDITH SLOAN is an actress, oral historian, writer and comedienne whose theatre work combines humour, pathos and a love of the absurd. A frequent guest lecturer and performer in universities, Sloan has had work produced in theatres, festivals and on radio throughout the USA and abroad. Her work has been supported by fellowships and grants from the National Endowment for the Humanities, the Paul Robeson Fund, the Puffin Foundation and the Franklin Furnace Performance Art Fund. She teaches Oral History, Performance and Character Development at New York University.

SARAH SILBERSTEIN SWARTZ works as a book editor, writer and translator from Yiddish. She is author of *Bar Mitzvah*, co-editor of and contributor to *Found Treasures: Stories by Yiddish Women Writers* and editor-in-chief for the two volume *Jewish Women in America: An Historical Encyclopedia*. She is currently preparing a groundbreaking volume entitled "Jewish Women in Canada: An Encyclopedia of Historical Biographies" to be published in the year 2000, as well as a children's book based on a Yiddish feminist theme.

RHEA TREGEBOV is the author of four collections of poetry, most recently *Mapping the Chaos*, as well as four picture books for children, including *The Big Storm*. Her poetry has won the Pat Lowther Award, the *Malahat Review* Long Poem Award and *Prairie Schooner*'s Readers' Choice Award. A fifth children's book, also set in the Depression, is forthcoming in fall 1999. She works as a creative writing instructor and editor in Toronto.

NANCY WECHSLER-AZEN was ordained in 1990 from the New York campus of the Hebrew Union College Jewish Institute of Religion. She is the founding rabbi of Temple Kol Ami in Thornhill, Ontario and is currently the spiritual leader of Congregation Adds Emuno in Leonia, New Jersey.

MARGIE WOLFE has worked in feminist publishing for more than twenty years, first at Women's Press and currently at Second Story Press. Wolfe has been a co-editor of several anthologies, including *Still Ain't Satisfied: Canadian Feminism Today*, *No Safe Place: Violence Against Women and Children* and *Found Treasures: Stories by Yiddish Women Writers*. She has also been an active member of the Canadian publishing community, and has recently completed her tenure as president of the Organization of Book Publishers of Ontario. Her next book project will focus on daughters of Holocaust survivors.